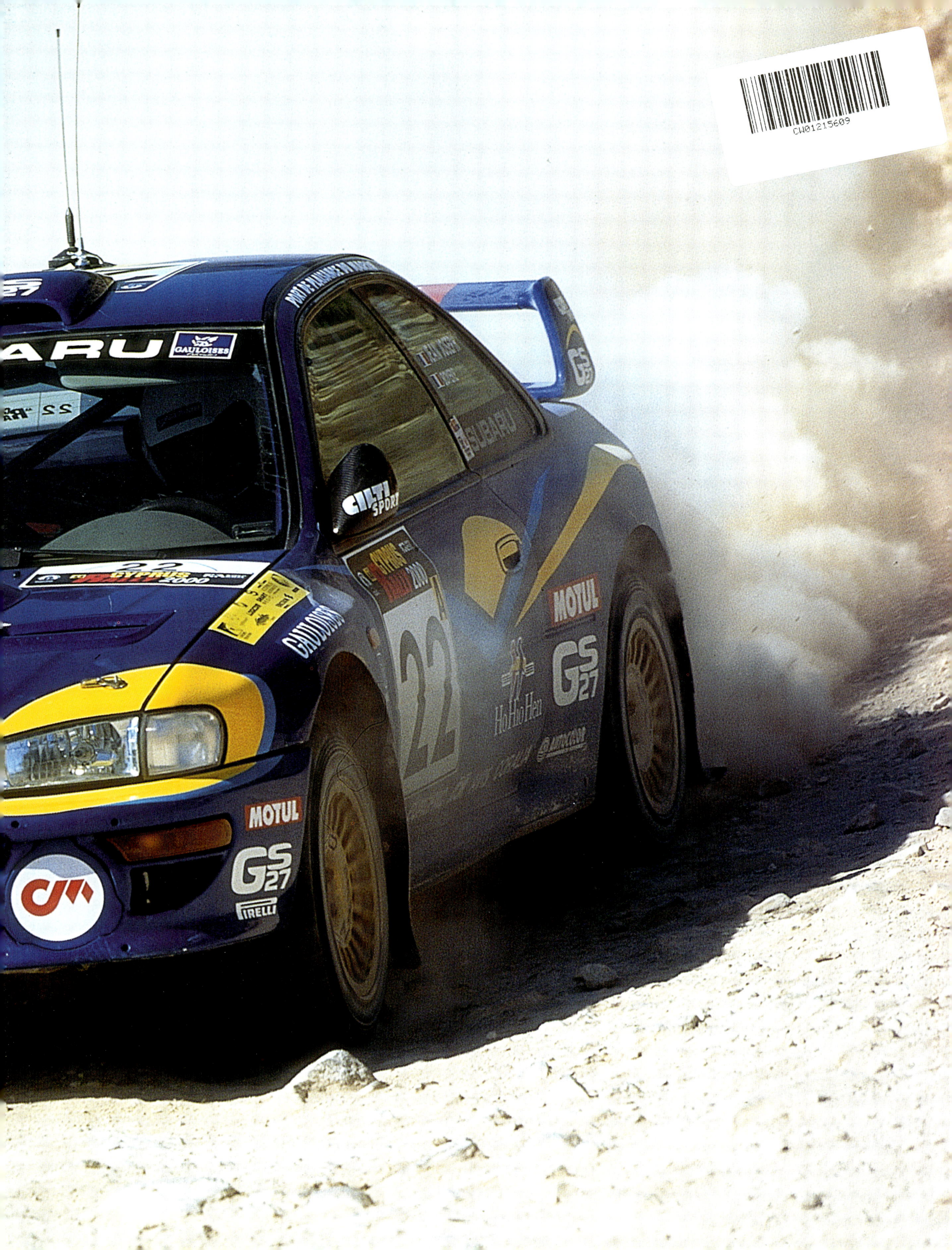
GAULOISES
SUBARU
22
MOTUL
GS 27
MOTUL
GS 27
PIRELLI

RALLY YEARBOOK
2000-2001

Nikon

All photos in this book were taken using Nikon equipment.
F5, AF-S 80-200f2.8, AF-S 28-70f2.8, AF-S 17-35f2.8, AF-S 600f4

NIKON France SA - 191, rue du Marché Rollay - 94504 Champigny sur Marne Cedex
www.nikon.fr

RALLY YEARBOOK
2000-2001

Pictures
Pascal Huit

Written by
Philippe Joubin

Statistics and results
Séverine Huit

ISBN 2-940125-72-4

© 2000, Chronosports Editeur
Jordils Park, Chemin des Jordils 40, CH-1025 St-Sulpice, Suisse. Tél. : (++41 21) 697 14 14. Fax : (++41 21) 697 14 16.
e-mail: info@chronosports.com   internet: www.chronosports.com
Printed in France by Imprimerie Sézanne, 11 rue du 35e Régiment d'Aviation, F-69500 Bron.

Esso
MICHELIN
KARJALA
ASG
PEUGEOT
M. GRONHOLM
NGK
SPARK PLUGS
sparco

FOREWORD

Uusi vuosisata, uusi vuosituhat, uusi kukoistus - nämä ajatukset mielessäni ja oppipojan palavalla innolla lähdin ensimmäiseen täyteen MM-sarjan kauteeni. Kauden alussa totesin itselleni, että tulen oppimaan valtavasti uutta tässä upeassa tiimissä, jonka tähtäimessä on sarjan mestaruus; pääsen tutustumaan kaikkiin minulle vielä uusiin ralleihin ja pääsen matkustamaan maailmojen ääriin. Huima ohjelma huimalla autolla!

Mestaruus kauden päätteeksi? No ei todellakaan; mahdollisesti sitten kolmen vuoden kuluttua, ajattelin..

Kunnioitan Peugeotin tiimin ammattitaitoa ja pyrkimystä täydellisyyteen sillä tuo tiimihän on mestaruuteni varsinainen räätäli ja haluan onnitella heitä koko sydämestäni. Maailmanmestaruus - aivan mieletöntä! Se oli pienen suomipojan päässä toinen unelma "Suurajojen" voiton ohella.

Kartturini Timon kanssa kiitämme myös kaikkia teitä innokkaita kannattajiamme, jotka olette rohkaisseet meitä ja olette nyt jakamassa tämän ilon kanssamme. Käyttäkää pieni hetki katsellen näitä kauden 2000 ikimuistoisia huippuhetkiä.

It's a new century, a new millennium and a new beginning. I was getting ready for my first full season in the world championship with all the enthusiasm of an apprentice. I told myself I would learn a lot, especially with a respected team which was aiming for the constructors' title. I would discover all the events that were new to me and travel to place as far away as the Antipodes. It was a major programme!
The title at the end of the year? No, I didn't believe in it. I told myself that it might be possible in three years. I salute the talent and perfectionism of the men from Peugeot, who were the architects of my success and I offer them my sincere thanks and congratulations. To be world champion was the second dream for a little Finnish lad, after that of winning the Thousand Lakes.
Along with my co-driver, Timo, I would like to thank all the fans who encouraged us along the way and shared our good fortune. Now is the time to ease off the throttle and enjoy all these memorable images of the 2000 season.

See you soon

Marcus Grönholm

RALLY YEARBOOK

48

30

22

14

9 > FOREWORD
12 > MILLENIUM
22 > MARCUS GRÖNHOLM
26 > HAPPY BIRTHDAY SUBARU
30 > MICHELIN IN THE CHAMPIONS
34 > THE STARS
42 > THE TEAMS
48 > WORLD CHAMPIONSHIP 2000
162 > STATISTICS

2000-2001

Pascal HUIT
Few photographers can claim such enthusiasm for the world rally championship. The 2000 edition of the San Remo was his 200th rally and he is unlikely to forget it, given how far the Italian event strayed from rallying philosophy.
He admits to an abiding passion for the Seventies and Eighties, a period he only knew through reading magazines when he should have been studying maths. His main regret is that he never witnessed at first hand the exploits of Munari in the Stratos and Waldegaard in a Porsche on the Safari.

Philippe JOUBIN
A 36 year old reporter for "L'Equipe" it was inevitable he would be smitten by motor sport, given that he was born in Mans. Along with rallying, he has a passion for sailing and his garage is home to an MG, a 2CV and a 306. He has spent the last four years following the rally circus around the globe.

ACKNOWLEDGEMENTS

The authors would like to thank all those who helped in the creation of this book. Special thanks to Tiina Lehmonen, Simo Lampinen, the press services at Ford, Hyundai, Mitsubishi, Peugeot, Seat, Skoda and Subaru; to Castrol, Piero Sodano of the FIA, Ayme Chatard, Andy Pope, Chris Williams and Dominique Bravy of Michelin, Nello Zoppe and all his team at Pro Nikon, the Laboratoires La Comete (Paris) and Picto (Lyon) as well as Bruno Jouanny of Asia (Lyon.) Thanks also to Marcus Grönholm, who was kind enough to write the preface to this book.
All the photographs in the book are the work of Pascal Huit with the exception of the Lancia Stratos photos of Mr. and Mrs. Morelli.

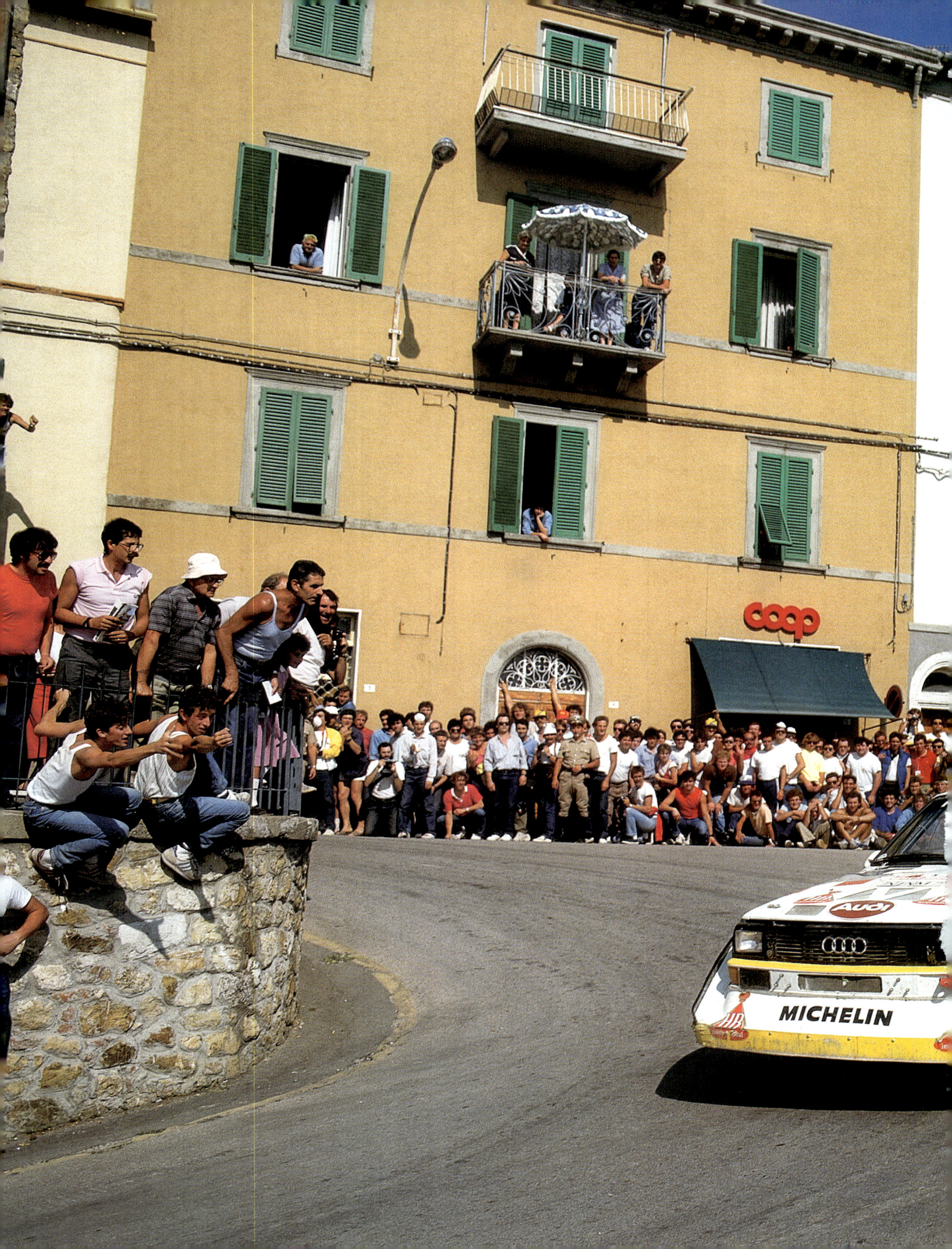
coop
Audi
MICHELIN

MILLENAIRE

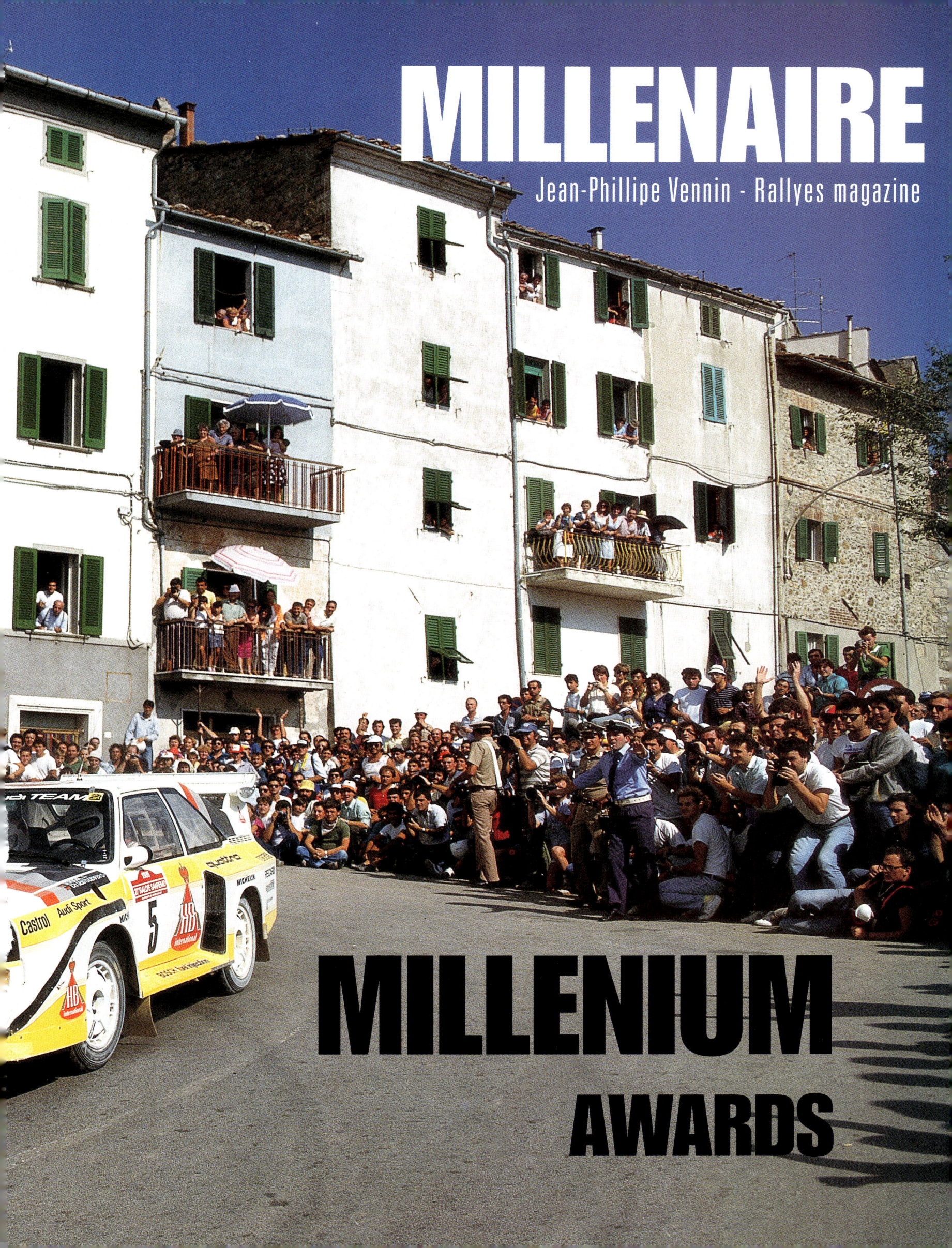

Jean-Phillipe Vennin - Rallyes magazine

MILLENIUM

AWARDS

DRIVER OF THE MILLE

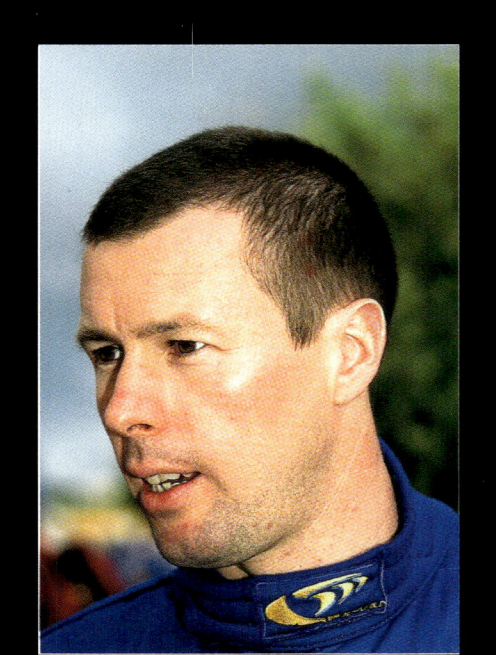

NNIUM

There are some who have won rallies which have passed into legend. Others never became world champion, but became the greatest drivers of all time.

Walter Rohrl was voted driver of the millennium by his peers. Jean-Pierre Nicolas, Jean Ragnotti and Miki Biasion had him as their all-time great, while four other voters featured him in their top three. This result is hardly a surprise, as the German was always considered the absolute reference point when he was at the height of his powers. One of the high points of an outstanding career was his four wins on the Monte Carlo Rally, with a different car each time.

As an official Fiat driver, Walter stamped his authority on the 1980 edition, at the wheel of a 131 Abarth. Two years later, he did it again in an Opel Ascona 400, which on paper was no match for the impressive Audi Quattro. He had a little bit of help from the weather gods on this occasion as it was dry for the entire duration of the event, which meant the four wheel drive Audis lost some of their advantage. He returned to the Fiat fold in 1983, this time driving a Lancia Rally 037. Once again the weather was kind and he left no room for hope to his team mate Markku Alen. Then, in 1984, he finally teamed up with Audi, having come close on several occasions. This time he outpaced his team-mates Blomquist and Mikkola in full winter conditions, which should have worked in favour of the two Scandinavians.

This series of victories was only interrupted in 1981 by Jean Ragnotti and Jean-Marc Andrie in the Renault 5 Turbo, when Rohrl did not compete. The German had decided to leave Fiat and join Mercedes. But as this constructor was suspected of cheating, it pulled out, just weeks after Rohrl had inked the contract. He had a sabbatical, with just an odd appearance or too, including a run on the San Remo in a Porsche 911.

He also won in Greece three times, including his first ever world championship event in 1975, driving an Opel Kadett. There were two victories on the San Remo, including the '85 rally, where at the wheel of an ageing Quattro, he wiped the floor with the Peugeot 205 and Lancias to record his final victory out of a total of fourteen. Rohrl never competed in the Thousand Lakes Rally, deeming it too dangerous and something of a Scandinavian speciality. He never bothered with the RAC either, not seeing the point of trundling around on mud in the fog. Those are the only two weak points in a legendary career.

However, a third place on the 82 Swedish remains one of the best finishes for a non-Scandinavian on this event. While he won "only" two world championships in 1980 and 1982, he could easily have picked up a third if he could have been bothered. Most notably in 1983, all he would have had to do was slightly increase the number of rallies he entered, which he himself had limited to just six.

WALTER RÖHRL

Rohrl reckons that today's drivers get as much pleasure out of the sport as they did in his heyday and that a win is as satisfying as it was in the 70s and 80s.

When he was asked who he thought was the best driver of the millennium, Rohrl picked Timo Makinen ahead of his old team-mate Marku Alen and Michele Mouton. She declined to answer the question, whereas Colin McRae picked himself! No surprises when Rohrl was asked to pick the best co-driver. He opted for his former partner, Christian Geistdorfer. What did you expect?

Over the past few years, Rohrl has taken part in several historic car rallies. He admitted that, if a world championship was organised for these cars, run over the old routes, he would be more than happy to take part. It's a nice idea. ∎

1	Henri Toivonen	52	8	Timo Makinen	24
	Walter Rohrl	52	9	Colin McRae	10
3	Juha Kankkunen	44		Bjorn Waldegaard	10
	Carlos Sainz	44		Jean-Luc Therier	10
5	Hannu Mikkola	42	12	Michéle Mouton	8
6	Markku Alen	36	13	Marcus Gronholm	6
7	Tommi Makinen	24	14	Stig Blomqvist	4

CAR OF THE MILLE

NIUM

From the over-the-top excesses of Group B, to the barely modified road cars of the early Seventies, back to the technical sophistication of the WRC, the rally cars have played their part in the making of the sport.

LANCIA STRATOS

Seventeen wins and three constructors' world championships, fifty wins and three European titles, seven national championships - four in Italy, two in France and one in Greece. These figures alone would be enough to make the Lancia Stratos the car of the millennium. Drivers of different generations such as Ove Andersson, Carlos Sainz and especially Sandro Munari whose career was inextricably linked to the car, all voted for it, not just for its successes and technical characteristics but also for the sheer look of the beast. It has entered the pages of legend as the car that embodied everything about the sport in its heyday.

"The Stratos really looked the business," wrote Patrick Michel in Rallyes Magazine in January 1999. "It looked great from any angle with that dynamic, angular shape, mixed with sinuous curves which flowed along the door line, its air ducts and the novel roof-mounted air intake for the V6 engine. In its Alitalia red, white and green livery it was almost too beautiful. And when you tipped the huge engine cover back, it got even better."

That was written twenty years after Bernard Darniche won the Monte, at the end of a memorable final night. Designed as a successor to the Fulvia and to challenge the Porsche 911 and Renault Alpine, the Stratos was born with the backing of Cesare Fiorio, who was then the boss of the Squadra Corse and it would radically change the face of rallying. It was not based on a road car, but was designed purely to go rallying, just like any prototype or single seater racing car. Low and short, based on the Bertone Carabo, a concept car shown at the 1970 Turin Motor Show, it had all round independent suspension and centrally mounted engine at the rear. It seemed too fragile to be a rally car. And yet, just one year after its debut on the 1972 Tour of Corsica, Sandro Munari and Jean-Claude Andruet took it to the first of a series of wins. The first in the world championship went to the Italian on the 1974 San Remo.

For the next three seasons, until 1976, the Stratos reigned supreme in the world of rallying. The works team collected a mass of wins and titles in the hands of Munari of course and also Waldegaard, Andersson, Darniche, Alen and Pinto. The end came with the merging of Fiat and Lancia's sporting aspirations. It had to make way for the Fiat 131 Abarth, which was equally effective but nowhere near as exciting.

In France, the importer Andre Chardonnet with Bernard Darniche at the wheel, continued to carry the torch until 1981 and a sixth win on the Tour of Corsica. Climbing to the top rung of the podium no less than forty one times, Darniche holds the record for the number of wins in a Stratos. ■

1	Lancia Stratos	50	14	Lancia Delta S4	10
2	Ford EscortRS	46		Mitsubishi Ev.3	10
3	Peugeot 205 T16 Ev2	44	16	Austin Metro 6R4	6
4	Audi Quattro	42		Fiat 131 Abarth	6
5	Peugeot 205T16	30		Subaru Impreza WRC	6
6	Lancia 037	20		Subaru Impreza 2000	6
7	Mini Cooper S	18		Toyota Celica 4WD	6
	Lancia Delta Integrale	18	21	Datsun Violet	4
9	Audi Quattro S1	16		Lancia Delta HF	4
	Alpine Renault A110	16		Mitsubishi Ev.5	4
	Ford Escort Cosworth	16		Renault 5 turbo Maxi	4
12	Peugeot 206WRC	14		Talbot Sunbean	4
	Porsche 911	14			

CO-DRIVER OF THE MIL

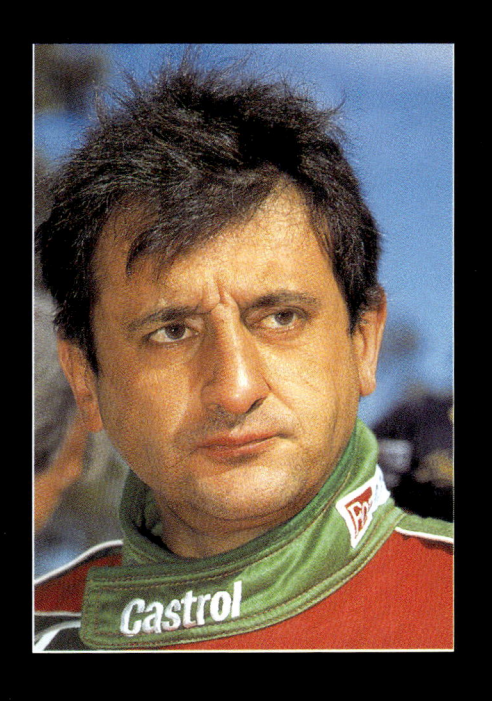

...NNIUM

Some have spent their lives riding shotgun alongside the best drivers, while others have become major players in the sport.

On the strength of his performances in the hot seat, Jean Todt deserves the title of co-driver of the millennium. Younger voters were no doubt also influenced by his success as Peugeot boss in rallies, rally raids and sports cars and more recently with Ferrari in Formula 1. But drivers of all generations voted for him as the best of the bunch. Walter Rohrl, Hannu Mikkola and Richard Burns all placed him third. Ove Andersson, Jean-Pierre Nicolas, Jean Ragnotti, Markku Alen, Juha Kankkunen, Michele Mouton, Francois Delecour and Colin McRae put him second. Shekhar Mehta, the king of the African tracks, where Todt was so successful put his name at the top of the list.

Jean Todt's Ferrari team won the F1 world championship in 2000 at the same time as his former driver Jean-Pierre Nicolas took the rally title with Peugeot and the 206 WRC. Although Todt's world is now far removed from the service areas and stages, he is still a rallyman. If one listens to his former colleagues and present friends, he still takes an interest in the progress of the Lion and its latest little pocket rocket.

Jim Clark and Dan Gurney were his first heros, but it was road cars that introduced him to the world of competition in 1964 at the wheel of a Mini-Cooper. Two years later he stood in for Guy Chasseuil's sick co-driver on the Criterium des Cevennes. While racing on the tracks, Todt became a respected rally navigator. Then, in 1969 he decided to stick to co-driving and his watchword was perfection. He would not allow himself a single mistake. The die was cast. The list of drivers whom he sat alongside is impressive and included, Jean-Francois Piot, Jean-Pierre Nicolas, Jean Vinatier, Jean-Claude Andruet, Jean-Luc Therier, Bernard Consten, Jean-Pierre Beltoise, Guy Frequelin were his principal French partners, while representing the rest of the world were Rauno Aaltonen, Ove Andersson, Hannu Mikkola, Achim Warmbold and Timo Makinen. The list of cars is equally long; Alpine, Fiat Abarth, BMW, Mercedes, Peugeot 304, 504, 504 V6 Coupe. So many kilometres in so many countries and several wins. The Constructors' Championship came with Talbot and Guy Frequelin at the end of 1981. Having accomplished that particular task, he immediately retired from the cockpit to take up a new challenge as the boss of Peugeot Talbot Sport, running the 205 Turbo 16 project. The rest is history. So is he the co-driver or team manager of the century? It does not really matter as the voting was mixed: Nicolas and Andersson voted for Todt, Rohrl for Geistdorfer, Munari for Manucci, Biaison for Siviero, Alen for Kivimaki, Sainz for Moya, Delecour for Grataloup, Michele Mouton for Fabrizia Pons and Tommi Makinen for Harjanne and Mannisenmaki. It is obvious that the key here is friendship and loyalty.

What was your favourite rally?
The 1978 Tour of South America.

What car did you like best?
In rallying, it was probably the Matra 650 with which, Jean-Pierre Beltoise, Patrick Depailler and myself won the Tour de France.

Is there a car that you would have liked to co-drive in?
I rode in so many that I don't think there is a single one that I did not manage to have a go in.

And what about a driver you would have liked to have worked with?
I think the answer is probably the same, although I would have been happy to do a rally with Walter Rohrl. I think I rode with almost all the best drivers in the world.

Were you tempted to be a driver?
Of course! At first I thought that co-driving would be a springboard to becoming a driver. Then, when this might have been possible, I had built up a level of credibility as a co-driver which could open up new horizons for me at the highest level. That's why I concentrated on co-driving.

Do you think rallies are easier today?
Rallying has changed a great deal. I think it was more of an adventure in my day. We sometimes went several days and nights without stopping and we spent longer on the recces. I think the modern rallies are less demanding than in my day.

Do you think a win today feels the same as back in the 70s and 80s?
A win at this level will always retain its prestige, but it is difficult to compare the two eras.

If a Historic Rally series was created, with events run the way they were, would you take part?
I would really love to take part in that type of event. Unfortunately, my current job means I do not have a moment to spare for anything else. ■

JEAN TODT

1	Jean Todt	70	Risto Mannisenmaki	10
2	Ilkka Kivimaki	42	Derek Ringer	10
3	Arne Hertz	40	Daniel Grataloup	10
4	Seppo Harjanne	38	Vincent Laverne	10
5	Luis Moya	30	Mario Mannucci	10
6	Christian Geistdorfer	24	17 Bruno Berglund	6
7	Fabrizia Pons	24	Bjorn Cederberg	6
8	Fred Gallagher	18	David Richards	6
9	Henry Liddon	16	Hans Thorzelius	6
10	Juha Piironen	10	21 «Biche»	4
	Tiziano Siverio	10	Terry Harryman	4

THE UNFORGETTABLE DRIVER

1. A Talbot driver for the 1980 and '81 seasons, he contributed to the team winning the constructors's world championship in 1981.

2. San Remo 1985 and one of his best results at the wheel of a Lancia 037.

3. An all-Finnish podium at the finish of the 1986 Monte Carlo.

4. He would achieve his greatest successes at the wheel of the Lancia Delta S4.

5. 20 years after his father won the event, Henri took victory in the Monte Carlo Rally in 1986.

Never crowned world champion, he only won three rallies, but Henri Toivonen made his mark on the history of rallying. Fifteen years after his death, his peers had no hesitation in electing him as "The unforgettable driver of the millennium."

HENRI TOIVONEN

He died in 1986, the golden age of rallying when the Group B cars meant that the sport had no trouble finding its way onto prime time television.

It happened on 2nd May and once again news bulletins featured rallying. This time however, the images on the screen were not those of action on the track or victory celebrations. For the second year running, Lancia had withdrawn its cars from the event in a gesture of mourning and respect; the team too distraught to continue. One year after the death of Attilio Bettega, Henri Toivonen and his co-driver Sergio Cresto had lost their lives during the rally of the thousand corners in Corsica. Henri was the son of Pauli, who had been the European Champion and winner of the Monte Carlo rally in the Sixties. Henri was a worthy successor to the list of Finns, long before Makinen and Gronholm.

The world of rallying was suddenly in mourning for this young man of 29, who had not yet built up a track record to rival a Rohrl or Blomquist or Alen. But his talent had exploded on the scene a couple of years earlier. Everyone who knew him recalls his kindness and charisma. At least, in the final six months of his life, he had started to fulfill his potential.

It had taken a long time. At the age of twenty four, he won the 1980 RAC Rally in a Talbot Sunbeam, just two years after following his father's footsteps in signing a contract with Citroen. Then, Henri's career appeared to stall. He did a second season with Talbot in the year when they won the constructors' title, then a further two with Opel alongside Rohrl and Vatanen. After that came a year in the European Championship at the wheel of a Porsche 911, which takes us to 1985 and his arrival in the prestigious Lancia team.

Life was not easy at first. He went off in Portugal, when he was setting fastest times and then came a big crash in the Costa Smeralda Rally in the European Championship. But then came the fabulous Delta S4 to replace the Rally 037, which had reached the end of its competitive life. He took a great win on the RAC with this real Group B car fitted with four wheel drive and a turbo, which was quite capable of chasing down the Peugeot 205 and Audi Quattro. 1986 started with an accident on a road section on the Monte, but then he staged an incredible comeback worthy of Vatanen's a year earlier or Darniche's back in 1979. This second consecutive win was accompanied by rumours of cheating, involving a change of car, but this did nothing to damage Toivonen's growing reputation and his position as a fancied runner for the title.

But then came Corsica and its eighteenth stage, from Corte to Taverna, which was run under heavy black clouds. In the seventeen previous stages, Henri had shown the others the way; the pursuing pack led by the 205 of Bruno Saby, who would go on take a sad win.

Coming as it did after the accidents involving Bettega, Surer, and the Santos crash in Portugal which had resulted in the death of spectators and a few other less serious incidents, Toivonen's crash signalled the end for the Group B cars as well as the Group S class which was due to succeed it. These monsters had become too quick and too hard to handle, as they were only barely adapted to the roads on which they performed. Toivonen had gone, so had Group B: nothing would ever be the same again.

Rallying entered one of its least interesting periods after losing a man who was set to be a hero of the sport. Markku Alen, Didier Auriol, Hannu Mikkola and Carlos Sainz, world champions all, voted for Toivonen as the most unforgettable driver. He deserved his place amongst them. ∎

All our thanks to those who voted:
Markku Alen, Ove Andersson, Didier Auriol, Miki Biasion, Stig Blomqvist, Richard Burns, François Delecour, Juha Kankkunen, Simo Lampinen, Colin McRae, Tommi Makinen, Shekhar Mehta, Hannu Mikola, Michèle Mouton, Sandro Munari, Jean-Pierre Nicolas, Jean Ragnotti, Walter Rohrl, Carlos Sainz, Timo Salonen, Ari Vatanen.

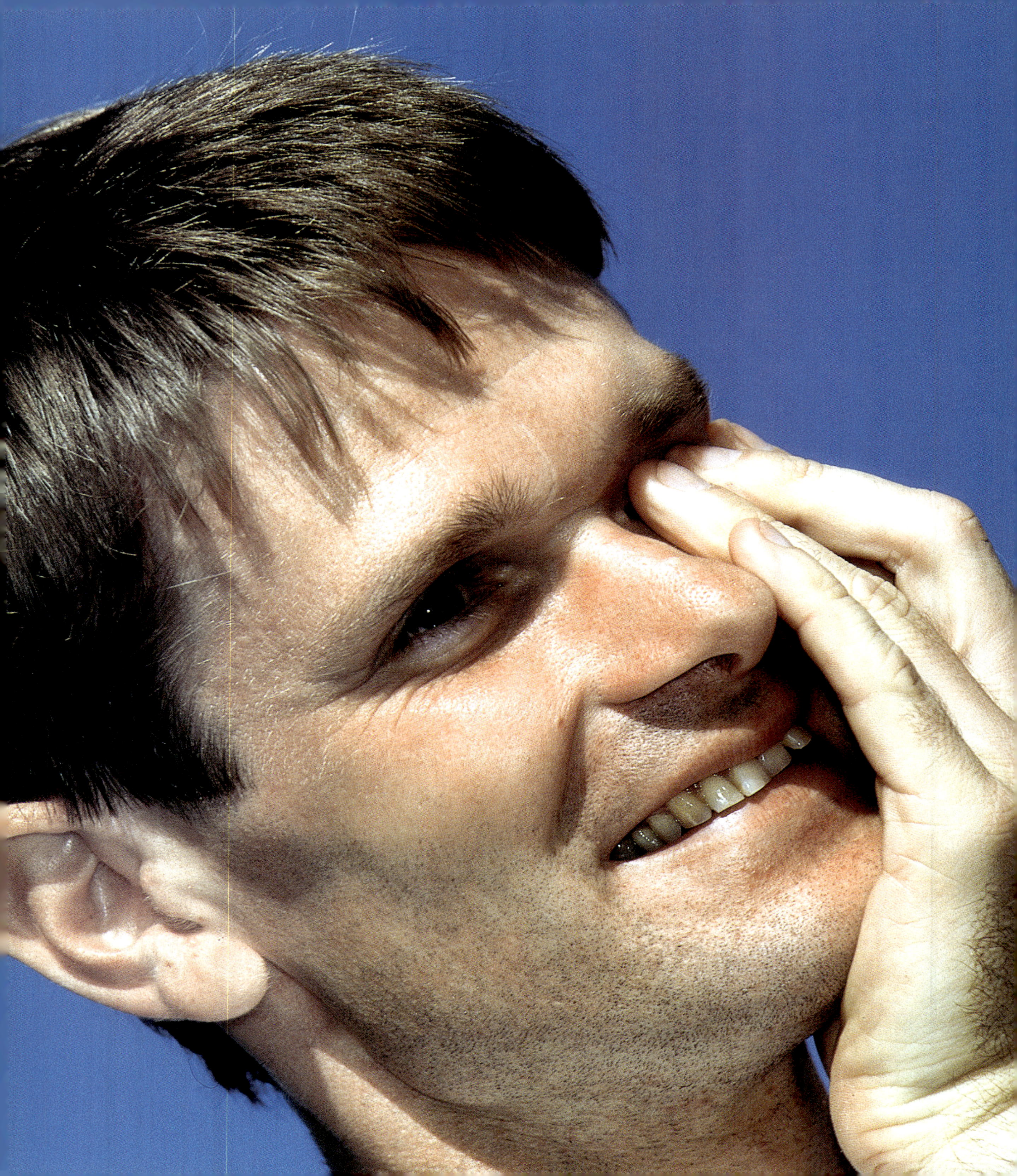

SUPERMARCUS

Marcus Gronholm is the 2000 world champion. Of that there is no doubt. But the marvellous paradox is that win or lose, it did not really matter. "Whatever happens, Marcus will be rated as the best driver of the year," reckoned an amazed Malcolm Wilson, one third of the way through the season. The Ford boss succinctly summed up the young man's surprising rise to stardom. He built his title piece by piece on this, his first ever complete round the world rally trip. He did it with style and talent, showing real conviction when the chips were down.

The fairytale really started on the Swedish Rally. His win was met with more than a simple accolade. He was inducted into a very exclusive private club and he was royally anointed by the masters of the sport, who had waited for him to emerge from the final stage. Tommi Makinen, the king of rallying was delighted for the youngster, hugging him and patting him on the back. Usually not very expansive, the four times world champion did not hold back from showing his feelings. It was not over emotional, because we are talking about Finns after all. Above all, it was a poignant moment.

On that February 13th, having just won his first ever world championship rally, the long man from Espoo had set out his stall and sent out a warning to all his rivals. It was especially impressive as he beat Makinen fair and square on an event that Tommi had virtually made his own in the past, stamping his authority on the event. "Marcus is a great driver," affirmed the beaten man, without any hint of hypocrisy. "Beating Tommi makes it even better," added the winner. For once the Finns were pretty chatty.

Two events later in Portugal, it was England's Richard Burns who won, to take the lead in the championship. Makinen realised his title was under threat. "Yes, Richard has shown he will be a dangerous rival for the title, maybe the most dangerous, but on an equal level with Marcus."

Taking the decision to sign up Gronholm showed amazing foresight on the part of Peugeot. "To be honest, I never stop congratulating myself for having signed up Marcus," admitted Jean-Pierre Nicolas, the boss of Peugeot's rallying department.

The first contact was made by telephone. That was back in the days when Peugeot was still dreaming of rally success and building up its team. "It was in the early summer of '98," recalled Gronholm. "I heard that the team was planning a world championship comeback. I asked a journalist for Nicolas' phone number and I called him immediately. "Ah yes.....Gronholm..." he answered, with a lot of long silences. I don't think he really had any idea who was calling. Gronholm, Radstrom, some guy from Scandinavia anyway. He said he was coming to Finland for the 1000 Lakes, so I immediately sent him my dossier. Then we met at the rally on the first day. I was third so I think it was a good time to talk, don't you agree?"
At the wheel of a semi-works Toyota, Gronholm had once again done enough to get himself noticed. So much so in fact, that offers rained down from the constructors, most notably Ford and Subaru. "But I decided to be loyal to Peugeot, who in the final analysis had been the first team to take a real interest in me. I had a better feeling about them on a human front. The only problem was that for the first year of the 206, Peugeot only wanted to offer me five rallies in 1999. Actually, I remembered what they had done in the Eighties. If they had been so good back then, I felt they could do it again and in a short space of time. I preferred to bet on the future."
All the same, it was an unusual return to grace in 1998. At exactly thirty years of age, he was at a key point in his career. It could have gone either way; success or anonymity, but Gronholm found the wherewithal to turn things around. "Back in 1996, I had given myself to the end of '98 to get myself a works drive. If I had not done it by then, I would have stopped. It really was my last chance."
He would have gone back to his farm at Inkoo, fifty kilometres from Helsinki, where the family worked its 63 hectares of wheat, wheat and more wheat. He would have donned his boots and returned to the quiet life, with no regrets." I don't do anything there anymore. Now I am a professional driver, I have rented my land to my cousin." Only rented mind, because all this is temporary, as one day he will go back to Inkoo on a full time basis, where his wife and three children await his return. "I took the farm on when I was nineteen, after I came out of agricultural college. The land had belonged to my father and ever since he died, when I was only thirteen, I was expected to take it over."

Even though he now had responsibilities, he started rallying that same year, after he had completed his education. "I had been driving for ages, but you are not allowed to compete until you are old enough to have a license. In the meantime, I tried my hand at motocross, but I was too tall and I had problems with my knees."
On the face of it, Marcus Gronholm could be yet another in a long line of Finns, who learned their art working the land, while driving down the dusty tracks in summer and across the frozen lakes in winter. In fact, he comes from a somewhat different mould to the Mikkolas, Makinens and Salonens of this world; not only because of his size, unusual in a sport more used to the jockey-like proportions of its Formula One colleagues, but also because of his background.
"His family comes from Finland's Swedish minority," explained Juha Piironen, long time co-driver to Juha Kankkunen and something of a historian on the sport of rallying. "They tend to be more open. Guys like Makinen and Kankkunen, you meet them in the street and they will only say hello if they have something to ask you. It comes from a certain coldness or shyness...whatever. But Gronholm will always stop for a chat. He's just a nice chap." The man whose surname means "green island" in Swedish is very approachable. Just ask Ove Andersson, a fellow Swede and, more importantly the boss of Toyota, who was the first to believe in him and gave him the odd drive whenever he could afford to do so. "He's not just a great guy, he's quick too."
Ask his current team and they will tell you they were immediately won over by his simplicity, his kindness and his availability. There are never any tantrums, no raised voices and never the slightest sign of any tension. It did not take long for his engineer, Francois-Xavier Demaison to realise the calibre of the man he was working with and he soon donned a cap in the colours of his driver (1.) This two man team was put together simply because Demaison speaks English and the relationship has worked out fine. "Marcus is demanding, but no more than is to be expected," said the engineer. "He is also very close to the team. We spend quite a lot of time together at work and outside office hours too. He is always with us." Apparently his driving style also sets him apart from his fellow Finns. "He doesn't slide the car very much. He has a delicate touch and is very precise," contined Demaison. "He spends as much time as possible in a straight line and so he spends more time on the limit, which

Sweden 1995: First rally in a mini-season of world championship events, which was overshadowed by too many mechanical problems.

1000 Lakes 1991: Alongside Juha Repo, Juha Kankkunen's current co-driver, he finished thirteenth at the wheel of an ancient Celica.

Finland 1997: Marcus is part of the official Toyota team as the new Corolla makes its debut.

1000 Lakes 1996: His first drive in the Celica GT-Four, he just misses out on third place.

Portugal 1999: Called in to replace Freddy Loix, who was injured in the Safari, he impressed the Mitsubishi team, before retiring with gearbox failure.

means he is always close to going off!" The Gronholm crew is a family affair as his long time co-driver, Timo Rautiainen is also his brother-in-law, having married Marcus's big sister. He knows him better than anyone and accepts he will be in for the odd scary moment now and again. "But his driving style is very natural and easy. It's not at all brutal, but is actually nice and flowing." Nevertheless, Timo sometimes has to calm Marcus down and he does not always succeed.

Another element that sets Gronholm apart, is that unlike the majority of the "Flying Finns," he does not come from anywhere near Jyvaskyla, home to the Thousand Lakes rally, with its bumps and yumps. As a kid, he never went and stood in the forests, to be eaten alive by the mosquitos and showered in mud, to see Aaltonen, Vatanen, Toivonen and others. He never had the support of Timo Jouhki, Finland's champion-maker, who thanks to Kankkunen and Makinen to name but two, brought no less than eight world championships back to Finland. This meant he was never part of the local "rally mafia" who would always put their hand in the pocket to find some funding for a new young hopeful.
In short, he was never really recognised or rated by his peers and fellow countrymen. He suffered accordingly, but he hides the fact. "I don't know why. Maybe because I have a different way of working. That's all I can think of. I do everything myself. Toni Gardemeister got a factory drive with Seat when he was twenty five. Good for him. I know how hard it is to get something like that. I have always been confident, because I knew I had the speed. But I get on fine with the rest of the boys. That's just the way it is and I had to do it myself." That included his first ever win in his first season of local events, which he tackled at the wheel of an old Ford Escort, which he drove when he was not at the controls of a combine harvester.
He won his first national title, in the Junior category in 1988, before taking the Finnish championship four times (1994, '96, '97 and '98) and he also shone on the Thousand Lakes. He does not say much about it as the subject seems to bore him. What he takes pride in is the fact he did it all himself - the self-made rallyman who followed in his father's footsteps.

Because Gronholm senior found time to do more than till the soil. He was a famous local driver, a national champion, who died a the wheel of a rally car while testing for Fiat in 1981. It is natural therefore, that part of what Marcus has already achieved was built on the desire to emulate and surpass his father's achievements; to honour him in this way. "The accident was nothing to do with rallying," was all Marcus would say about it, when he won his first world championship event on 13th February 2000, when he dedicated the win to his father. It is his justification for saying that if his four year old son wants to follow in his footsteps, he will neither encourage nor discourage him.
He knows the real cost of danger and it has not put him off joining the list of on the limit racers like Vatanen and Makinen and the President for Life of this exclusive club, McRae, who have built their careers on their willingness to push to the outer edge of the envelope.

Back in November 1999, Gronholm's face betrayed despair and anger after yet another massive accident on the Rally of Great Britain, where he was as sad as the miserable autumn day in Wales. A momentary lapse of concentration, a corner which came up too quickly, a heavy right foot and one, two, three, six rolls. The 206 was destroyed and the driver was beside himself with bitterness. "It was the biggest accident of my career." It was also one of the most stupid, given that he was lying third at the time. "That accident, which came after a similar one in San Remo, two months earlier, followed by his first win, completely changed him," claimed Jean-Pierre Nicolas. "From that point on, he put his rallies together more carefully. He has matured from the impetuous charger he was before." The 1999 RAC and the 2000 Swedish were therefore the key moments in his career as a professional. He was always quick, but he soon proved how good he was, by learning rapidly on the unknown that was a tarmac surface. "This is my weak point, I have to improve on tarmac." Looking at his 2000 results, that particular task has already been completed. There is more to come. "Marcus will be quicker in 2001," reckoned Timo Rautiainen. If he continues in this vein, then he will stamp his authority on the championship for years to come. How do you say "a star is born" in Finnish?

1.- One third into the season, the Peugeot management pointed out to its mechanics and engineers that it was not the done thing to wear a cap in the colours of one particular driver. They should wear the official team headgear instead. A sad case of uniformity.
2.- The Mantta Rally, the first official win for the 206 WRC. ■

1. Acropolis 1990, Markku Alen
2. Sweden 1996, Didier Auriol
3. Acropolis 1994, Colin McRae

HAPPY SUBARU
Prodrive's spirit of rallying

4. Australia 1993, Colin McRae
5. Acropolis 1990, Markku Alen and Ilkka Kivimaki
6. 1000 Lakes 1993, Ari Vatanen
7. Sweden 1993, Hannu Mikkola

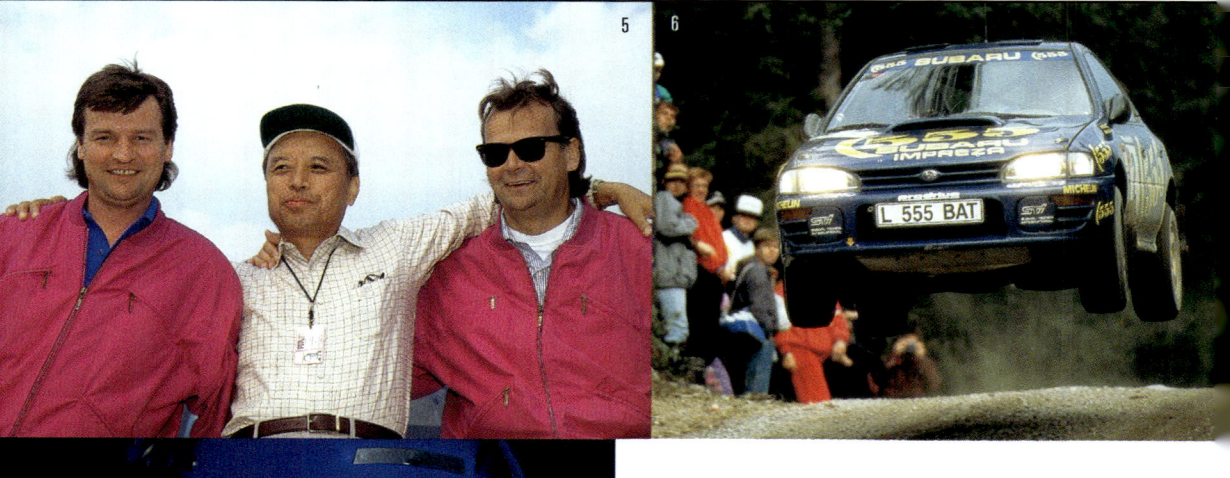

BIRTHDAY

8. RAC 1995, 1st world championship for Subaru
9. 1000 Lakes 1993, Ari Vatanen
10. Australia 1997, Colin McRae

Twenty years of rallying since 1980 and four world titles have definitely changed Subaru's image. Cars that made their name as farmers' unbreakable runabouts have been transformed into undoubted thoroughbreds. Proof that competition improves the breed.

It has been a well orchestrated and remarkably successful campaign. In the course of twenty years, one of the smallest Japanese constructors has built up an incredible performance portfolio.

For the record, the marque with the constellation emblem decided to take part in its first world championship rally back in 1990, in the Safari, which has always been an important event for the Japanese. As the only constructor with an entirely four wheel drive range of cars, it was a logical move and Audi would go on to prove the worth of all wheel drive.

Subaru forged its link with Prodrive in 1989. The English company started by preparing a Legacy, which Markku Alen took to fourth place on the 1990 Thousand Lakes. Much of the marque's success was due to David Richards' brave decision to take on a wild young man in 1991. Two years later, Colin McRae gave Subaru its first ever win on a world championship event in New Zealand. The team progressed from then on. With an Imprezza 555, the Scotsman and the Japanese company took the title in 1995, before the constructor went on to repeat that feat in 1996 and '97. Recently, Subaru took the decision to stick with Prodrive until 2005. The current Impreze WRC P 2000 will be replaced by the WRX, starting with the 2001 Monte Carlo Rally. The story is not over yet! ∎

1. Spain 1995, Carlos Sainz
2. Monte-Carlo 1997, Piero Liatti

3. Safari 1997, 1st African win
4. Finland 1999, Juha Kankkunen

Simon Jean-Joseph

«I'm made up!»

Simon Jean-Joseph had a surprising season. Having started out on the roads of France, he ended up in style on those of the world. His return proved the merits of talent and efficiency.

Simon Jean-Joseph, how do you rate this surprising 2000 season?

This has been a dream season for me and on various different levels. I came out of 1999 feeling destroyed, after what happened with Ford. Life was difficult and I had to rebuild it. Thanks to the help of a lot of friends and supporters, starting with Motul, who came back to rallying after a long absence, I was able to put together an interesting and worthwhile programme.

At first, it was a case of tackling the French tarmac championship. It was a difficult time, especially as we experienced a few technical problems with the Subaru Impreza WRC on the first two rallies of the season and later. Then, when it started to come together, on rallies like the Alsace-Vosges, our main rivals in the Citroen team had made a lot of progress. Whenever we took a step forward, they took two!

But, the programme was a good one, in terms of experience and emotionally. There was a lot of satisfaction from managing the project. But in the long run, we were not on the pace and were just making up the numbers, which was of no interest to me, or my sponsors. Usually they are in business to win, fighting with equal equipment, but this was not the case.

So we had to look elsewhere and we turned our attention to the French loose surface championship. We did three of these events and won each time and on top of that, I really enjoyed myself. I fell in love with driving on the loose and with the series. In fact, these days when there is so much talk of promoting young drivers, what we need is a mixed championship and not just a tarmac one. Our roads have nothing to be ashamed of and this series should be created. It should be given more recognition so that more good drivers are attracted to it.

But at the same time, you worked with the factory Subaru team...

Yes, starting in January 2000. I had the pleasure and the honour of helping them with the P 2000 project. I drove both cars, the WRC 99 and the P 2000; thirty to forty kilometres with one and then with the other in back to back comparisons. It was an important job, but great fun as well. The first time I did it, I said to my co- driver Jack Boyere, "pinch me, because I think I'm dreaming! All this, just for us." We did an enormous amount of work. That helped me to progress a great deal in terms of my driving and my sensitivity to what the car was doing. It was great. Then, I did the Tour of Corsica and the San Remo for them, knowing that the Monte and Catalunya were both too early in the season. Whatever people think about my results, I feel I did exactly what was expected of me. I got better and quicker and on the San Remo, I was more aggressive. There was also a real feeling of confidence around me, which was completely different to 1999. All in all, in the space of two years I lived through two nice experiences, working with two different factory teams, with two different cars, using different tyres.

And what about 2001?

We are working on it. Subaru and Hyundai are two of the possibilities, maybe in the French Championship. We will see. ∎

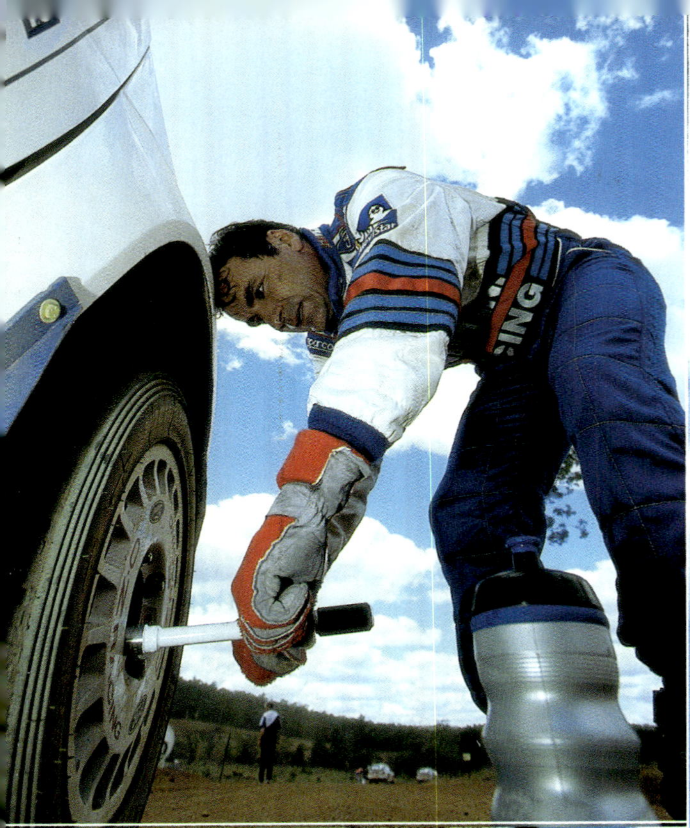

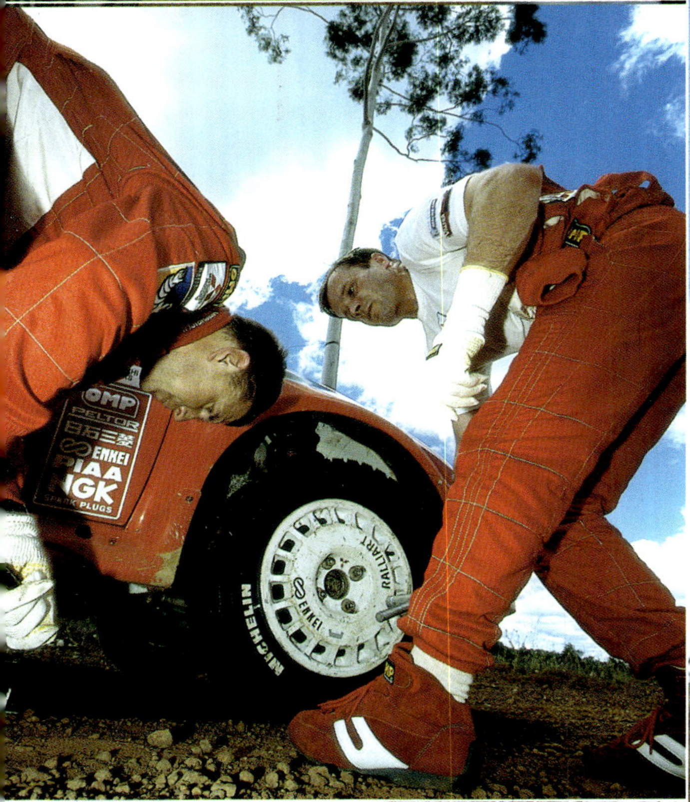
OMP
PELTOR
ENKEI
NGK
MICHELIN

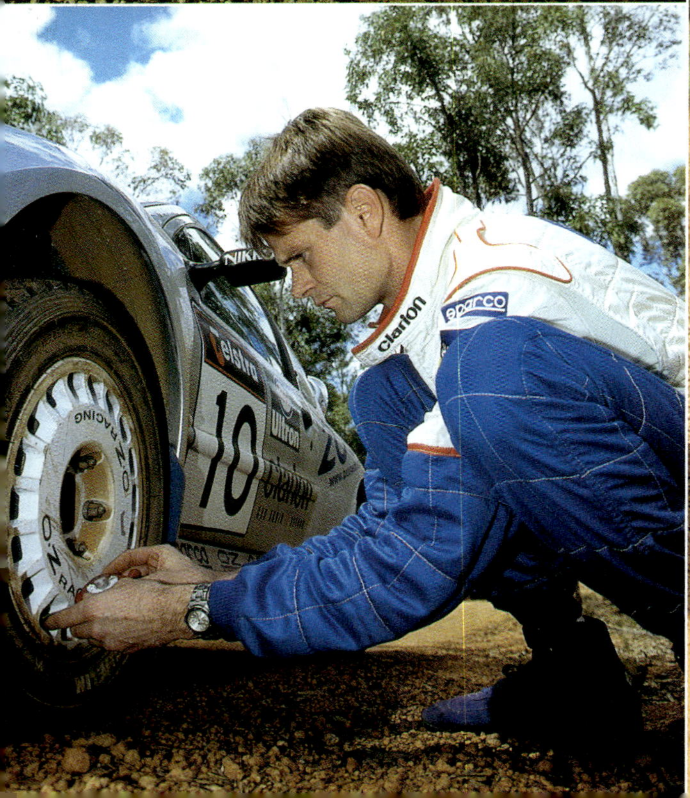
sparco
clarion
10

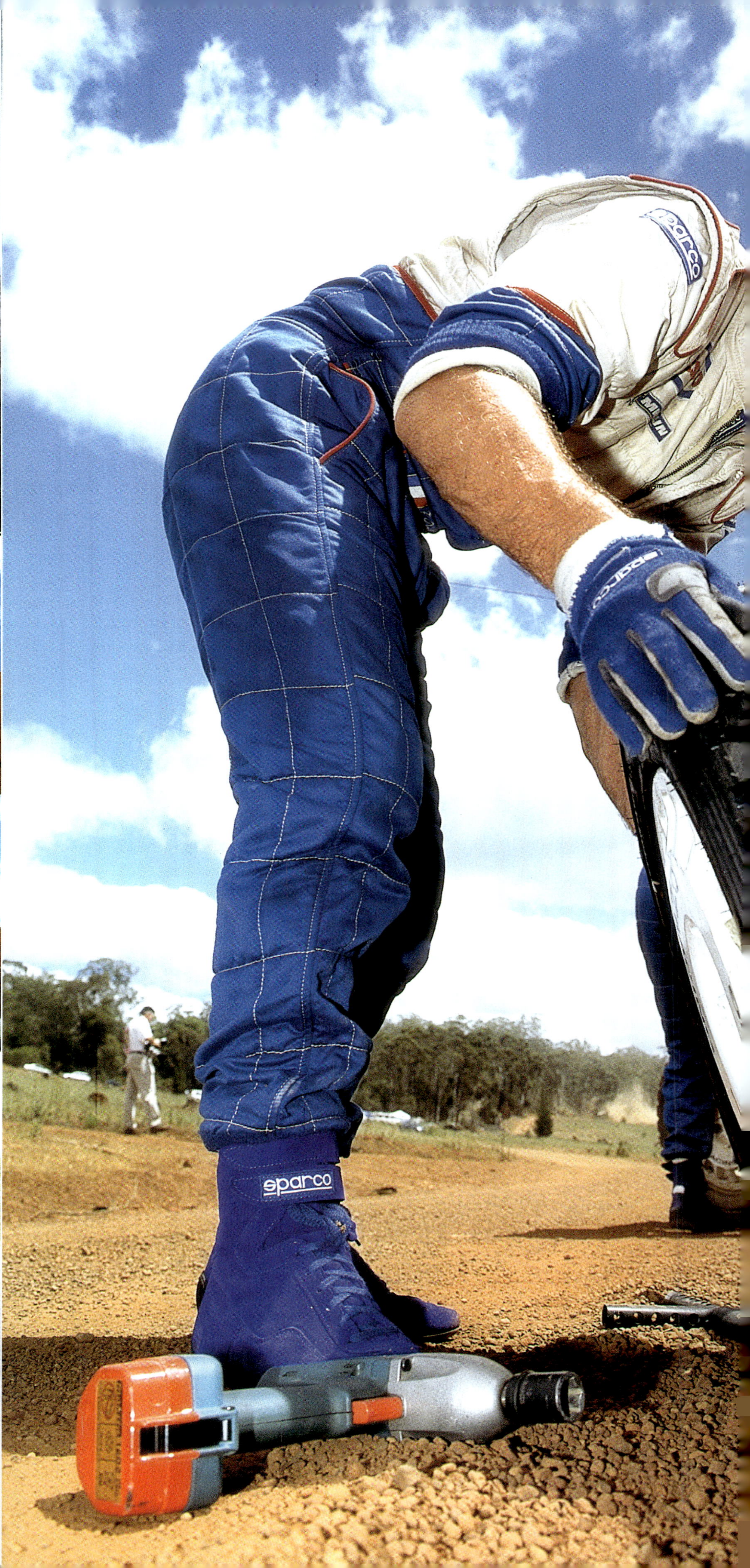
sparco

MICHELIN CHAMPION

At the end of one of the most closely fought World Rally Championships for years, Michelin won, taking its total to 30 titles; 15 drivers' and 15 constructors, including eight drivers' crowns and seven constructors' in the last ten years. These results reflect Michelin's continued presence at the very highest level of the sport.

When the teams left their European homes for the penultimate rally in Australia, the situation could not have been closer, with three teams, Peugeot-Michelin, Ford-Michelin and Subaru all in the hunt and no less than four drivers, Marcus Gronholm, Richard Burns, Colin McRae and Carlos Sainz, separated by just six little points. Victory for Peugeot in Perth tipped the title into the French constructor's lap with one event to go, while the drivers' crown would go down to the wire in Great Britain, where another strong performance from Marcus Gronholm saw him take the title in his first full season in the world championship.

One of the most important factors to emerge this season was the gain in performance from the WRC-Michelin, across a wide range of surfaces tackled in the course of the year. Not only did the Michelin tyres score yet another Grand Slam on tarmac with wins in the windswept Monte Carlo and on the very dry Catalunya event, as well as in Corsica and on the San Remo, it also won on a variety of loose surfaces, including two one-two finishes on the toughest of the European events, in Greece and Cyprus.

The only negative point this year came on Kenya's Safari Rally, where Michelin was unable to add to its total of seven wins since 1991 on African soil. Competitions Director Pierre Dupasquier affirmed that Michelin was determined to address this problem as soon as possible.

Despite this, with ten victories from the fourteen events of the 2000 championship, the company can rightly be proud of its record this year; a record which confirms Michelin's success on all surfaces and on two and four wheels.

Moya
Sainz
Telefonica MoviStar
www.fordracing.net
MARTINI
6
Valvoline
MICHELIN

MICHELIN
Clarion
16

8
Infineon
MICHELIN

SUCCESS ON ALL FRONTS

No other tyre manufacturer is as deeply involved in so many different forms of motorised sport at an international level. Without making any claims of false modesty, Michelin can well and truly claim to be at the top of the pyramid on both two and four wheels.
In 2000, Michelin yet again picked up an impressive array of titles, from the World Rally Championship to the 500 Motorcycle Grand Prix, the Le Mans 24 Hours, the World Superbike Championship and various off road motor cycle series, as well as a host of national titles, race and rally wins.
On top of all this, Michelin spent much of its time working throughout 2000 on entering Formula 1 in 2001.
Over the next twelve months, the battle in the top disciplines of motor sport are likely to be as closely fought as they were in 2000, with tyres as usual playing a decisive role, just as they did this year.

LE MANS 24 HOURS - 9 OUT OF 9!

The 2000 Le Mans 24 Hours saw Michelin shod cars take the top nine places, giving the manufacturer from Clermont Ferrand its most convincing result ever in this legendary French endurance race.
An all-Audi top three was also Michelin's third consecutive win at La Sarthe, each achieved with a different constructor, after an all-BMW top four in 1999 and a one-two finish for Porsche-Michelin in 1998. The win for Frank Biela/Tom Kristensen/Emmanuele Pirro last June was Michelin's ninth, since the race began back in 1923 and its seventh from the last twelve races.
Under this year's hot sun, which pushed track temperatures up to 42 C, Michelin's race team was delighted with the performance of its tyres throughout the race, especially the fact that their hot weather tyres were able to do three stints during the hottest part of the race. In fact, the performance and durability of the tyres was without a doubt the cornerstone of Michelin's success. Naturally, the tyres stood up even better in the cool of the night. As the track temperature dropped to 20 C, all the sports cars running on Michelin, were able to put three stints together during the night, which meant they could make up a lot of time during the pit stops, by not bothering to change tyres.

FORMULA 1,

Just over twelve months after officially announcing its plans to return to the fold, Michelin will once again compete in Formula 1, for the first time since 1984. Its first race will be the 2001 Australian Grand Prix in March. The French manufacturer understands better than most just what a challenge it is facing. It has a good track record to lean on with three drivers' titles, two constructors' and 59 wins from 112 grands prix starts between 1977 and 1984. Its return is eagerly awaited.
At the time of going to press, Michelin has already announced partnerships for this new phase in its history, with BMW-Williams, Jaguar, Benetton and Prost, with Toyota due to join in 2002. The first two mentioned have already been involved in a probing test programme over the past twelve months. Driving a 1999 Stewart and a Williams respectively, test drivers Tom Kristensen and Jorg Muller have done over 10,000 kilometres on a variety of tracks around Europe, developing and collecting data for next year's tyres.

MOTOR BIKES - GLOBAL SUCCESS ON TWO WHEELS

The 500 cc world championship has brought Michelin a great deal of success in 2000, celebrating not only its 250th win in a 500 grand prix, thanks to Alex Criville (Honda-Michelin) in May, but also its twelfth championship title with Kenny Roberts winning the 500 class on a Suzuki-Michelin. The championship provided one of the most spectacular and close fought series of the past few years. No fewer than eight riders were in the running for the crown, which finally went to the American in the penultimate race of the sixteen round series. ∎

THE STARS...

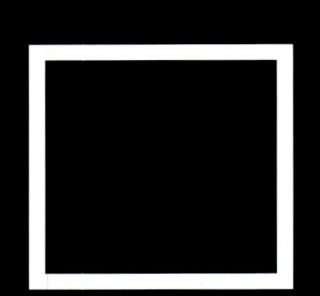

There were seven teams entered in 2000 and yet there were no less than 23 drivers who took their turn in the cockpit. Here we present a short tour of the main protagonists among the masters of sideways motoring.

MARCUS GRONHOLM
PEUGEOT

He was thirteenth in the 1999 championship and this year, the tall boy from Espoo was in contention throughout the year, finally taking the title at the final event. Everyone knew he had potential, but it was a big step from there to filling Tommi Makinen's shoes. Neither he nor his indefatigable partner Timo Rautiainen dared dream of doing it. But in this, the final season of the century, he bestrode the championship like a young colossus. He did not escape the crippling blow which saw all the Peugeots and Burns's Subaru freeze in the cold in Gap. But revenge was spectacular when he beat Makinen in Sweden, the four times champion's favourite playground. After that, he had to mark time for a while, while the Subarus held court and a few technical worries halted his progress. Then the summer finally went his way. He won in New Zealand and Finland, getting through the tarmac trials of Corsica and San Remo unscathed before winning Australia on a technicality. He was on his way to the top and a mature drive in Great Britain saw him take the title. The headstrong driver evolved considerably during the season, tempering his enthusiasm for bending bodywork and benefiting from the odd helping hand from Lady Luck. He showed great intelligence in the way he went about building his wins. Marcus really changed in 2000 as a driver, but the man remains the same.

IDENTITY CARD
- Nationality: Finnish
- Date of birth: 5 february 1968
- Place of birth: Espoo (Finland)
- Resident: Inkoo (Finland)
- Marital status: Married
- Children: 3 (Jessica, Johanna and Niclas)
- Hobbies: -
- Co-driver: Timo Rautiainen (Finnish)

CAREER
- First Rally: 1989
- Number of Rallies: 43
- Number of victories: 4

1996 - 10th in championship
1997 - 12th in championship
1998 - 16th in championship
1999 - 15th in championship
2000 - WORLD CHAMPION

RICHAR[D]
SUBARU

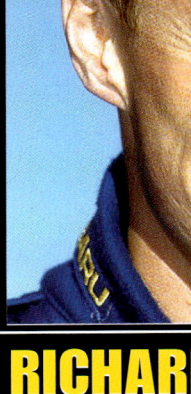

He thought he had [...]
easily. Runner up in [...]
Englishman must ha[ve...]
Tommi Makinen's s[...]
him felt the champi[on...]
be Makinen's main [...]
reckoned David Ric[hards...]
Portugal. Certainly, [...]
after the hiccough [...]
Impreza refused to s[...]
drove an intelligent [...]
yet his speciality. Th[...]
title with both hand[s...]
second place in Ca[...]
Richard was flying [...]
looked bright. Afte[r...]
six points coming [...]
enough for a cham[pionship...]
usually safe hands [...]
couple of bad crash[es...]
while, Gronholm wa[s...]
unwelcome pressur[e...]
he still had a great [...]
Still under thirty, h[e...]
maturity. Once he g[...]
bound to follow.

IDENTITY CARD
- Nationality: British
- Date of birth:
  17 january 1971
- Place of birth: Readi[ng] (England)
- Resident: Reading (England)
- Marital status: Single
- Hobbies: Motorbikes[,] Mountain-bike
- Co-driver: Robert Re[id] (British)

COLIN McRAE
FORD

McRae had a strange 2000 season. At first, it seemed the bad luck that had dogged him throughout 1999 was still lingering in the cockpit of his Focus. But then he won in Catalunya and again in Greece. He racked up several second places, including Finland where, in the past, he had found it hard to even stay on the road. This prompted some serious discussions with the Peugeot team. Then we came to Corsica. Highlander stuck his wheels in his kilt with an almighty crash. Despite having to undergo surgery and struggling to get back in the groove, he still managed to keep his title hopes alive up until his engine gave up the ghost in Australia. His turn will surely come again.

IDENTITY CARD
- Nationality: British
- Date of birth: 5 august 1968
- Place of birth: Lanark (Scotland)
- Resident: Scotland, Monaco
- Marital status: Married, 1 daughter
- Hobbies: Water-skiing, motocross
- Co-driver: Nicky Grist (British)

CAREER
- First Rally: 1986
- Number of Rallies: 101
- Number of victories: 20

1992 - 8th in championship
1993 - 5th in championship
1994 - 4th in championship
1995 - WORLD CHAMPION
1996 - 2nd in championship
1997 - 2nd in championship
1998 - 3rd in championship
1999 - 6th in championship
2000 - 4th in championship

TOMI MAKINEN
MITSUBISHI

It's not easy being a four times world champion. Having won so much, having won nearly everything, what more can a man do? Tommi Makinen lifted off a bit this year. His car was getting old, despite an umpteenth makeover and towards the end of the year, the Finn seemed to lack motivation. However, it all got off to the best possible start with a win on the Monte. After that came disappointment and despair. Right at the end though, some of the old spark returned. But The Cat had to suffer the pain of disqualification after winning in Australia. Let's hope the team find him a car worthy of his talent and his reputation as the best driver in the world.

IDENTITY CARD
- Nationality: Finnish
- Date of birth: 26 june 1964
- Place of birth: Puuppola (Finland)
- Resident: Puuppola and Monaco
- Marital status: Single
- Children: 1 son (Henry)
- Hobbies: Golf, Skiing, Hiking
- Co-driver: Risto Mannisenmaki (Finnish)

CAREER
- First Rally: 1987
- Number of Rallies: 97
- Number of victories: 20

1990 - 20th in championship
1991 - 29th in championship
1993 - 10th in championship
1994 - 10th in championship
1995 - 5th in championship
1996 - WORLD CHAMPION
1997 - WORLD CHAMPION
1998 - WORLD CHAMPION
1999 - WORLD CHAMPION
2000 - 5th in championship

FRANÇOIS DELECOUR
PEUGEOT

He would mumble the same mantra rather too often: "I don't know the stages as well as the others." There were few rallies that escaped this lament from the lips of Father Francois. It was true that he lacked experience when held up against the masters of the universe. However, although he was never supposed to do the full season, he actually only missed out on the Safari. Delecour did what was expected of him, whether on the first leg in New Zealand or during his duels with Panizzi in Corsica and San Remo. He scored points for Peugeot but found it hard to accept his role as Gronholm's lieutenant and on two occasions, that of number two to Panizzi. It was not easy for the ambitious and emotional lad.

IDENTITY CARD
- Nationality: French
- Date of birth: 30 august 1962
- Place of birth: Cassel (France)
- Resident: Plan de la Tour (France)
- Marital status: Single
- Children: 2 (Anne-Lise, Gabriel)
- Hobbies: Jet-ski, mountain-bike
- Co-driver: Daniel Grataloup (French)

CAREER
- First Rally: 1984
- Number of Rallies: 71
- Number of victories: 4

1991 - 7th in championship
1992 - 6th in championship
1993 - 2nd in championship
1994 - 8th in championship
1995 - 4th in championship
1997 - 17th in championship
1998 - 10th in championship
1999 - 16th in championship
2000 - 6th in championship

PETTER SOLBERG
FORD . SUBARU

Youngsters can be ungrateful. That's what Malcolm Wilson must have been thinking late last summer, when the young man he plucked from obscurity at home, reneged on his long term contract with Ford to join Subaru. After a nondescript 1999 season, Solberg proved this year that he really is the bright young hope. He picked up a few fastest stage times, some points and was always on the attack. He did all he could to get himself noticed, especially as the team had told him not to worry about how many cars he broke! It worked and he emerged to pocket a sizeable amount of dollars from Subaru, along with a major programme for 2001.

IDENTITY CARD
- Nationality: Norwegian
- Date of birth: 18 november 1974
- Place of birth: Spydeberg (Norway)
- Resident: Norway
- Marital status: Single
- Co-driver: Phil Mills (British)

CAREER
- First Rally: 1996
- Number of Rallies: 18
- Number of victories: 0

1999 - 18th in championship
2000 - 10th in championship

DIDIER AURIOL
SEAT

Is there a stranger driver than Didier Auriol? A perfectionist to his fingertips, in the past he was often incapable of driving the car, if it was not set up to the nearest micron. This year however, he gave his all, hustling around in a Cordoba WRC E2. To say the Spanish car was less than perfect is an example of the art of understatement. Numerous problems with power steering gave the Frenchman a serious work-out and the differentials often made the car handle like a drunken donkey. The little yellow coupe hardly ever ran completely trouble free. It was impressive therefore to see the man fight the machine as if the outcome of the championship depended on it, determined as he was to prove that age had not withered him. He rebuilt his reputation with a zen like attitude to the job in hand. His reward was a Peugeot contract for 2001.

IDENTITY CARD
- Nationality: French
- Date of birth: 18 august 1958
- Place of birth: Montpellier (France)
- Resident: Millau (France)
- Marital status: Married
- Children: 2 (Robin and Diane)
- Hobbies: Golf, mountain bike
- Co-driver: Denis Giraudet (French)

CAREER
- First Rally: 1984
- Number of Rallies: 122
- Number of victories: 19

1988 - 6th in championship
1989 - 4th in championship
1990 - 2nd du championnat
1991 - 3rd in championship
1992 - 3rd in championship
1993 - 3rd in championship
1994 - WORLD CHAMPION
1995 - Excluded (Toyota)
1996 - 25th in championship
1997 - 11th in championship
1998 - 5th in championship
1999 - 3rd in championship
2000 - 12th in championship

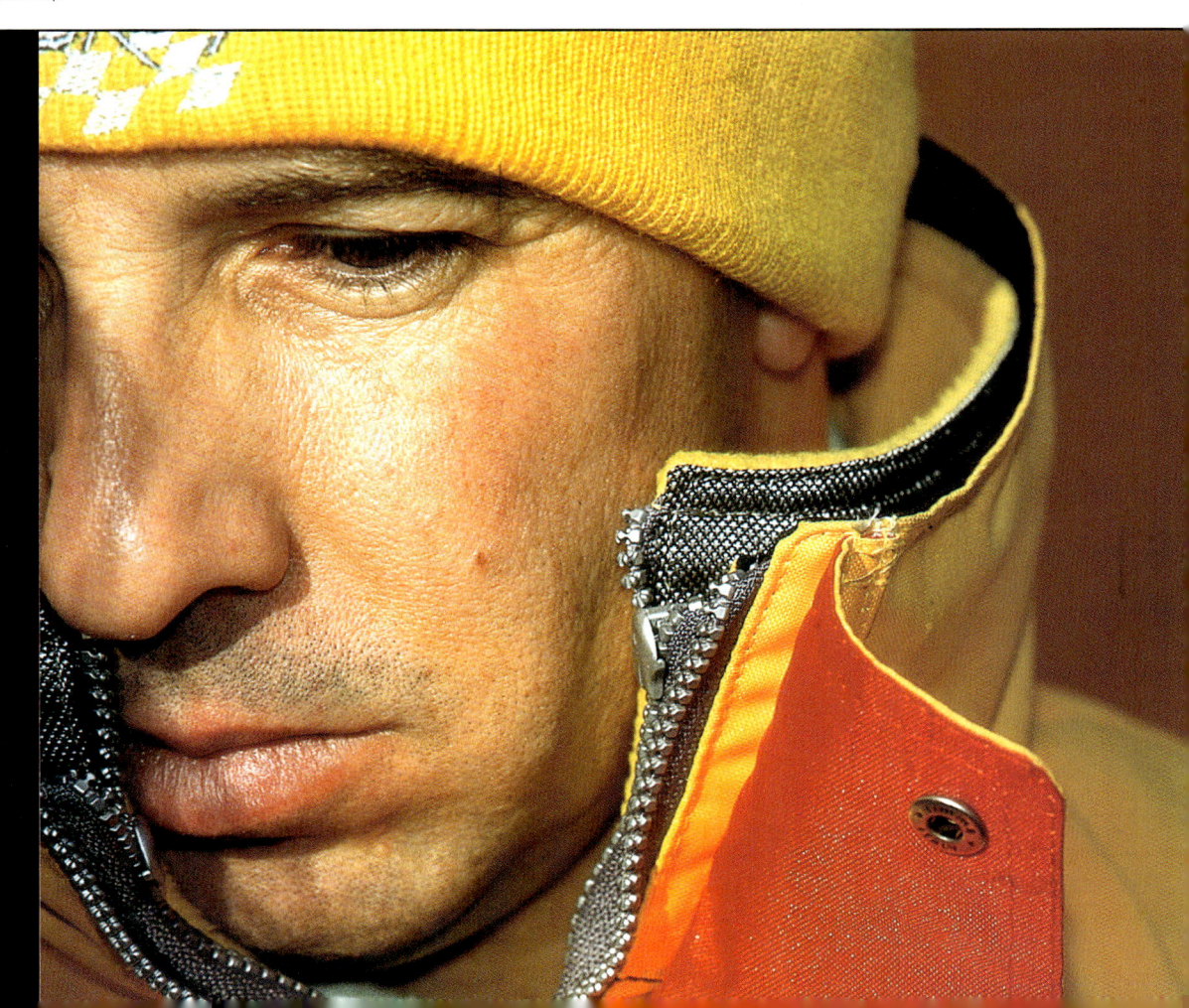

JUHA KANKKUNEN
SUBARU

This year, there was something about the big Mr. K, which reminded one of an old boxer who had climbed into the ring once too often. In 1999, the four times world champion had managed to win twice, but this year, he was but a shadow of his former self. At the wheel of the Subaru, he was never able to match his team-mate's performance. He was generally lacklustre, which proved costly for his team, who needed him to finish in the points to bolster their title challenge. Hating tarmac rallies, he even handed his car over to Jean-Joseph. But that's typical KKK; laid back as ever as he puffs on a cigarillo. With the young guard knocking on the Subaru door, he might not compete that often in 2001.

IDENTITY CARD
- Nationality: Finnish
- Date of birth: 2 april 1959
- Place of birth: Laukaa (Finland)
- Resident: Laukaa
- Marital status: Married, 1 son (Tino)
- Hobbies: Golf, fishing
- Co-driver: Juha Repo (Finnish)

CAREER
- First Rally: 1979
- Number of Rallies: 152
- Number of victories: 23

1983 - 16th in championship
1984 - 24th in championship
1985 - 5th in championship
1986 - WORLD CHAMPION
1987 - WORLD CHAMPION
1989 - 3rd in championship
1990 - 3rd in championship
1991 - WORLD CHAMPION
1992 - 2nd in championship
1993 - WORLD CHAMPION
1994 - 3rd in championship
1995 - Excluded (Toyota)
1996 - 7th in championship
1997 - 4th in championship
1998 - 4th in championship
1999 - 4th in championship
2000 - 8th in championship

TONI GARDEMEISTER
SEAT

He was promoted as the latest little wonder to emerge from the stable of star maker Timo Joukhi, but Toni Gardemeister had difficulty living up to that reputation in his first world championship season with a works team. It was not really his fault as his Spanish mount had all the integrity of a paella dish. He tried to make up for its deficiencies by over-driving, with occasional disastrous consequences. On the Safari and in New Zealand he destroyed the car and almost his co-driver Paavo Lukander and himself along the way. But sometimes, just like his team leader, when the car was going well he managed to put in some good times.

IDENTITY CARD
- Nationality: Finnish
- Date of birth: 31 march 1975
- Place of birth: Kouvola (Finland)
- Resident: (Finland)
- Marital status: Single
- Co-driver: Paavo Lukander (Finnish)

CAREER
- First Rally: 1997
- Number of Rallies: 30
- Number of victories: 0

1999 - 10th in championship
2000 - 12th in championship

SIMON JEAN JOSEPH
SUBARU

After a disastrous time with Ford in 1999, there were few who rated the world championship chances of the young man from Martinique. They were not counting on his tenacity and his desire to prove that, given a good car, he deserved a drive. Subaru asked him to work on the development of the Impreza P2000 on tarmac. Jean-Jo did the job so well, he was offered Kankkunen's car for two events. In Corsica and San Remo, he did exactly what was expected of him; he brought home the points. He was happy, David Lapworth was happy and the mechanics were also happy. But behind all the smiles, there was a doubt as to whether he would hang onto the drive for 2001.

IDENTITY CARD
- Nationality: French
- Date of birth: 9 june 1969
- Place of birth: Fort de France (Martinique)
- Resident: Fort de France (Martinique)
- Marital status: Married, 3 childrens
- Co-driver: Jack Boyere (French)

CAREER
- First Rally: 1993
- Number of Rallies: 10
- Number of victories: 0

1999 - Not classified
2000 - Not classified

ALISTER McRAE
HYUNDAÏ

Brought up in the overpowering shadow of his big brother Colin and pushed along by his father Jimmy, Alister McRae had finally got a works drive in a WRC after struggling last year with a Kit-Car Coupe. His Accent WRC was neither reliable nor quick. There was the odd occasion, like in New Zealand, where McRae Junior managed to get something out of this promising car. It is futile therefore to judge him in terms of points scored or fastest stage times. But he proved he has the determination to succeed. At least he merits a place in the record books for finishing seventh in Argentina, scoring the Korean firm's first ever world championship point.

IDENTITY CARD
- Nationality: British
- Date of birth: 20 december 1970
- Place of birth: Lanark (Scotland)
- Resident: Lanark
- Marital status: Single
- Hobbies: Motocross, mountain bike
- Co-driver: David Senior (British)

CAREER
- First Rally: 1988
- Number of Rallies: 42
- Number of victories: 0

1995 - 10th in championship
2000 - Not classified

GROUP N

The Group N category had not been this interesting for many a long year. Up against Gustavo Trelles, Manfred Stohl arrived on the scene from Austria with his own team. He was determined to upset the Trelles applecart which had dominated this category since 1996, without any real challengers. The fight was soon underway, both psychologically and on the stages. In Australia for example, the man from Uruguay was convinced that Finland's Paasonen, who won this class in Sweden and Finland, had only been taken on by his Austrian rival's team so that the two men could conspire against him. If this annoyed him, it turned into a positive doubt, as it spurred Trelles to victory and he posed a real threat to the Austrian. Group N was also livened up this year, by an excellent gang of youngsters from Argentina, like Menzi, Pozzo and Sanchez; the first of these two winning their events in Kenya and the Acropolis. They are both worth watching in the future, when they will have gained the same level of experience as Trelles, Stohl, Paasonen and even the returning Nittel, as well as Portugal's Campos. Thanks to all these drivers, Mitusbishi completely annihilated the opposition in the category for standard cars.

TEAM'S CUP

There was greater diversity in the FIA team's cup reserved for private teams. Up against the Toyota Corollas of Bakhashab and Yazici were the Subaru Imprezas of Dor and Arai and they were all pretty evenly matched. But despite the amount of time and energy invested in this category, it seemed to attract little interest outside those who were taking part.

FREDDY LOIX
MITSUBISHI

It went from bad to worse. After a catastrophic 1999 season, his second year with Mitsubishi was even worse, if that was possible. Admittedly, the car was not at the height of its powers, but the Belgian kept tripping over his shoelaces. There was the odd mechanical melt down, but there was also a fair quota of stupid mistakes, such as Corsica, when he crashed out on the first corner of the rally. Freddy appears to be drifting, although he set a few good times, especially in Cyprus. Mitsubishi had thought of sacking him, but he keeps his drive for 2001. It's another chance, courtesy of long time supporter Marlboro. Freddy is a great guy, charming, funny and brilliant, but currently he is possibly the worst of the factory drivers.

IDENTITY CARD
- Nationality: Belgian
- Date of birth: 10 november 1970
- Place of birth: Tongres (Belgium)
- Resident: Millen (Belgium)
- Marital status: Single
- Children: -
- Hobbies: Squash, mountain-bike
- Co-driver: Sven Smeets (Belgian)

CAREER
- First Rally: 1993
- Number of Rallies: 50
- Number of victories: 0

1996 - 8th in championship
1997 - 9th in championship
1998 - 8th in championship
1999 - 8th in championship
2000 - 12th in championship

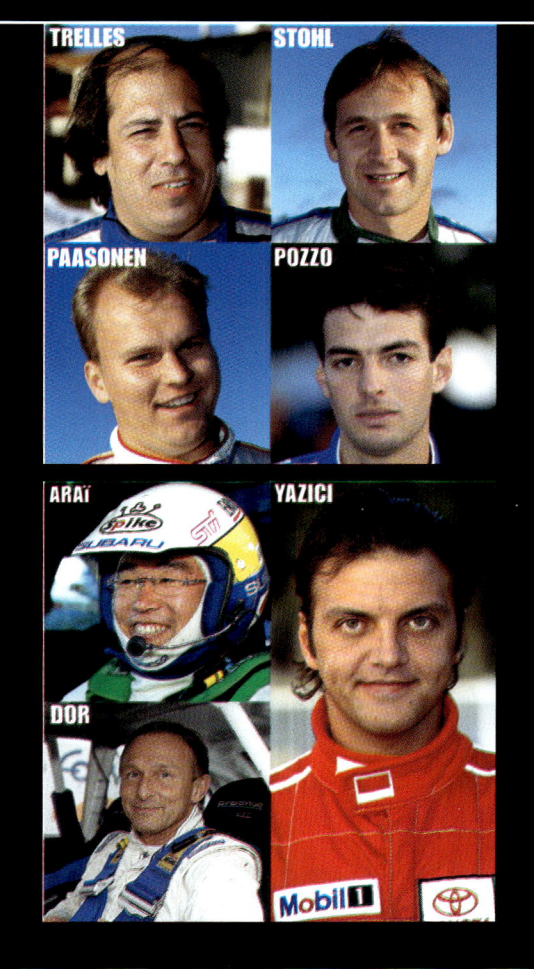

GILLES PANIZZI
PEUGEOT

His season appeared to get off to a great start on the first leg of the Monte. However, just as that event ended in disappointment, so too the rest of Panizzi's season was blighted with chaos, errors, fights and fines, as happened in the Safari. There was disappointment in Catalunya and he got on the wrong side of his team. But the man known as Zebedee had enough spring in his step to bounce back to win in both Corsica and San Remo, bringing his team a very valuable 20 points. Apart from rumours regarding illicit recceing, he proved he had a right to be in the championship; on tarmac at least, as his performance on the loose was not exactly breathtaking. A hard worker, he knows his limitations, so as long as there are drives available there is always hope.

IDENTITY CARD
- Nationality: French
- Date of birth: 19 sept. 1975
- Place of birth: Roquebrune Cap Martin (France)
- Resident: Monaco
- Marital status: Married, 1 daughter
- Children: -
- Hobbies: -
- Co-driver: Hervé Panizzi (French)

CAREER
- First Rally: 1990
- Number of Rallies: 23
- Number of victories: 2

1997 - 9th in championship
1998 - 12th in championship
1999 - 10th in championship
2000 - 7th in championship

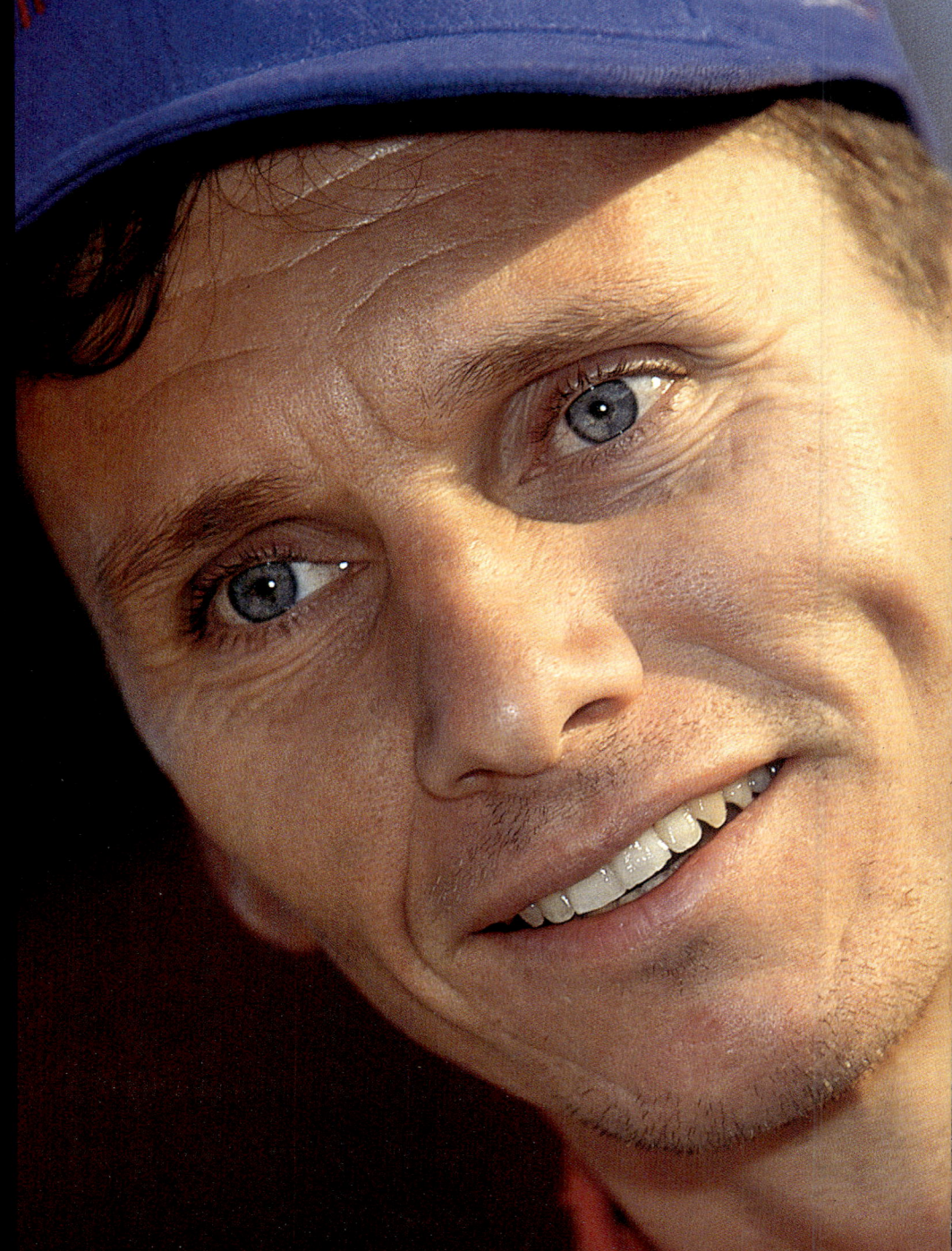

ARMIN SCHWARZ
SKODA

Armin Schwarz is known for his happy nature, but this year he was often caught in flagrante delicto, sporting a dark scowl while ranting and raving, not against his team, but against his Octavia WRC. It was too heavy, too big and never had enough power. But he fought like a madman and his reward was to score the Czech firm's first ever fastest stage time in the championship on the Catalunya Rally. But his ardour also saw him fly off into the scenery, in keeping with his headstrong reputation. He was one of the first to crash out of the San Remo for example. The years go by, but the German never changes.

IDENTITY CARD
- Nationality: German
- Date of birth: 16 july 1963
- Place of birth: Oberreichenbach (Germany)
- Resident: Monaco
- Marital status: Single
- Children: -
- Hobbies: Water-skiing, music
- Co-driver: Manfred Hiemer (Germany)

CAREER
- First Rally: 1988
- Number of Rallies: 64
- Number of victories: 1

1991 - 6th in championship
1994 - 7th in championship
1995 - Excluded (Toyota)
1997 - 8th in championship
1999 - Not classified
2000 - 17th in championship

LUIS CLIMENT
SKODA

What is there to say about Luis Climent? In truth, not a lot, as he was almost invisible this season. Much was expected of the man who had won the Teams' Cup in 1999, now that he had a works drive. The Spaniard owed his Octavia drive to his sponsor, who apparently never seemed too keen to cough up the money to Skoda. The Czech team colours might be green, but they never saw many greenbacks! Climent never shone and was completely off the pace. Towards the end of the year, the team started to give him a hard time about his lack of results, while admitting he was a nice enough bloke.

IDENTITY CARD
- Nationality: Spanish
- Date of birth: 12 november 1966
- Resident: Requena (Spain)
- Marital status: Single
- Hobbies: Television, Relaxing
- Co-driver: Alex Romani (Spanish)

CAREER
- First Rally: 1986
- Number of Rallies: 36
- Number of victories: 0

2000 - Not classified

KENNETH ERIKSSON
HYUNDAÏ

"Old soldiers never die," is the phrase often trotted out in defence of ancient and worthy campaigners with one foot in the grave. Eriksson seemed destined to be a man with only a past, after leaving Subaru in 1997, but for Hyundai he was a man with a future. He spent two miserable years battling with the infuriating Kit Car Coupe, before tackling this season at the wheel of the Accent WRC. 44 years old, the taciturn Swede proved he still knew how to do the job, setting up the car well enough to sneak the odd fifth place here and fourth spot there. Despite the fact he would have been willing to carry the car across the line if asked, it seems his employers are considering showing him the door.

IDENTITY CARD
- Nationality: Swede
- Date of birth: 13 may 1956
- Place of birth: Appelbo (Sweden)
- Resident: Appelbo, Monaco
- Marital status: Single
- Hobbies: fishing, hunting, plane
- Co-driver: Staffan Parmander (Swede)

CAREER
- First Rally: 1977
- Number of Rallies: 116
- Number of victories: 6

1986 - 10th in championship
1987 - 4th in championship
1989 - 6th in championship
1991 - 5th in championship
1993 - 7th in championship
1995 - 3rd in championship
1996 - 4th in championship
1997 - 5th in championship
2000 - 11th in championship

BEST PRIVATEERS

MARKO MARTIN

Once again this year, Markko Martin made an impression. The young Estonian, with the look of an angry duck, only turned twenty five this year and he worked wonders at the wheel of his private Toyota Corolla WRC, to such an extent that, come the end of the summer, he had a Subaru contract in his pocket. This classy performer seems destined to be a star of the future.

SEBASTIEN LOEB

Is this man France's great white hope? Maybe. That's certainly what the French Federation believes, as it helped him to compete in Corsica and San Remo with the Grifone team, who were impressed by his two top ten results. The man from Alsace also put in an appearance in Finland and on the RAC at the wheel of a Saxo, primarily to learn about these events. Already 28 years old, he has not got much time to show what he can do.

HARRI ROVENPERA

Kicked out like a criminal by Seat at the end of 1999, having hustled for them at the wheel of an Ibiza and then a Cordoba since 1997, the thin Finn with a voice deeper than a V8, attempted a timid return in Sweden at the wheel of a private Seat. He was in better form in Portugal and Finland, where he was a frontrunner. It was a case of starting all over again to prove he has the talent. In this, he succeeded.

THE
TEAMS

Never in the history of the championship had so many teams embarked on such major programmes as they did in 2000. This year also saw the appearance of several excellent private teams, making up a field of outstanding quality.

PEUGEOT
206 WRC

Alpine-Renault had done it back in 1973, when they took the title in their first year of world championship competition. It was inevitable, given this was the first ever year the championship had been run. But the team had been around for a while before then. So Peugeot can well and truly claim to have repeated their own achievement established in 1985 with the 205, by winning at their first attempt with the 206. No other team has ever done it. After a tricky start to the season, with victory in Sweden and Gronholm's consistency, the second part of the year was a grandiose performance, with a host of wins, kicking off in New Zealand. With more wins than any other team, Peugeot richly deserved the 2000 title. It was the first for the 206, and probably not the last.

Position (*= 2 litre)

Engine
Type: 4 cylinders in-line, 16 valves
Bore x stroke: 85,0 x 88,0 mm
Capacity: 1997,5 cm3
Turbo: Garrett - Allied Signal
Max. power: 300 bhp
Max. torque: 53,5 kg/m > 3500 rpm

Transmission
Type: Permanent 4-wheel drive
Gearbox: 6-speed sequential

Suspension
Front: McPherson strut
Rear: McPherson strut

Dampers
Peugeot

Steering
Power-assisted rack

Brakes
Ventilated discs with 4 piston calipers

Tyres
Michelin

Dimensions
Length: 4005 mm
Width: 1770 mm
Height: 1370 mm
Weight: 1230 kg
Wheelbase: 2468 mm
Front/rear track: 1510 mm/1505 mm

Position

Year	Position
1973	3rd
1973	15th
1974	13th
1975	5th
1976	8th
1977	13th
1978	8th
1979	11th
1980	8th
1981	9th
1982	-
1983	10th
1984	3rd
1985	1st
1986	1st
1987	-
1988	10th
1993*	3rd
1994*	5th
1995*	1st
1996*	4th
1997*	3rd
1998*	2nd
1999	6th
2000	1st

FORD
FOCUS WRC

There was an impressive presentation prior to the Monte Carlo Rally, the sole aim of which was to prove that Ford was back. After a '99 season which brought two wins, but also a raft of technical problems, the Focus had been further modified by M-Sport and should have been the ultimate rally weapon. It wasn't far off thanks to the efforts of McRae and Sainz, two drivers who are always capable of getting into the points and winning two or three rallies between them. Then came Australia: a broken engine for the Scotsman and Sainz disqualified meant that all hope was lost. When Makinen's Mitsu was disqualified, the rejigged points meant Peugeot took the title. But for Ford, it had been an honourable defeat.

Engine
Type: 4 cylinders, 16 valves
Bore x stroke: 84,8 x 88 mm
Capacity: 1995 cm3
Turbo: Garrett
Max. power: 300 bhp > 6500 rpm
Max. torque: 55 kg/m > 4000 rpm

Transmission
Type: Permanent 4-wheel drive
Gearbox: 6-speed sequential

Suspension
Front: McPherson strut
Rear: McPherson strut

Dampers
Reiger

Steering
Power-assisted rack and pinion

Brakes
Ventilated discs
4 piston calipers (front) - 4 pistons (rear)
8 piston calipers (front) - 4 pistons (rear)

Tyres
Michelin

Dimensions
Length: 4152 mm
Width: 1770 mm
Height: 1425 mm
Weight: 1230 kg
Wheelbase: 2635 mm
Front/rear track: 1550 mm/1550 mm

Position

Year	Pos	Year	Pos	Year	Pos
1973	3rd	1981	3rd	1991	4th
1974	3rd	1982	4th	1992	3rd
1975	6th	1983	-	1993	2nd
1976	3rd	1984	12th	1994	3rd
1977	2nd	1985	11th	1995	3rd
1978	2nd	1986	5th	1996	3rd
1979	1st	1987	5th	1997	2nd
1980	3rd	1988	2nd	1998	4th
		1989	13th	1999	4th
		1990	8th	2000	2nd

MITSUBISHI
LANCER EVO6

The year got off to a great start for the team which was aiming mainly for the drivers' title. Winning the Monte will forever remain a major achievement for them. On the following event, a second place for Makinen was almost like a victory as it was Gronholm who had upset the winning machine. The rest of the year held little but disappointment. One can pretty much ignore Loix, who was incapable of doing anything, even when the team gave in to his whims when it came to setting up his Carisma. Of more concern were the woes which befell Makinen. The Lancer was approaching retirement and the team was concentrating more on developing its replacement than on the current car. Makinen eventually returned to the ranks of front runner towards the end of the summer. Finally, just when Mitsubishi thought they were back on track, Makinen's car was disqualified after winning in Australia. It was a year to forget.

Engine
Type: 4 cylinders, 16 valves, DOHC
Bore x stroke: 85,0 x 88,0 mm
Capacity: 1997 cm3
Turbo: Mitsubishi
Max. power: 300 bhp > 6000 rpm
Max. torque: 52 kg/m > 3500 rpm

Transmission
Type: Permanent 4-wheel drive
Gearbox: 6-speed sequential (INVECS)

Suspension
Front: Independent - McPherson struts with helicoidal springs
Rear: Independent with pull rods and helicoidal springs

Dampers
Ohlins

Steering
Power-assisted rack

Brakes
Front - Ventilated discs with 6 piston calipers
Rear - Ventilated discs with 4 piston calipers

Tyres
Michelin

Dimensions
Length: 4350 mm
Width: 1770 mm
Wheelbase: 2510 mm
Front/rear track: 1510 mm/1505 mm

Position

Year	Pos	Year	Pos	Year	Pos
1973	3rd	1981	14th	1992	5th
1973	16th	1982	8th	1993	5th
1974	11th	1983	16th	1994	-
1975	11th	198	14th	1995	2nd
1976	10th	1985	-	1996	2nd
1977	10th	1986	-	1997	3rd
1978	13th	1987	-	1998	1st
1979	13th	1988	14th	1999	3rd
1980	15th	1989	4th	2000	4th
		1990	3rd		
		1991	3rd		

SEAT CORDOBA EVO3 WRC

The team were all at sea and there was no one at the helm. By employing Auriol and Gardemeister at the end of 1999 and putting together a big budget, Seat's avowed intention for this year was to haul itself up into the ranks of the top teams and to win at least one event. It was not to be and the Spanish outfit had a disastrous time. The Cordoba suffered with several power steering failures, it was incapable of getting through a ford, its differentials had a mind of their own and its engine was nothing special. Before Cyprus, the team paid the penalty as the company announced it was pulling out of the sport and the end of the year. The joke was that the official reason for the withdrawal was to allow the Seat Sport experts to work on the marque's road cars. No, don't laugh!

Engine
Type: 4 cylinders, 16 valves
Bore x stroke: 83 x 92,1
Capacity: 1995 cm3
Turbo: Garrett
Max. power: 300 bhp > 5300 rpm
Max. torque: 55 kg/3500 rpm

Transmission
Type: Permanent 4-wheel drive
Gearbox: 6-speed sequential (INVECS)

Suspension
Front: McPherson strut
Rear: McPherson strut

Dampers
Ohlins

Steering
Power-assisted

Brakes
Ventilated discs

Tyres
Pirelli

Dimensions
Length: 4150 mm
Width: 1770 mm
Height: 1500
Weight: 1230
Wheelbase: 2443 mm
Front/rear track: 1520 mm/1520 mm

Position
1977.........14th
1993*......12th
1994*......10th
1995*......4th
1996*......1st
1997*......1st
1998*......1st
1999.........5th
2000.........5th

SUBARU IMPREZA 2000 WRC

The Impreza WRC was already an excellent car and the P 2000 which succeeded it as from the Portuguese rally was even better. Under similar bodywork, the mechanical parts had been seriously overhauled. It was enough to make the team dream of another title, something they had not achieved since 1997. Sadly there were too many reliability issues, as seen in a pitiful double retirement in New Zealand and Kankkunen's performance was not up to the job. Even Burns hit the wrong pedal now and again. There was one major change to the management, in that David Richards was no longer involved on a day to day basis, choosing to concentrate on setting up the television project: just one reason why Subaru appeared to lose its way this year.

Engine
Type: Flat-4
Bore x stroke: 92,0 x 75,0 mm
Capacity: 1994 cm3
Turbo: IHI
Max. power: 300 bhp > 5500 rpm
Max. torque: 48 kg/m > 4000 rpm

Transmission
Type: Permanent 4-wheel drive
Gearbox: Manual/semi automatic 6 speed (PRODRIVE)

Suspension
Front: McPherson strut
Rear: McPherson strut avec bras longitudinal et transversal

Dampers
Bilstein

Steering
Power-assisted rack and pinion

Brakes
Ventilated discs, 4 piston calipers

Tyres
Pirelli

Dimensions
Length: 4172 mm
Width: 1770 mm
Height: 1400 mm
Weight: 1230 kg
Wheelbase: 2520 mm
Front/rear track: 1590 mm/1590 mm

Position
1983.........7th
1984.........9th
1985.........12th
1986.........8th
1987.........10th
1988.........9th
1989.........12th
1990.........4th
1991.........6th
1992.........4th
1993.........3rd
1994.........2nd
1995.........**1st**
1996.........**1st**
1997.........**1st**
1998.........3rd
1999.........2nd
2000.........3rd

GROUP N and TEAM'S CUP

Rounder than ever, less motivated than ever, Gustavo Trelles nevertheless set off for another crack at Group N in the hope of winning a fifth consecutive title, even if his heart was not in it. But, just as Hamed Al Wahaibi had mounted a challenge in 1999, this time it Manfred Stohl who was attempting to upset the apple cart. The Austrian had a dream start to the season, pulling out an advantage over the Uruguayan. Then it went pear shaped. "Uncle Gustavo" found a new lease of life after winning in Argentina. There were others who shone briefly, including Paasonen and the promising Argentinians, Pozzo, Menzi and Sanchez, who occasionally interfered with the duel. But Stohl could see Trelles looming large in his mirrors, to the extent that, before the Rally of Great Britain, only one point separated them. Stohl held fast and thus was the first man to take the title that Trelles had monopolised since 1996. Well done.

The FIA prize for teams, known as the Team's Cup is reserved for private teams and it never really caught the public's imagination. This year, it quickly settled into a four way fight between Abdullah Bakhashab, the Saudi Arabian (Toyota Corolla WRC,) Japan's Toshihiro Arai (Subaru Impreza WRC and Group N) with backing from Allstar and Subaru Prodrive, the Frenchman Frederic Dor (Subaru Impreza WRC) and Turkey's Serkan Yazici (Toyota Corolla WRC) who was part of the ever efficient Scuderia Grifone. These last two soon lost touch with the leaders, leaving Bakhashab and Arai to fight it out, despite a late win for Yazici in Australia. All the Japanese driver had to do to win was start the Great Britain event, which he managed to do, taking the title in the process.

SUBARU IMPREZA

MITSUBISHI EVO 6

MITSUBISHI EVO 6

YOYOTA COROLLA WRC

HYUNDAÏ ACCENT WRC

Starting eleven of the fourteen events on the calendar, Hyundai did even better than Skoda, as far as the minor teams are concerned. Its Accent WRC, created, developed and run by the English firm MSD, no doubt has a greater potential than the Czech car, even if this did not translate in terms of standings in the championship. As things turned out, the two pretty little cars entered for Alister McRae and Kenneth Eriksson were held up too often by multiple mechanical worries, which affected just about every bit of the car. There is work to be done to ensure the same thing does not happen again in 2001. This is a serious and hardworking team and it if can sort out the technology, then it could be a serious irritant to the front runners in the near future.

Position
1996*	7th
1997*	6th
1998*	5th
1999*	2nd
2000	6th

Engine
Type: 4 cylinders, 16 valves
Bore x stroke: 84 x 90 mm
Capacity: 1998 cm3
Turbo: Garrett
Max. power:
300 bhp > 5200 rpm

Transmission
Type: Permanent 4-wheel drive
Gearbox: 6-speed sequential

Suspension
Front: McPherson strut/Proflex
Rear: Proflex

Dampers
Ohlins

Brakes
Gravel - Ventilated discs with 4 piston calipers (front) – Discs with 4 piston calipers (rear)
Asphalt - Ventilated discs with 6 piston calipers (front) – Discs with 4 piston calipers (rear)

Tyres
Michelin

Dimensions
Length: 4340 mm
Width: 1770 mm
Height: 1313 mm
Weight: 995 kg
Wheelbase: 2475 mm
Front/rear track:
1465 mm/1450 mm

SKODA OCTAVIA WRC

This was the second year of participation for the Octavia WRC and it was still incapable of taking part in the whole season. Never mind. The valiant little Czech team did what it could with the means at its disposal. A fastest stage time, in Catalunya courtesy of Schwarz was the equivalent of a win for Pavel Janeba and his boys. During the year, the big and overweight car gradually evolved, but its performance was never sparkling. The German driver was not helped by the poor showing of his team-mate, Luis Climent, who got the drive courtesy of his wallet. In the final analysis, Skoda was almost equal with Seat in terms of points, even though it had a much smaller budget. Now, what if the men at VAG were to dig into their pockets for this deserving cause?

Position
1993*	2nd		1996*	3rd
1994*	1st		1997*	2nd
1995*	3rd		1999	7th
			2000	6th

Engine
Type: 4 cylinders, 20 valves
Bore x stroke: 82,5 x 93,5 mm
Capacity: 1999 cm3
Turbo: Garrett
Max. power:
296 bhp > 6000 rpm
Max. torque:
50,1 kg/m > 3250 rpm

Transmission
Type: Permanent 4-wheel drive
Gearbox: 6-speed sequential

Suspension
Front: McPherson strut/Proflex
Rear: McPherson strut

Dampers
Proflex

Steering
Power-assisted rack

Brakes
Ventilated discs

Tyres
Michelin

Dimensions
Length: 4511 mm
Width: 1770 mm
Height: 1429 mm
Weight: 1230 kg
Wheelbase: 2512 mm
Front/rear track:
1580 mm/1576 mm

WORLD CHAMPIONSHIP RALLIES

MONTE CARLO	48 | 106	NEW ZEALAND
SWEDISH	56 | 114	FINLAND
SAFARI	64 | 122	CYPRUS
PORTUGAL	74 | 130	FRANCE
CATALUNYA	82 | 138	SAN REMO
ARGENTINA	90 | 146	AUSTRALIA
ACROPOLIS	98 | 154	GREAT BRITAIN

2000

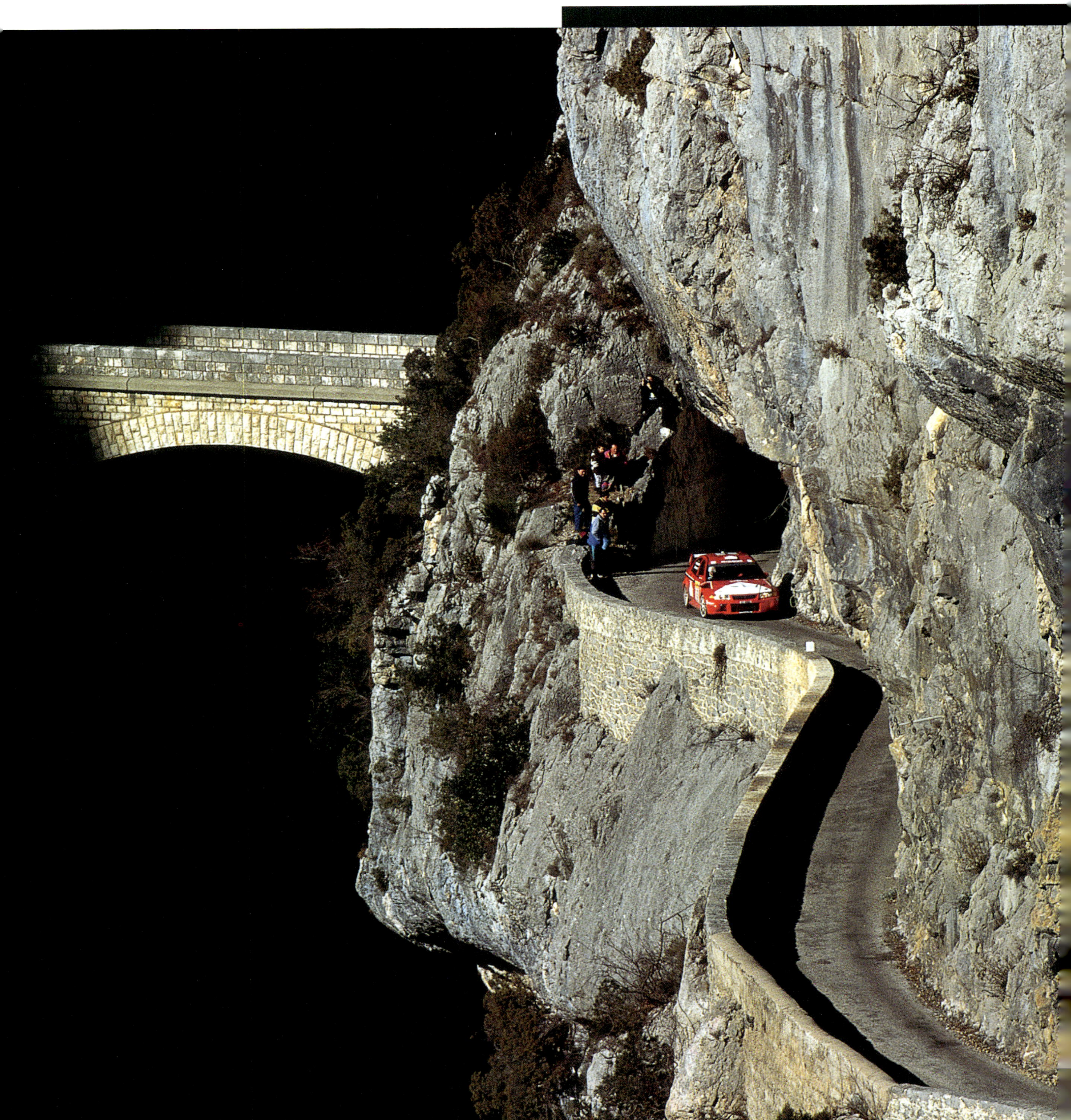

monte carlo

Robbed of any substance by the surprising and simultaneous retirements of the three Peugeots and Burns' Subaru, the first event of the year was handed to Makinen on a plate.

THE RALLY

Peugeot hands it to Makinen

It's cold in Gap in the winter time, very cold in fact. Everything is icy and freezing, making it hard to get up in the mornings and that applies to the cars as well.

It's seven in the morning and the onlookers are already gathered to see the competitors get underway, before they head off to fight it out in the mountains as they tackle the stages. It is still dark and steam rises on the spectators' breath, which is what you would expect as the thermometers are stuck on minus eight. There is no sign of the 206s. Gilles Panizzi and Francois Delecour both try and fire up their WRC cars, but the little rocket ships are not playing ball as they are completely frozen. "Pap, pap, pap," is the only sound the starter motors can manage. Herve Panizzi, brother and co-driver to Gilles, tries to push the Peugeot along a narrow downhill street in the hope of bringing the beast to life. But it achieves absolutely nothing. The same scenario plays out for Delecour. As for Gronholm, he manages to find a spark, but the engine runs for just 90 seconds before switching to permanent shut-down.

Further along, Richard Burns' Subaru Impreza also refuses to respond to the early morning alarm call. The Englishman, who had been lying in second place, is facing the serious possibility of missing out on a great result. But for Peugeot, it is a catastrophe. The Lion had been roaring right from the start of the season opener as it headed for the Monegasque citadel. At the end of the first leg, Panizzi was third, 30.6 seconds down on leader Makinen, while Burns was second, 12.3 behind the world champion. Delecour had been slowed by a bad dose of flu and had been unable to mix it with the leaders. Gronholm was here to learn the stages and he had acquitted himself well in tenth place.

The stage seemed set for a final showdown, with several legendary stages on the menu of this second leg, including the Sisteron-Thoard stage and a run over the Turini.

Instead of a battle royal, we were faced with a miserable retreat. "It's ridiculous," wailed the men from Peugeot. "We are ridiculous." With three cars out at the same time, they were going to make it into the pages of rallying history for all the wrong reasons. It had happened before of course; Saby had found his R5 Turbo engine refusing to play ball one equally cold morning in Gap. It happened to Sainz in Catalunya in '91, costing him the rally and the championship and more recently in the same event in 1999, Puras was leading until his Xsara refused to fire up. But never three cars before. Three identical cars, at the same time and place with the same problem. It was something for the record books.

Ridicule was rife and spectators out on the stages feigned mock concern at the prospect of starting up their own Peugeot road cars. The press needless to say, had a field day: "206 is the wrong number!" was the lead headline in "L'Equipe" the next day, alongside a cartoon of a little boy having broken his toy. The French constructor found it a bitter pill to swallow, after clearly stating its intentions with no sense of modesty, as to its ambitions for this car.

As far as the sport was concerned, it had taken the fire out of the 2000 season opener and had short changed those expecting a thrilling contest after the opening Monaco to Gap leg. Back on that first Thursday 20th January, the entry list was indeed impressive and the Monte seemed to suggest a dream season in store. For Makinen, Burns and Panizzi, there was no question of a gentle introduction feeling their way back into the sport and they were immediately trading times down to the nearest tenth of a second. After just three stages, this rapid trio had already taken off into the distance, one stage apiece and a substantial 1m 15 lead over the rest of the pack, which was being pulled along by the surprising Toni Gardemeister, setting a blistering pace in his Seat. "What I really cannot explain," complained Ford's technical director, Gunther Steiner, whose Focus cars were unable to match the leaders, "is why they are so quick." There was a sense of impotence in the Ford camp.

Of course there was the usual litany of feeble excuses, but nothing convincing enough to explain why the leading trio was already driving round Mars, while the rest of the field had apparently failed to even fire up their rockets. Makinen was especially neat and impeccable, brave enough to risk a daring tyre choice, by running with fewer studs than his timorous opponents, who would not match his cat-like progress over the ice. On the fourth stage from Selonnet to Breziers across the Savoyons, a stage on which according to the old hands, you were not allowed to think of your safety, he stole an amazing fastest time before repeating the feat on the final one of the day. He therefore led the first leg in dominant form. "Tommi was perfect," admitted Burns, who was determined to knock the Finn off his perch. Panizzi was also still in the fight. That Thursday evening, the cat had scratched the mice, but there was life in the rodents yet! But by the next morning, they were well and truly deceased.

The 68th Monte Carlo rally was well and truly over. In real terms, Makinen's lead was so great, he had no real opposition. He won the first rally of the year pretty much as he pleased. "It has to be said, we were helped quite a bit by others," said co-driver Risto Mannisenmaki. "From the start of the second leg, we didn't have much to do in the car," added the driver.

Nevertheless, this second consecutive win in the Principality was not entirely down to luck as he had shown what he could do on the first leg. Makinen had thus made a very strong start to the season and if the title was not already his, he certainly had to be regarded as a favourite. "I've now got twenty wins to my name," mused the World Champion. "The year could not have got off to a better start!"

While Makinen cruised the second leg, the rest of them had their work cut out. As it got underway, second place was up for grabs between Gardemeister, Sainz and McRae. The young Finn paid dear for his lack of experience: bad tyre choice, a knock and a spin. He did not end with a flourish, leaving the door open for McRae and maybe even Kankkunen.

There were no team orders between the two Ford men. "I think we could see this situation a few times during the season," smiled the Spaniard. The Scotsman was tackling the Alps as though they were the Scottish Highlands and was putting Sainz under serious pressure. Then, having overcome some gearbox niggles, McRae's engine expired on the climb to the Turini, the final stage of the rally, which allowed Juha Kankkunen into third place.

ANALAYSIS

The sadness of the Lion

Once they had got over the mockery and jibes, the Peugeot men turned away from the anger created by the ghastly Gap misfortune and set about working out what had happened, to ensure it never happened again. There was no suspicion of sabotage in the case of the three 206s which had failed to wake up that fateful morning. It was not a repeat of what happened to the Lancias in 1970. At that year's San Remo rally, three of the four Fulvia's, those of Ballestrieri, Lampinen and Barbosa, never got out of parc ferme. Not long after, plastic was discovered in the fuel tanks. Team manager Cesare Fiorio was convinced it was a criminal act.

No, the Peugeot incident was nothing of the sort, but the comments were deeply hurtful to the team which had thrown its heart and soul into the project. What made it worse is the fact there is such a close link between a rally machine and a road car. When a

On his first outing with Ford, Carlos Sainz delivered them a second place finish. Not bad.

The Panizzi brothers, (Gilles on the left and Herve) have reason to sulk as their 206 refused to start for the second leg, when they were lying third.

DISAPPOINTMENT
Ford looks long and hard

Ford had been expected to put on a somewhat more sparkly and pertinent show in the opening event of the season. Sure, Carlo Sainz's second place meant he could congratulate himself on having taken the right decision in choosing the blue oval in preference to Seat at the end of 1999, but as he clambered out of the cockpit at the end of the event, he looked haunted and grumpy. As Ford motor sport boss Martin Whitaker offered his congratulations, the Spaniard, with his usual grasp of what is pertinent, could only reply that he was "sorry for Colin." McRae had retired yet again, making it the ninth rally on the trot that he had failed to see the finish.

Actually, the team new boy could not give a stuff about the fate of his Scottish team mate. He was only interested in his own performance and he knew it had not been that great. He might have finished second, but he was 1.25 behind Makinen. This gap amounted to an eternity, given that before the start, Ford had claimed it had its sights set firmly on the constructors' and drivers' titles.

Sainz had never been on the pace, because when the Peugeots and Burns in the Subaru had still been in the running, neither he nor McRae had ever shown signs of menacing the leaders. Even worse, the man from Madrid felt powerless to do anything about it. "The car's handling was alright and I didn't have any problems. But there is still a lot of work to do and I am keen to see some new and important evolutions find their way onto the car." The fact is that the Focus had a fantastic chassis with effective suspension, but its engine was sadly lacking in the power department. Sainz was in the right place to see that for himself: up until 1999, he had driven for Toyota, whose engine was reckoned to be the cream of the crop. On top of that, McRae's retirement with engine bothers had done nothing to reassure His Emminence. That winter, Sainz knew better than anyone that one swallow on the podium would not make a champions's summer.

THE REVELATION
A testing baptism for Gardemeister

This was his first rally as a full time works driver for Seat, or with any team for that matter, and Toni Gardemeister had made a strong impression. It's true that his competitive nature and his speed was not a secret, but to go from that to calling everyone's bluff in the Monte Carlo rally was quite a step, given it is one of the toughest events on the calendar. But he had made the grade. Of course, he won the two litre- two wheel drive category in 1999, right from his very first try at the event, but mastering a World Rally Car is a different story.

In 1999, he made a few appearances for the Spanish team, including a third place in New Zealand to give the Cordoba its first ever podium. It certainly propelled the youngster up the ranks, allowing him to slide into the seat previously occupied by his compatriot Rovanpera. In the meantime, Italy's Piero Liatti handed his car over to Didier Auriol.

Right from the start of the Monegasque event, he got himself noticed, thanks to his incredible times (second on the seventh stage.) His style was also worth watching and his aggression was a big hit with the spectators who appreciated his over the limit approach on the ice covered corners. At the end of the first leg, he was sixth, right behind Francois Delecour. The next day, making the most of the disappearance of the front runners, he was lying third and he tackled the final leg, determined to dislodge Sainz from Makinen's slipstream. Then, a bad tyre choice meant he had an off and a spin, which lost him the remarkable rhythm he had built up as he tried to get on the podium. Of course, the entire Spanish team was delighted with this performance, except perhaps his team mate, Didier Auriol, who encountered mechanical bothers throughout the rally. He had a broken diff right from the start which led to erratic handling. The Frenchman rapidly dropped down the running order, before having to retire with an oil pressure problem. He did not have a car which allowed him to fight, but nevertheless, to be jostled in the team built around him by this upstart youngster, could not have been easy to live with for an established champion. ∎

---

grand prix car stalls on the grid as the lights go out on a Sunday afternoon, there is no immediate link to a Mercedes C180 or a Honda Accord. In road events, there is a much closer connection between those taking part and the spectators. In Monaco, those who had driven their Peugeots to the spectator points had to endure the taunts and jibes of others. It was all the worse, because having achieved a degree of success in six of the previous year's events, the French constructor arrived in Monaco with its colours and ambitions nailed firmly to the mast. This failure was enough to make them look pretty silly.

In their Velizy workshop, a major post mortem was the first appointment in the diary. Even before the rally was over, the 306s were back in the Peugeot Sport factory, in the Paris suburbs. After several meetings, it was decided that from the very next day, tests would be carried out in the climatic chamber used to test road cars in the Peugeot R and D centre in La Garenne-Colombes. The matter was urgent to say the least, because the problem had to be sorted in time for the Swedish Rally a fortnight later. Even if the parc ferme in Karlstad was located in an underground car park, Scandinavia was not exactly famous for its palm trees and boiling hot sun.

As things turned out, the root of the problem was easy to trace. Gronholm's car was a slightly different case. "It was connected with the link between engine and gearbox," explained Peugeot Sport director Claudio Provera. "It was no doubt a manufacturing fault. If his car had started, he would certainly not have gone much further."

The two other cars had suffered from a lack of power between the starter motor and the battery. "They had actually been charged up the night before," continued Provera. "All the indications were that they were in tip top condition. The problem is therefore one of electronics rather than an electrical one and concerns the power available to fire up the engine, which involves the spark plugs and other elements in the circuit."

It was a problem which had cropped up during pre-season testing, especially when the team had taken the 206 to Sweden. "We thought we had fixed it," concluded a distraught Provera. Nevertheless, several of the team's technicians would later admit they had been worried about this sword of Damocles during the first leg. The Peugeot team was anxious to put this sad incident and its three zero scores behind it as quickly as possible.

The big revelation of this rally was Toni Gardemeister, who proved he richly deserved his first works drive.

MONTE CARLO

MONTE-CARLO

The night shift at Mitsubishi. It is time for the greats to gird their loins before setting off to tackle the mountains once again. Once his main rivals, Burns and Panizzi were out of the way, Tommi Makinen only had to make it to the finish to take his second consecutive Monte win.

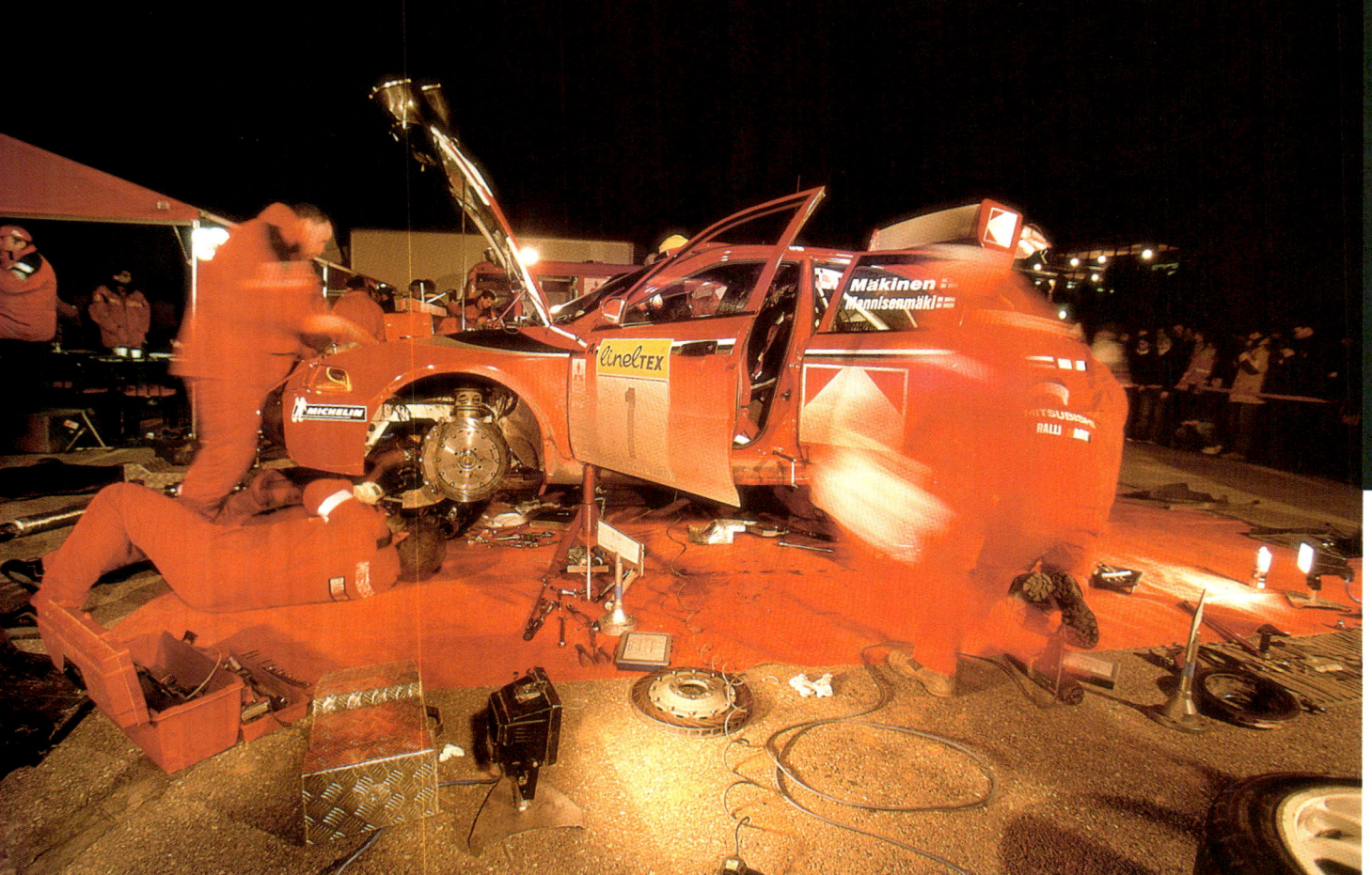

MONTE-CARLO

No matter how much it is cut up, shortened and messed with, the Monte will always be a unique event. The winter, the mountains the rocky passes, the icy peaks are all part of the character of this most famous of events and it cannot deny its roots and its sheer quality. The Monegasque rally is a dream and in 2000, it provided the final opportunity for the amateurs to rub shoulders with the best drivers in the world. It will never be the same again.

MONTE-CARLO

68th MONTE-CARLO RALLY

1st leg of the 2000 world rally championships for constructors and drivers
1st leg of the production car drivers' and team's world cups
Date 20 - 23 january 2000
Route 1468,57 km divided into 3 legs
15 stages on tarmac roads (412,71 km) two of which neutralized (381,31 km)
1st leg Thursday 20 january: Monaco - Gap, 5 stages (112,83 km)
2nd leg: Friday 21 january: Gap - Gap, 5 stages and 4 stages ran (131,04 km)
3rd leg: Saturday 22 january: Gap - Monaco, 5 stages (137,55 km)
Starters - Finishers: 91 - 58
Conditions: Good weather, cold, roads were dry, damp and icy.

This version of the Monte-Carlo will forever be remembered as the one where the Peugeots refused to start. Delecour, seen here in action, would not escape the collective failure.

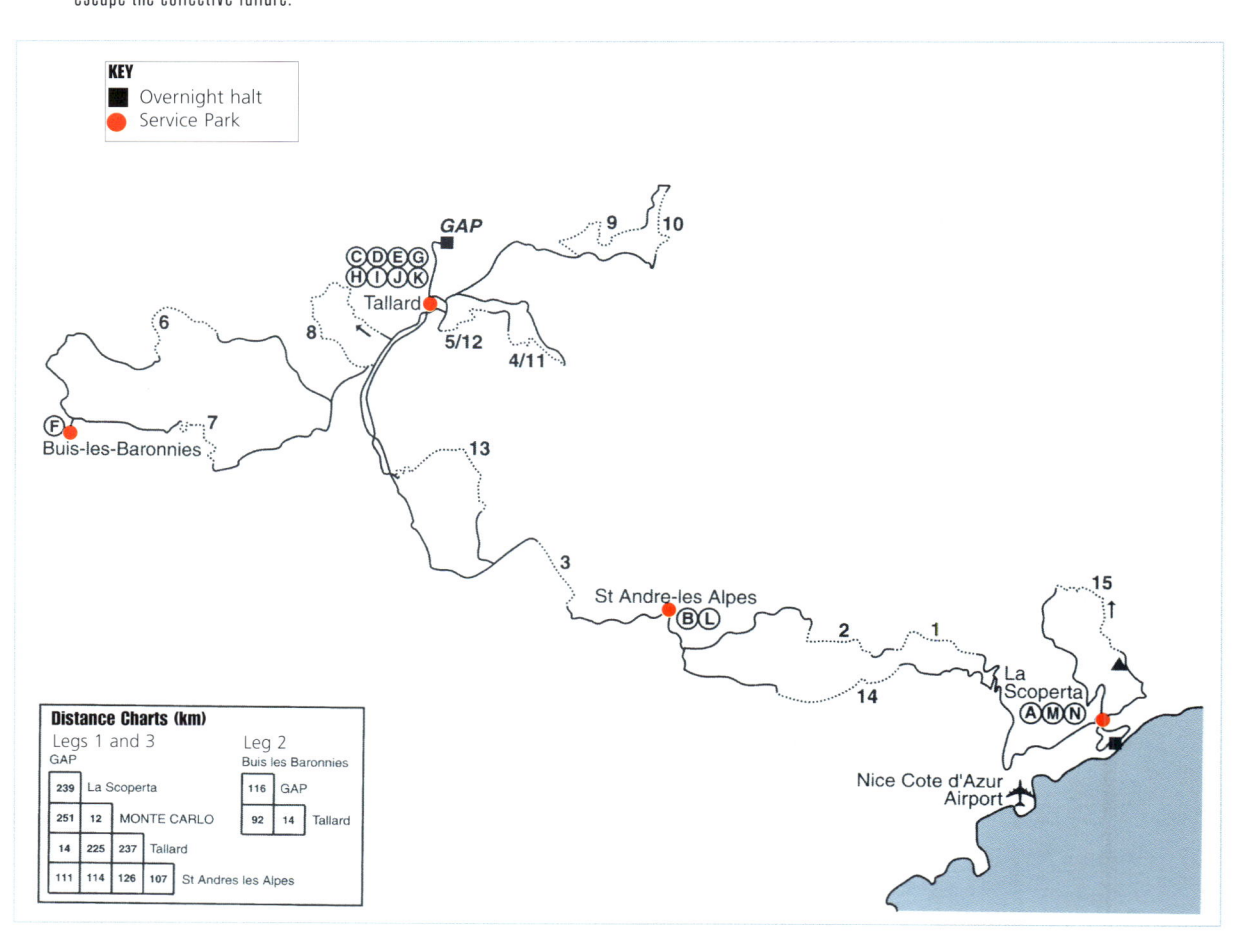

TOP ENTRIES

1 Tommi Makinen - Risto Mannisenmaki
   MITSUBISHI LANCER Evo 6

2 Freddy Loix - Sven Smeets
   MITSUBISHI LANCER Evo 6

3 Richard Burns - Robert Reid
   SUBARU IMPREZA WRC

4 Juha Kankkunen - Juha Repo
   SUBARU IMPREZA WRC

5 Colin McRae - Nicky Grist
   FORD FOCUS WRC

6 Carlos Sainz - Luis Moya
   FORD FOCUS WRC

7 Didier Auriol - Denis Giraudet
   SEAT CORDOBA WRC Evo 2

8 Toni Gardemeister - Paavo Lukander
   SEAT CORDOBA WRC Evo 2

9 François Delecour - Daniel Grataloup
   PEUGEOT 206 WRC

10 Gilles Panizzi - Hervé Panizzi
   PEUGEOT 206 WRC

11 Armin Schwarz - Manfred Hiemer
   SKODA OCTAVIA WRC

12 Luis Climent - Alex Romani
   SKODA OCTAVIA WRC

16 Gustavo Trelles - Jorge Del Buono
   MITSUBISHI LANCER Evo 6

17 Marcus Gronholm - Timo Rautiainen
   PEUGEOT 206 WRC

18 Bruno Thiry - Stéphane Prévot
   TOYOTA COROLLA WRC

19 Henrik Lungaard - Jen Christian Anker
   TOYOTA COROLLA WRC

20 Olivier Burri - Christophe Hofmann
   TOYOTA COROLLA WRC

21 Manfred Stohl - Peter Muller
   MITSUBISHI LANCER Evo 6

22 Uwe Nittel - Detlef Ruf
   MITSUBISHI CARISMA Evo 6

25 Gianluigi Galli - Guido D'Amore
   MITSUBISHI LANCER Evo 5

74 Jürgen Barth - Jean-Claude Perramond
   SEAT IBIZA TDI

KEY
■ Overnight halt
● Service Park

Distance Charts (km)

Legs 1 and 3
GAP

239			La Scoperta
251	12		MONTE CARLO
14	225	237	Tallard
111	114	126	107	St Andres les Alpes

Leg 2
Buis les Baronnies

| 116 | | GAP |
| 92 | 14 | Tallard |

SPECIAL STAGE TIMES

ES.1 Tourette du chateau - St Antonin (24,81 km)
1. Panizzi 17'58"2; 2. Burns 18'03"3; 3. Thiry 18'10"4; 4. Gardemeister 18'14"0; 5. Makinen 18'16"6; 6. Delecour 18'19"5; Gr.N Galli 19'16"7

ES.2 St Pierre - Entrevaux (30,63 km)
1. Makinen 22'17"7; 2. Burns 22'24"8; 3. Panizzi 22'38"7; 4. McRae 22'58"2; 5. Kankkunen 23'04"3; 6. Delecour 23'12"4; Gr.N Nittel 24'00"3

ES.3 Norante - Ets Thermal (19,75km)
1. Burns 12'49"8; 2. Panizzi 12'51"3; 3. Makinen 12'52"4; 4. Gardemeister 12'58"2; 5. Sainz 13'00"9; 6. Auriol 13'00"9; Gr.N Nittel 13'53"2

ES.4 Selonnet - Breziers 1 (17,94 km)
1. Makinen 12'47"6; 2. Panizzi 13'01"6; 3. Burns 13'01"9; 4. Sainz 13'07"1; 5. Delecour 13'13"1; 6. Kankkunen 13'17"4; Gr.N Nittel 13'42"7

ES.5 Rochebrune - Urtis (19,70 km)
1. Makinen 16'19"8; 2. Burns 16'26"6; 3. Panizzi 16'34"9; 4. Sainz 16'36"8; 5. Gronholm 16'41"6; 6. Delecour 16'45"4; Gr.N Nittel 17'22"2

ES.6 L'Epine - Rosans (31,4 km)
Cancelled, too many spectators.

ES.7 Ruissas - Eygalayes (27,7 km)
1. Kankkunen 17'01"6; 2. Gardemeister 17'05"5; 3. Sainz 17'08"7; 4. Loix 17'10"0; 5. Makinen 17'13"2; 6. Thiry 17'17"4; Gr.N Stohl 18'10"9

ES.8 Plan de Vitrolles - Fayes (48,55 km)
1. Makinen 31'06"1; 2. Sainz 31'18"0; 3. Gardemaister 31'18"6; 4. Mc Rae 31'29"3; 5. Kankkunen 31'42"9; 6. Loix 31'56"9; Gr.N Nittel 33'05"4

ES.9 Prunières - Embrun (34,12 km)
1. Mc Rae 20'09"5; 2. Sainz 20'17"3; 3. Schwarz 20'24"9; 4. Gardemeister 20'25"9; 5. Kankkunen 20'28"5; 6. Auriol 20'33"7; Gr.N Galli 21'13"6

ES.10 St Clément - St Sauveur (20,58km)
1. Makinen 13'44"1; 2. McRae 13'46"1; 3. Gardemeister 13'54"3; 4. Thiry 13'56"6; 5. Kankkunen 14'04"9; 6. Sainz 14'05"3; Gr.N Stohl 15'04"0

ES.11 Selonnet - Breziers 2 (17,94 km)
1. Mc Rae 12'46"1; 2. Sainz 12'51"2; 3. Schwarz 12'52"3; 4. Makinen 12'58"3; 5. Kankkunen 12'59"7; 6. Auriol 13'03"6; Gr.N Stohl 13'16"0

ES.12 Rochebrune - Urtis (19,70 km)
1. Makinen 16'16"1; 2. McRae 16'19"6; 3. Kankkunen 16'21"3; 4. Sainz 16'22"6; 5. Gardemeister 16'34"2; 6. Schwarz 16'35"2; Gr.N Stohl 17'06"1

ES.13 Sisteron - Thoard (36,94 km)
1. Kankkunen 25'04"0; 2. Makinen 25'07"1; 3. McRae 25'13"0; 4. Loix 25'23"2; 5. Schwarz 25'28"2; 6. Thiry 25'28"4; Gr.N Gillet 27'10"5

ES.14 St Auban - Roqueseron (29,17 km)
1. Sainz 19'23"9; 2. McRae 19'26"3; 3. Thiry 19'40"6; 4. Makinen 19'48"8; 5. Kankkunen 19'50"7; 6. Loix 19'51"6; Gr.N Stohl 20'45"7

ES.15 Sospel - La Bollène (33,80 km)
1. Sainz 23'34"2; 2. Thiry 23'55"4; 3. Gardemeister 23'56"9; 4. Makinen 24'00"9; 5. Kankkunen 24'14"3; 6. Burri 24'42"5; Gr.N Trelles 25'57"2

RESULTS AND RETIREMENTS

	Driver/Co-Driver	Car	Gr.	Total Time
1	Tommi Makinen - Risto Mannisenmaki	Mitsubishi Lancer Evo 6	A	4h23m35,2s
2	Carlos Sainz - Luis Moya	Ford Focus WRC	A	4h25m00,7s
3	Juha Kankkunen - Juha Repo	Subaru Impreza WRC	A	4h26m57,2s
4	Tony Gardemeister - Paavo Lukander	Seat Cordoba WRC Evo 2	A	4h27m20,9s
5	Bruno Thiry - Stéphane Prévot	Toyota Corolla WRC	A	4h28m24,2s
6	Freddy Loix - Sven Smeets	Mitsubishi Lancer Evo 6	A	4h30m39,9s
7	Armin Schwarz - Manfred Hiemer	Skoda Octavia WRC	A	4h33m24,1s
8	Olivier Burri - Christophe Hofmann	Toyota Corolla WRC	A	4h34m17,2s
9	Manfred Stohl - Peter Muller	Mitsubishi Lancer Evo 6	N	4h44m17,6s
10	Luis Climent - Alex Romani	Skoda Octavia WRC	A	4h44m25,3s
ES.6	Richard Burns - Robert Reid	Subaru Impreza WRC	A	Electronics
ES.6	Gilles Panizzi - Hervé Panizzi	Peugeot 206 WRC	A	Electronics
ES.6	François Delecour - Daniel Grataloup	Peugeot 206 WRC	A	Electronics
ES.6	Marcus Gronholm - Timo Rautiainen	Peugeot 206 WRC	A	Electronics
ES.10	Uwe Nittel - Detlef Ruf	Mitsubishi Lancer Evo 6	N	Electronics
ES.13	Henrik Lundgaard	Toyota Corolla WRC	A	Accident
ES.14	Didier Auriol - Denis Giraudet	Seat Cordoba WRC Evo 2	A	Engine
ES.15	Colin McRae - Nicky Grist	Ford Focus WRC	A	Engine

EVENT LEADERS

ES.1	Panizzi
ES.2 > ES.3	Burns
ES.4 > ES.15	Makinen

BEST PERFORMANCES

	1	2	3	4	5	6
Makinen	6	1	1	3	2	-
Sainz	2	3	1	3	1	1
McRae	2	3	1	2	-	-
Kankkunen	2	-	1	1	7	1
Burns	1	3	1	-	-	-
Panizzi	1	2	2	-	-	-
Gardemeister	-	1	3	3	1	-
Thiry	-	1	2	1	-	2
Schwarz	-	-	2	1	1	-
Loix	-	-	-	2	-	2
Delecour	-	-	-	-	1	3
Gronholm	-	-	-	-	1	-
Auriol	-	-	-	-	-	3
Burri	-	-	-	-	-	1

CHAMPIONSHIP CLASSIFICATIONS

Drivers
1. Tommi Makinen — 10
2. Carlos Sainz — 6
3. Juha Kankkunen — 4
4. Toni Gardemeister — 3
5. Bruno Thiry — 2
6. Freddy Loix — 1

Constructors
1. Mitsubishi — 12
2. Ford — 6
3. Subaru — 4
4. Seat — 3
5. Skoda — 1

Group N
1. Manfred Stohl — 10
2. Gustavo Trelles — 6
3. Gianluigi Galli — 4

Team's cup
no finishers

PREVIOUS WINNERS

1973	Andruet - "Biche"	Alpine Renault A 110
1975	Munari - Mannucci	Lancia Stratos
1976	Munari - Maiga	Lancia Stratos
1977	Munari - Maiga	Lancia Stratos
1978	Nicolas - Laverne	Porsche 911 SC
1979	Darniche - Mahé	Lancia Stratos
1980	Rohrl - Geistdorfer	Fiat 131 Abarth
1981	Ragnotti - Andrié	Renault 5 Turbo
1982	Rohrl - Geistdorfer	Opel Ascona 400
1983	Rohrl - Geistdorfer	Lancia rally 037
1984	Rohrl - Geistdorfer	Audi Quattro
1985	Vatanen - Harryman	Peugeot 205 T16
1986	Toivonen - Cresto	Lancia Delta S4
1987	Biasion - Siviero	Lancia Delta HF 4WD
1988	Saby - Fauchille	Lancia Delta HF 4WD
1989	Biasion - Siviero	Lancia Delta Integrale
1990	Auriol - Occelli	Lancia Delta Integrale
1991	Sainz - Moya	Toyota Celica GT-Four
1992	Auriol - Occelli	Lancia Delta HF Integrale
1993	Auriol - Occelli	Toyota Celica Turbo 4WD
1994	Delecour - Grataloup	Ford Escort RS Cosworth
1995	Sainz - Moya	Subaru Impreza 555
1996	Bernardini - Andrié	Ford Escort Cosworth
1997	Liatti - Pons	Subaru Impreza WRC
1998	Sainz - Moya	Toyota Corolla WRC
1999	Makinen - Mannisenmaki	Mitsubishi Lancer Evo 6

ESSO
SWEDISH RALLY
10
NIKKO
MICHELIN
MAGNETI MARELLI
206 MVB 75
Esso
COMPUTER ASSOCIATES

swedish

Beating the world champion fair and square on his favourite surface is quite an achievement. That is exactly what Marcus Gronholm did to take both his and the 206's first world championship victory.

THE RALLY

Gronholm the Great

Organising a winter rally in a country called Varmland, literally "warm land," is asking for trouble. Inevitably, once or twice it has to happen that the sun comes out to chase winter away with a few penetrating rays up the backside. It happened in 1990, when General Winter was unable to muster his troops, leading the organisers of the Swedish leg of the world championship to cancel their event. This year, it was a close call, as a sudden rush of mild weather melted much of the ice and snow which gives the event its character.

It is out of the question to run the stages without their protective covering, because of the damage it entails on the tracks. Luckily, the temperature dropped just as suddenly just before the start and again during the rally. The event went ahead with just a few timed miles amputated from the original route, including the super-stage in the middle of the first leg.

Before the start, Francois Delecour predicted in professorial tones the cocktail of surfaces which awaited them: "20% ice, 50% ice and loose mixed, 10% of ice and mud alternating every 50 metres and 20% slush." It was not much to look forward to as the stages would lack the familiar walls of snow which lined the tracks. They provide a safety barrier stopping you from going off the road," explained Colin McRae, an expert in these matters.

The event, the second of the season, began under sunny skies, with Tommi Makinen installed as pre-rally outright favourite. It was not his home event, but the King of the World, who arrived fresh from victory in Monte Carlo, had for several years now made this event his own, winning three out of the last four Swedish rallies. However, right from the start, it was local boy Radstrom who was quickest on the first stage at the wheel of his private Toyota Corolla entered by Toyota Team Sweden. It was a form of revenge for the red faced lad who had been shown the door by Ford at the end of 1999, who was showing that his win in the 1994 edition of this rally had not been a fluke.

Marcus Gronholm fought hard to score his first ever world championship win.

Nevertheless, the good Thomas was under no illusions and he was soon eaten up raw by a hungry wolf who likes nothing better than to stalk the forests of the frozen north. Marcus Gronholm was also eating up the icy stage miles and was quickest on the second stage, which put him in the lead. "I'm not surprised to be leading," he explained calmly in the middle of the day. "It's what I wanted. I knew that the car was just fantastic." He managed to maintain his position throughout the leg, setting a total of four fastest times out of the eight stages on the programme that day. He even claimed one of them at the staggering average speed of 122.93 km/h despite the tricky conditions. The big man from Espoo left the rest to fight over the crumbs from his table. These included Radstrom and also Burns, McRae and Makinen. The surprise of the day was the fact that Tommi did not seem to be on his usual Swedish form. The World Champion was grumpy, angry with his car for not being up to what he demanded from it. "The engine is down on power at high revs," explained Mitsu's chief engineer, Bernard Lindauer. "That means we are lacking top speed, but we are playing with the electronics to sort it out." Makinen's anger almost cost him dear, but he escaped with just a damaged rim after a moment on Bjalverud, halfway through the leg. He managed to hang onto third place, 3s behind Radstrom and 18 down on Gronholm. At least he knew that in the second leg, he would be able to count on Jutbo.

If Sweden is his enchanted forest, then Jutbo is his secret garden. This stage has attained mythical proportions and it well deserves it. Jutbo is 47.65 km without any let up or respite; around 48 kilometres of ice and mud, with tracks no wider than the cars, setting its traps in the middle of dense forest peppered with a multitude of blind corners and savage yumps. It is 47650 metres that demand every last drop from the driver. It has to be driven while holding one's breath almost, while also concentrating on looking after one's tyres. It was on this widow-maker of a stage that Makinen intended making up all or most of his deficit to the valiant Gronholm. But here's the rub; the intensity with which he launched himself at Jutbo almost saw Makinen miss the target. "In a right hand corner, not a very quick one as I was in fourth, I lost control. The car went into a slide and hit a huge rock very hard." It tore a big chunk out of the front right rim and the risk of finishing on two punctured tyres might have been asking a lot of the anti-puncture foam in his Michelins. "So I had to slow up a bit," he sighed with disappointment. McRae for his part had managed to step up the pace to such an extent that he emerged with the best time on this monumental stage. "I am rather surprised," he explained afterwards. "Because I didn't think I was going that quickly." His Focus bore the scars of battle with slashed tyres and the front guard bashed about.

As for Gronholm, he had worried about how the studs would stand up to this long stage and he was clearly physically tired. But he had found the right compromise and emerged unscathed. But to make the point he was in charge here, big Marcus set the fastest time on the next stage and kept the lead as they came in to finish the second leg in Karlstad, having stuck a further 8 s on Makinen, who was second. McRae was 29.6 behind.

On this event, where a driver's skill outweighs the intrinsic qualities of his car, a hard charging Tommi Makinen was powerless against a peerless Gronholm.

It looked as though everything was in place for the final five stages of the last leg, despite a worry on stage 16, Malta, where the leader hit a rock hard enough to show up signs of weakness in the dampers on his 206.

All through the day, which had seen the return of the snows, the Peugeot driver managed to contain Makinen's charge by stepping up his efforts. At the same time, Radstrom and McRae were burning up the snow as they fought for third place, which went down to the wire in favour of the Scotsman.

As Gronholm stopped at the finish of the final stage, he wanted to see with his own eyes that Makinen had not made up the 15.9 s which had been the gap before this section. It was not until he was warmly congratulated by the world champion that he finally understood that here in Sweden he had finally won. It was his first world rally championship victory and also the first for the 206. A more extraordinary outcome would have been hard to imagine. "To win ahead of Tommi makes it even better." At that moment, no one could really be sure if they had witnessed a change in the pecking order of this sport.

First rally for the Hyundai Accent WRC of Eriksson and Alister McRae, which they just about managed to finish in thirteenth and fourteenth places.

Colin McRae takes revenge for the injustice of the Monte by taking third place. It was his first finish in ten rallies!

THE WINNER
Marcus Gronholm's marvellous journey

This is a wonderful and poetic tale. By flying in Sweden on a Marvellous Journey every bit as worthy as that of Nils Holgersson, Marcus Gronholm had reached out and touched with his fingertips at least part of his personal ambitions. Up until now, he had come close, very close and sometimes the fall from grace had been hard to bear. For some time now, all the regulars on the world championship trail had grown used to seeing Gronholm lead a rally, but they also knew it tended not to last very long. He was often a victim of over enthusiasm, bending his car in a ditch somewhere, lurking to catch out the unwary. In the roll call of car breakers, he was not quite in the Vatanen or McRae league or even a match for Makinen in his early days, but he did have a certain talent for it. There was a good reason why his mechanics nicknamed him Full Pedal.

His Scandinavian demonstration proved beyond doubt that the boy had reached maturity, while keeping his speed. Having competed in 34 world championship rallies, eleven of them since he first tackled the Thousand Lakes in 1989, he has finally made it into the exclusive winners club, his card now marked with number 60.

The way he did it was more than impressive. Of course the 206 WRC had a hand in his success, but this rally is regarded as one where the quality of the driver outweighs that of his mount. From the very start of the first leg, he attacked like a mad thing, taking the lead off Radstrom by the end of the second stage, never to lose it to the very end of the event. In total, he set seven fastest times out of nineteen stages. However, his lead never exceeded 27s. It was a measure of the new Gronholm that he managed to stay on the road, avoiding the risk of putting himself out of contention, while standing up to the pressure he was put under by the rest of the pack, led by a hard charging Makinen. The remarkable way he dealt with Jutbo - "that's where I lost it as we had not prepared well," admitted the world champion - is what propelled him inexorably towards the top step of the podium. "Everything in the car was calm," according to his co-driver Timo Rautiainen, speaking after the event. "All through the rally, I never felt we were going over our limit." This from a man who is known to get a bit twitchy when his driver goes a bit too far and heads into the danger zone. For his part, Gronholm never had any doubts, except in the very final stage, when he started to get anxious. "I didn't stop asking Timo if I was running at the right pace or if I was going too fast." If he had eased off too much he could have lost everything. This was another trap the Peugeot man avoided. It would have been impossible not to admire this demonstration and his main rival was fulsome in his praise. "Marcus deserves this win," said Makinen, who appeared genuinely delighted for his fellow countryman. "I am sincerely very happy for him. He is a great driver who had an excellent car. Marcus has got over the hardest part now that he has won his first rally!" Like the good farmer he is, the Espoo giant had no wish to put an end to this promising harvest, especially as Peugeot immediately decided to offer him a drive for the whole season, which had not been part of his original deal. It was a great present and a just reward.

THE RETURN
Peugeot sweeps aside the past

RAC 1986 - Sweden 2000. Fourteen barren years had elapsed between these two rallies. It was easy to explain, as Peugeot had abandoned the sport of rallying for almost all of those years. All the same, this was win number 22 for the blue team, since the start of the world rally championship in 1973. The 206 was the natural successor to the African Queen that was the 504 and then the unstoppable 205 T16, which swept all before it.

Evidently, the 1999 mini campaign when the Lion tackled six rallies had speeded up the development process of its WRC, but the French firm failed to get back into its winning ways straight away, most notably on the San Remo rally. It had to wait until the Swedish event, neatly washing away the huge disappointment, not to say embarrassment of Monte Carlo three weeks earlier. "This win has wiped away a bitter memory," explained Jean-Pierre Nicholas, from Paris where he had just undergone an operation. "We felt the Monegasque situation was an injustice. Yes, we had a problem but the price we paid was too steep. This Swedish result is a good feeling. The team needed it and there is nothing like it to keep the troops motivated."

This long awaited result did more than that as it meant that in 2000, the team could stick to its avowed aim of challenging for the constructors' title. It looked on the cards. The 206 WRC had finally and explosively shown what it could do. In the middle of the rally, the beaten Makinen had expressed the anxiety this car raised for him. "Of course there is Marcus. He drove faultlessly. He knows the stages and we know he is always quick. But you also have to look at Delecour's times. It's been a long time since he tackled this event and I think his performances have been first class (slowed by technical problems, the Frenchman finished 7th.) This proves the 206 is really strong." All Makinen's fellow drivers agreed with this assessment and knew the car was especially quick on tarmac and even though it looked to have some promise on loose surfaces, very few expected the Lion cub to win in the Kingdom of Sweden. There were still a few question marks over its reliability, as the Scandinavian event is not exactly kind on the cars. The gearbox especially is still a bit fragile," admitted Gronholm. "But the driving style needed on ice or snow puts it under much less strain that on tarmac for example." Delecour was not exactly delighted with life, cursing the incessant differential problems which had slowed him yet again and once too often. The victor's laurels were reassuring but they were not comfortable enough to rest on! ∎

SWEDISH

Marcus Gronholm fought like a lion to win in Sweden. His first championship success coincided with that of the 206 WRC, on only its eighth rally. Above all, it made up for the disappointment of Monte Carlo, when all three cars retired at the same time. A star is born on the Scandinavian ice.

Subaru played a waiting game and did not have the best of times. Burns (above) came fifth as he was still getting to grips with the winter rally. As for Juha Kankkunen (below) a sixth place was not what one had come to expect. It seemed that the young Englishman was claiming the upper ground over the Finn.

49th RALLY SWEDISH

SWEDISH RALLY 2000

2nd leg of the 2000 world rally championships for constructors and drivers
2nd leg of the production car drivers' and team's world cups
Date: 10 - 13 february 2000
Route: 1708,62 km divided into 3 legs
20 special stages on snow covered tracks (399,39 km)
of which three were shortened and one was cancelled (376.68 km.)
Start: Thursday 10th february: Karlstad, 0 stage
1st leg: Friday 11 february: Karlstad - Torsby - Karlstad, 9 stages et 8 stages ran (127,29 km)
2nd leg: Saturday 12 february: Karlstad - Borlange - Karlstad, 6 stages (153,21 km)
3rd leg: Sunday 13 february: Karstad - Hagfors - Karlstad, 5 stages (96,1 km)
Starters - Finishers: 78 - 54
Conditions: sunny weather with covered skies, icy roads with very little snow.

In ninth place, the young Estonian, Markko Martin, once again proved his worth.

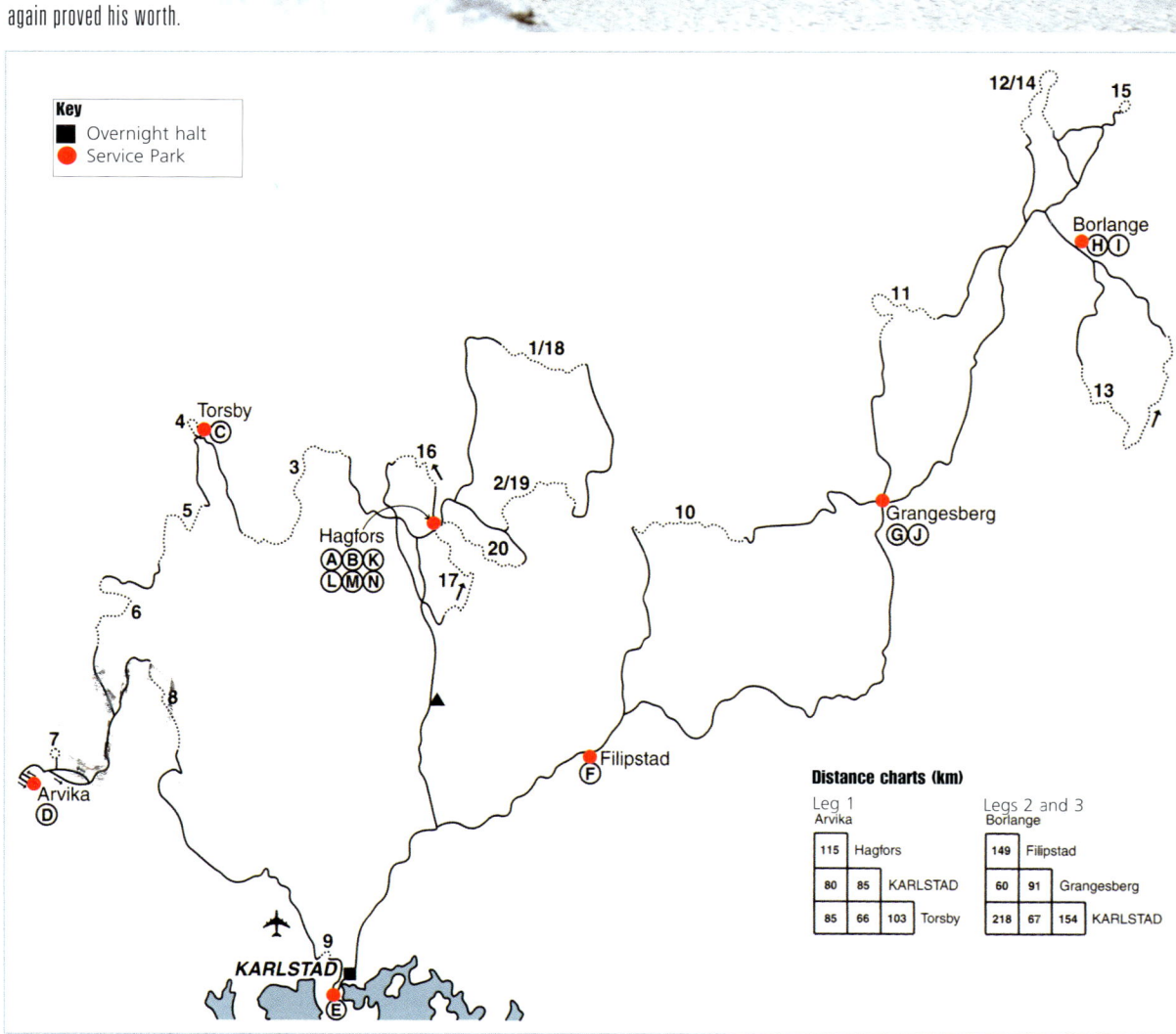

TOP ENTRIES

1 Tommi Makinen - Risto Mannisenmaki
   MITSUBISHI LANCER Evo 6

2 Freddy Loix - Sven Smeets
   MITSUBISHI LANCER Evo 6

3 Richard Burns - Robert Reid
   SUBARU IMPREZA WRC

4 Juha Kankkunen - Juha Repo
   SUBARU IMPREZA WRC

5 Colin McRae - Nicky Grist
   FORD FOCUS WRC

6 Carlos Sainz - Luis Moya
   FORD FOCUS WRC

7 Didier Auriol - Denis Giraudet
   SEAT CORDOBA WRC Evo 2

8 Toni Gardemeister - Paavo Lukander
   SEAT CORDOBA WRC Evo 2

9 François Delecour - Daniel Grataloup
   PEUGEOT 206 WRC

10 Marcus Gronholm - Timo Rautiainen
   PEUGEOT 206 WRC

14 Kenneth Eriksson - Staffan Parmander
   HYUNDAI ACCENT WRC

15 Alister McRae - David Senior
   HYUNDAI ACCENT WRC

16 Harri Rovanpera - Risto Pietilainen
   SEAT CORDOBA WRC Evo 2

17 Thomas Radstrom - Tina Thorner
   TOYOTA COROLLA WRC

18 Markko Martin - Michael Park
   TOYOTA COROLLA WRC

19 Pasi Hagstrom - Tero Gardemeister
   TOYOTA COROLLA WRC

20 Mats Jonsson - Johnny Johansson
   FORD ESCORT WRC

22 Krzysztof Holowczyc - Jean-Marc Fortin
   SUBARU IMPREZA WRC

23 Janne Tuohino - Miikka Anttila
   TOYOTA COROLLA WRC

25 Stig-Olov Walfridsson - Lars Backman
   MITSUBISHI LANCER Evo 6

26 Kenneth Backlund - Tord Andersson
   MITSUBISHI LANCER Evo 6

27 Jani Paasonen - Jakke Honkanen
   MITSUBISHI CARISMA GT

28 Juuso Pykalisto - Esko Mertsalmi
   MITSUBISHI CARIMA GT29

29 Uwe Nittel - Detlef Ruf
   MITSUBISHI CARISMA Evo 6

30 Manfred Stohl - Peter Muller
   MITSUBISHI LANCER Evo 6

31 Abdullah Bakhashab - Bobby Willis
   TOYOTA COROLLA WRC

32 Jonas Kruse - Per Schlegel
   RENAULT MAXI MEGANE

Key
■ Overnight halt
● Service Park

Distance charts (km)

Leg 1
Arvika

115	Hagfors
80	85	KARLSTAD
85	66	103	Torsby

Legs 2 and 3
Borlange

149	Filipstad
60	91	Grangesberg
218	67	154	KARLSTAD

SPECIAL STAGE TIMES

ES.1 Sagen 1 (14,76 km)
1. Radstrom 7'57"7; 2. Sainz 7'58"8; 3. Gronholm 7'59"7; 4. Makinen 8'00"2; 5. Kankkunen 8'02"4; 6. McRae 8'05"4; Gr.N Paasonen 8'33"0

ES.2 Rammen 1 (23,44 Km)
1. Gronholm 12'10"3; 2. Kankkunen 12'16"6; 3. Radstrom 12'18"4; 4. Makinen 12'18"8; 5. McRae 12'20"1; 6. Sainz 12'20"5; Gr.N Paasonen 13'02"0

ES.3 Hamra (28,59 km)
1. Burns 15'03"1; 2. McRae 15'04"4; 3. Radstrom 15'05"6; 4. Gronholm 15'07"1; 5. Makinen 15'11"6; 6. Kankkunen 15'15"3; Gr.N Pykalisto 16'05"4

ES.4 Torsby (2,79 km)
1. Makinen 2'05"9; 2. Gronholm 2'06"1; 3. Sainz 2'06"6; 4. McRae 2'06"8; 5. Burns 2'07"2; 6. Kankkunen 2'07"4; Gr.N Walfridsson 2'16"1

ES.5 Bjalverud (21,58 km)
1. Gronholm 10'43"1; 2. Burns 10'43"2; 3. Radstrom 10'44"4; 4. Makinen 10'45"4; 5. Sainz 10'45"8; 6. McRae 10'52"7; Gr.N Walfrisson 11'31"6

ES.6 Mangen (13,29 Km)
1. Gronholm 6'51"8; 2. Burns et McRae 6'52"7; 4. Radstrom 6'53"0; 5. Makinen 6'55"0; 6. Kankkunen 6'55"9; Gr.N Paasonen 7'22"6

ES.7 Arvika (2 Km)
Cancelled

ES.8 Langjohanstorp (19,44 km)
1. Gronholm 9'29"3; 2. Makinen 9'30"0; 3. McRae 9'33"5; 4. Radstrom 9'35"2; 5. Sainz 9'36"6; 6. Burns 9'37"9; Gr.N Walfridsson 10'20"1

ES.9 I2 (3,40 km)
1. McRae 1'55"9; 2. Kankkunen 1'57"4; 3. Gardemeister 1'57"5; 4. Sainz 1'57"6; 5. Radstrom 1'58"1; 6. Makinen 1'58"4; Gr.N Backlund 2'10"5

ES.10 Fredriksberg (27,39 km)
1. Gronholm 15'43"0; 2. McRae 15'47"8; 3. Delecour 15'53"0; 4. Burns 15'53"3; 5. Makinen 15'55"7; 6. Radstrom 15'56"1; Gr.N Paasonen 16'41"5

ES.11 Nyhammar (27,79 km)
1. Gronholm 14'34"7; 2. Makinen 14'37"1; 3. Burns 14'37"9; 4. McRae 14'38"3; 5. Radstrom 14'39"5; 6. Delecour 14'46"9; Gr.N Paasonen 15'35"1

ES.12 Skog 1 (24,19 km)
1. McRae 12'49"6; 2. Makinen 12'50"5; 3. Radstrom 12'52"6; 4. Burns 12'53"0; 5. Gronholm 12'54"4; 6. Martin 13'00"6; Gr.N Paasonen 13'47"0

ES.13 Jutbo (47,65 km)
1. McRae 26'30"9; 2. Makinen 26'35"6; 3. Burns 26'37"0; 4. Gronholm 26'39"1; 5. Radstrom 26'39"6; 6. Kankkunen 26'48"5; Gr.N Walfridsson 28'45"7

ES.15 Lugnet (2 km)
1. Makinen 1'53"8; 2. McRae 1'55"1; 3. Radstrom 1'55"3; 4. Gronholm 1'55"9; 5. Burns et Eriksson 1'56"3; Gr.N Backlund 2'05"4

ES.16 Malta 11,8 km)
1. Radstrom 5'44"3; 2. Makinen 5'46"7; 3. McRae 5'50"4; 4. Burns 5'50"8; 5. Gronholm 5'50"9; 6. Kankkunen 5'54"8; Gr.N Pykalisto 6'15"0

ES.17 Ullen (24,62 km)
1. Burns 12'05"4; 2. Makinen 12'10"3; 3. Gronholm 12'12"8; 4. McRae 12'14"7; 5. Radstrom 12'16"3; 6. Kankkunen 12'23"9; Gr.N Paasonen 13'08"4

ES.18 Sagen2 (14,76 km)
1. Radstrom 7'45"9; 2. Makinen 7'47"4; 3. McRae et Gronholm 7'47"9; 5. Burns 7'49"7; 6. Delecour 7'51"1; Gr.N Paasonen 8'22"9

ES.19 Rammen2 (23,44 km)
1. Radstrom 11'52"8; 2. Makinen 11'53"3; 3. McRae 11'53"5; 4. Burns 11'56"0; 5. Gronholm 11'56"7; 6. Kankkunen 12'03"5; Gr.N Ekstrom 12'49"9

ES.20 Hagfors (21,21 km)
1. McRae 11'22"9; 2. Radstrom 11'24"5; 3. Makinen 11'27"9; 4. Burns 11'35"5; 5. Gronholm 11'37"0; 6. Eriksson 11'39"1; Gr.N Backlund 12'24"1

RESULTS AND RETIREMENTS

	Driver/Co-Driver	Car	Gr.	Total time
1	Marcus Gronholm - Timo Rautiainen	Peugeot 206 WRC	A	3h20m33,3s
2	Tommi Makinen - Risto Mannisenmaki	Mitsubishi Lancer Evo 6	A	3h20m40,1s
3	Colin McRae - Nicky Grist	Ford Focus WRC	A	3h20m47,0s
4	Thomas Radstrom - Tina Thorner	Toyota Corolla WRC	A	3h20m48,2s
5	Richard Burns - Robert Reid	Subaru Impreza WRC	A	3h21m08,3s
6	Juha Kankkunen - Juha Repo	Subaru Impreza WRC	A	3h23m20,9s
7	François Delecour - Daniel Grataloup	Peugeot 206 WRC	A	3h24m05,2s
8	Freddy Loix - Sven Smeets	Mitsubishi Lancer Evo 6	A	3h25m41,6s
9	Markko Martin - Michael Park	Toyota Corolla WRC	A	3h25m47,3s
10	Didier Auriol - Denis Giraudet	Seat Cordoba WRC Evo2	A	3h25m39,2s
16	Krzysztof Holowczyc - Jean-Marc Fortin	Subaru Impreza WRC	A	3h34m46,0s
17	Jani Paasonen - Jakke Honkanen	Mitsubishi Carisma GT	N	3h36m02,1s
ES11	Toni Gardemeister - Paavo Lukander	Seat Cordoba WRC Evo2	A	Engine
ES11	Carlos Sainz - Luis Moya	Ford Focus WRC	A	Engine

PREVIOUS WINNERS

1973	Blomqvist - Hertz Saab 96 V 4		1987	Salonen - Harjanne Mazda 323 Turbo
1975	Waldegaard - Thorszelius Lancia Stratos		1988	Alen - Kivimaki Lancia Delta HF 4WD
1976	Eklund - Cederberg Saab 96 V 4		1989	Carlsson - Carlsson Mazda 323 4WD
1977	Blomqvist - Sylvan Saab 99 ems		1991	Eriksson - Parmander Mitsubishii Galant VR-4
1978	Waldegaard - Thorszelius Ford Escort RS		1992	Jonsson - Backman Toyota Celica GT-Four
1979	Blomqvist - Cederberg Saab 99 Turbo		1993	Jonsson - Backman Toyota Celica Turbo 4WD
1980	Kullang - Berglund Opel Ascona 400		1994	Radstrom - Backman Toyota Celica Turbo 4WD
1981	Mikkola - Hertz Audi Quattro		1995	Eriksson - Parmander Mitsubishi Lancer Ev.2
1982	Blomqvist - Cederberg Audi Quattro		1996	Makinen - Harjanne Mitsubishi Lancer Ev.3
1983	Mikkola - Hertz Audi Quattro		1997	Eriksson - Parmander Subaru Impreza WRC
1984	Blomqvist - Cederberg Audi Quattro		1998	Makinen - Mannisenmaki Mitsubishi Lancer Ev.4
1985	Vatanen - Harryman Peugeot 205 T16		1999	Makinen - Mannisenmaki Mitsubishi Lancer Ev.6
1986	Kankkunen - Piironen Peugeot 205 T16			

EVENT LEADERS

ES.1 — Radstrom
ES.2 > ES.20 — Gronholm

BEST PERFORMANCES

	1	2	3	4	5	6
Gronholm	7	1	3	3	4	-
McRae	4	4	4	3	2	2
Radstrom	4	1	5	3	4	1
Makinen	2	9	1	3	3	1
Burns	2	2	3	5	3	1
Kankkunen	-	2	-	-	1	7
Sainz	-	1	1	1	2	2
Delecour	-	-	1	-	-	2
Gardemeister	-	-	1	-	-	-
Eriksson	-	-	-	-	1	-
Loix	-	-	-	-	-	1
Martin	-	-	-	-	-	1

There was little snow or ice, but Freddy Loix still managed to find a snowdrift. It was not enough to explain why he could do no better than eighth.

CHAMPIONSHIP CLASSIFICATIONS

Drivers
1.	Tommi Makinen	16
2.	Marcus Gronholm	10
3.	Carlos Sainz	6
4.	Juha Kankkunen	5
5.	McRae	4
6.	Gardemeister	3

Constructors
1.	Mitsubishi	18
2.	Peugeot	11
3.	Ford	10
4.	Subaru	9
5.	Seat	3
6.	Skoda	1

Group N
1.	Manfred Stohl	13
2.	Jani Paasonen	10
3.	Gustavo Trelles	6

Team's cup
1.	Turning Point Racing Team (Holowczyc)	10
2.	Toyota Middle East (Bakashab)	6

MICHELIN

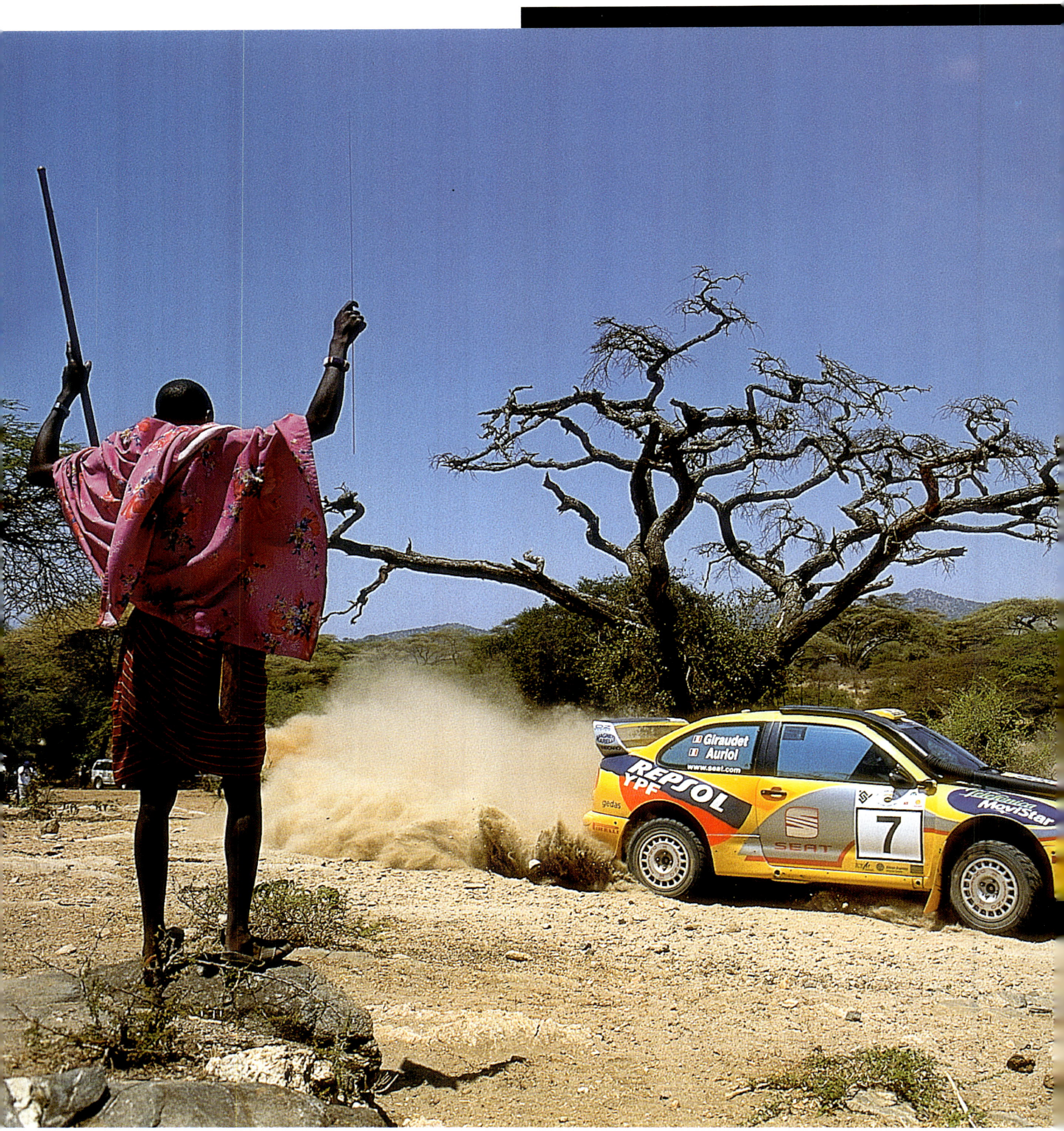
Giraudet
Auriol
www.seat.com
REPSOL
YPF
7
SEAT
MoviStar

Safari

The wheel of fortune turned in favour of those fitted with Pirellis. The result was a one-two for Subaru, courtesy of Burns and Kankkunen ahead of a hard charging Auriol. The Michelin runners have still not wiped away their tears.

Didier Auriol and Richard Burns proved that it was better to be running Pirelli rubber than Michelin in Kenya this year.

THE RALLY

Richard the Lion King

It was a painful time in the scrubland, with plenty of long faces which appeared to mirror the sad demeanour of the wildebeest. One look at the strained expressions of the Michelin technicians on the opening day of the Safari, there at Whistling Thorns, as they watched the cars roll in one by one on their rims, was enough to show that all was not well on the vast and wind blown savannah. This despite the fact that the tyre men like their magic circles of black rubber, they know how to look after them, mollycoddle them almost. But in this, the last Safari of the century, their tyres had cried enough. They were incapable of standing up to the torture meeted out to them on the infinitely long East African tracks, seeded with rocks and thorns, where the ground temperature hit the 50 degree mark. There was an atmosphere of mass suicide, as audible as the hissing of a tyre valve.

The first notable victim was Marcus Gronholm, who was in trouble right from the first stage. At the hastily erected finish control, just outside the tiny hamlet of Isinya, near the church with its metal roof banging in the equatorial breeze, the 206 grinds to a halt in a cloud of dust. Beside himself with rage and pent up frustration, the giant Finn is out of the car almost before it has stopped. He waves two fingers in the air, not as a victory salute, nor even as a rude gesture. "Two punctures," he shouts to reinforce the hand signals. "I didn't hit anything. I don't understand. Two, two!" It was as though he felt shouting about it would exorcise the pain. Then he was off again, in search of his service crew. Farewell Mr. Gronholm and good luck with your African adventure.

It was only the start of the troubles for the cars shod with French rubber. In the next three stages, the epidemic had engulfed the rally like a herd of zebras swarming across the Rift Valley.

In the second timed section, Mitsubishi lost its brightest star, Tommi Makinen. "I had three punctures," related the Finn in disbelief. "We stopped every time to change the wheel, except the third time as we only had two spare wheels. I managed to get out of the stage, but I had run too long on the rim and the rear suspension was destroyed. After that, I couldn't make it to the service area."

In the course of the day, McRae, Sainz, Loix and countless others fell victim to this problem which affected all the teams. The world champion, who is not the sort to attack anyone, knew where to lay the blame. "I know how much I owe Michelin, but ever since I have been competing in the Safari, the Pirellis have been better. It's only on this rally. It's a real problem, but that's the way it is." Stern criticism indeed, but Makinen reckoned he knew the root of the problem. "Generally, the rally got off to a much faster start than last year and the Michelins were not up to it."

It was not as though they had not been aware of the situation. The drivers themselves know better than anyone that, in the Safari, you have to drive with your head and not just your right foot. You must not get carried away by the beautiful scenery and those infinitely long straights that the cars eat up like hungry lions. However, the fact remained that the Pirelli-shod runners were able to maintain this devilish pace without, for the most part getting caught out with punctures. The only ones who had to get the jacks out were the Seat drivers, starting with an aggressive Auriol, who was quickest on the first section and was actually leading overall; something unheard of for the Spanish cars. Gardemeister was not really in the rally long enough to be a part of this equation. He had already suffered a major crash in the preliminary testing and now, the young Finn had ripped the left hand door off his coupe, forced to drive 100 kilometres with dust swirling round the cockpit. It was yet another hardship for co-driver Lukander, who was already complaining of a bad back, after their pre-event roll. He could go no further as the pain had become unbearable.

Sailing on this sea of adversity, it was a piece of cake for Subaru to take the lead. With his solid Pirellis, allied to the sort of road holding which the Cordoba lacked, hence its punctures, Burns set three fastest times and calmly led into Nairobi at the end of the first leg. He had a 4.24 lead over team-mate Kankkunen and a 7.37 advantage over Auriol. "Having the Pirellis helped," explained the young Englishman. "But my Subaru also ran perfectly and I

Despite picking up three punctures in one stage, Makinen managed to finish this one after changing two wheels, but he broke the suspension on his Mitsubishi.

SAFARI

never had to drive in a way that would risk damaging the car. It's true that this year, we set off at a cracking pace. We have managed to get this far. Let's wait and see." Because it was not just the tyres which were giving the other teams a headache. The Fords were being slowed with broken suspension and dampers and Panizzi retired at the end of the day with broken rear suspension.

Nevertheless, as the second day dawned, the future looked rosy for the Subaru crew. It has to be said that the event became rather boring from then on. The gaps were so big and the Imprezas so dominant that only a dramatic change of fortune could affect the outcome. The marathon had become a game of patience. There was one moment of drama, but it did not affect the overall classification. At the end of the Morendat stage, an amazing 93 kilometres, run through the centre of Kenya across farm land all belonging to Lord Delamere, Burns stalled. Nothing to worry about under usual circumstances, but this time the engine refused to fire up. Without any sign of panic, even if he appeared to have turned white as a sheet with the tension of it all, Burns contacted his team by radio. With a workshop manual by his side and spanners in his hands, the Englishman and co-driver Robert Reid tried to bring the beast back to life. The driver plunged his hands into the engine entrails, feeling his way around, impatience written all over his face and the clock carried on ticking. "If that doesn't work, then what do I do?" he kept asking over the radio. Then finally, he poured some water over the offending part, fiddled around some more and jumped back in the car. The starter churned over and finally the four cylinder boxer engine fired into life. It had been a close call and it would have been a bitter blow if their rally had ended there. Unjust even, as despite the fact that Sainz had set three fastest times out of four that day, the Englishman had so much in hand, he could afford to look after his car, slowing the pace without giving away too much time. As he said himself before starting the third leg, "I'll drive quickly enough to maintain concentration, but slowly enough to avoid any problems." He still led from Kankunnen and Auriol; the only change being that Sainz had caught up and passed Solberg for fourth.

In fact, the final 350 kilometres had no affect on the order and Burns cruised to his second Safari win with team-mate Kankkunen making it a Subaru one-two, the first of the season. Didier Auriol struggled home in third spot, having struggled yet again with the Cordoba's eternal Achilles heel, a broken power assisted steering. It was a remarkable achievement in an event that was full of them, but more importantly, Subaru now led the Constructors' classification.

THE WINNER
Burns back in contention

The Englishman drove an intelligent and brilliant rally to build this success, the second of his career on African soil, the fourth by a British driver in the magical former colony of Kenya. Once his rivals had fallen by the wayside, the man they call "Camel-Face" had only to get on with the job in hand. He did it with panache, making the most of his quick and rock solid Subaru, fitted with Pirelli tyres. "Looking at it from the outside, with Kankkunen finishing second, it might seem as though this was an easy event for us," was the winner's analysis back in Nairobi at the finish. "But the Safari is never easy. But, if you go through a meticulous preparation and a lot of recces, then you have a good base to build on." A job well done placed the driver and team firmly at the top of the pecking order. For Burns, it was a breakthrough after an average start to the season spent chasing an on-form Makinen. As for the Anglo-Japanese team, it was now leading the Constructors' classification. "Believe me, it's a great feeling to be in this position," said an ecstatic team boss David Lapworth. "It means we have started the season in much better shape than in '99," added Kankkunen. "It gives us reason to be hopeful." All this was due of course to the Impreza. Kenya was its last outing in its current WRC form and for the next round in Portugal, everyone was awaiting the arrival of the new version, the P2000. Going out with a win in Africa was certainly a stylish way to retire.

A HARD KNOCK
Tough times for Michelin

The tyre manufacturer's lament is well known: "People are only interested in our product when it goes wrong!" It is heard so often that there has to be an element of truth in the complaint. Sadly for Michelin, the 2000 Safari was no exception to the rule. But for the avalanche of punctures which buried all the runners using the French product, the rally might have had a different outcome. There was plenty for the Clermont Ferrand folk to fret about. Facing his accusers, the company's competition boss Pierre Dupasquier did not deny the allegations and took the responsibility on board. "We don't know exactly what has happened," he admitted without preamble. "The rally was run at a very fast pace this year. We did not come here to do any specific testing beforehand. Our tyres seemed to be more prone to losing pressure than the Pirellis. Our rivals must have worked harder." That might have been true, but it was not the whole truth. Back in 1999, the Italian product had already proved to be clearly superior on these unique roads. "We have to produce more specialised tyres, which are more puncture resistant," added Dupasquier. "We will work on it and we will carry out at least two test sessions later this year, aimed specifically at the Safari." No one doubted Michelin's ability to fight back from injury and put on a good show next year.

THE COMEBACK
The silent lion

Africa, the Safari, the Paris-Dakar, the Bandama...Peugeot had built its reputation on the dark continent. So its return to the Kenyan stomping grounds was eagerly awaited. In fact, the French team had not done much Safari-type testing and it landed with cars that were not quite as ready as the team's engineers would have liked. Michel Nandan, its technical director, would have liked to have skipped this event. The team's only preparation had consisted of a test in France at Chateau Lastours and a trip to Senegal, where the roads have little in common with those in East Africa, because of the difference in altitude.

As things turned out, it was a disastrous event for the 206. First off, Gilles Panizzi appeared to be overawed by the whole African experience. He made a beginner's mistake, failing to adjust his pace, breaking a suspension arm which

The Lion was not at home in Africa. Panizzi went out on the first leg, to be joined by Gronholm on the second.

eventually led to his retirement. Worse still, he panicked when stuck behind a slower car, getting too close so that his car was enveloped in a cloud of smoke and dust. It was while driving blind that he failed to spot a pothole and damaged the suspension, which would finally give up the ghost in the next stage.

Furious with the unfortunate Sanchez, who had held him up, no sooner had they arrived at the time control than Panizzi shot over to the Argentinian's car. An unseemly exchange and ruck ensued. The FIA was not impressed and fined the Frenchman a whopping 50,000 dollars! Peugeot looked away, leaving the driver to open his own wallet to settle the debt.

As for Marcus Gronholm, after his initial bother with multiple punctures, the second day saw him crippled with a loose steering rack and soft brakes, before a jammed clutch caused him to retire, while lying eighth. "Every stage here is an adventure," concluded the Finn, who like Panizzi was having his first taste of this unique event. It had a been a tough apprenticeship and Peugeot promised to return better prepared next year. Before the rally had even reached its conclusion, they had planned for a test session in late autumn of 2000. ∎

SAFARI

Solidly built and well prepared for this terrain, the two works Skodas of Schwarz and Climent made it to the finish, reaching Nairobi in 7th and 8th places respectively. The Czech constructor left Africa with three more points in the bank.

Merciless Africa. The Safari often causes carnage. McRae's Ford Focus and his hopes were drowned in a ford. Thankfully, Carlos Sainz managed to finish fourth, the highest placed Michelin runner.

SAFARI

The prairie express was running on full steam. The Subaru team had no real opposition on this event. A strong, fast car with excellent tyres; the combination was perfect, allowing the blue coupes to score the first one-two finish of the season. It signalled a comeback for Burns, who had retired early in Monte Carlo, just as Gronholm had done.

SAFARI

Rally after rally, Petter Solberg proved that Malcolm Wilson had made the right decision in bringing him into the Ford team. The Norwegian paced himself well and made it to the finish, avoiding the pitfalls of the mud holes.

SAFARI

SAFARI

Didier Auriol was not spared on the Safari. Of course he had punctures, but he also suffered suspension failure and a broken power steering. This was not enough to stop the Frenchman from finishing a remarkable third. He was briefly in the lead, having been quickest on the first stage.

Marcus Gronholm will not remember this Safari with any pleasure. His clutch let him down and he had to retire at the mid point, when an honourable finish seemed to be his for the taking. Peugeot was not well prepared and will have to improve their equipment for the African event.

SAFARI

TOP ENTRIES

1. Tommi Makinen - Risto Mannisenmaki
   MITSUBISHI LANCER Evo 6

2. Freddy Loix - Sven Smeets
   MITSUBISHI LANCER Evo 6

3. Richard Burns - Robert Reid
   SUBARU IMPREZA WRC

4. Juha Kankkunen - Juha Repo
   SUBARU IMPREZA WRC

5. Colin McRae - Nicky Grist
   FORD FOCUS WRC

6. Carlos Sainz - Luis Moya
   FORD FOCUS WRC

7. Didier Auriol - Denis Giraudet
   SEAT CORDOBA WRC Evo 2

8. Toni Gardemeister - Paavo Lukander
   SEAT CORDOBA WRC Evo 2

9. Gilles Panizzi - Hervé Panizzi
   PEUGEOT 206 WRC

10. Marcus Gronholm - Timo Rautiainen
    PEUGEOT 206 WRC

11. Armin Schwarz - Manfred Hiemer
    SKODA OCTAVIA WRC

12. Luis Climent - Alex Romani
    SKODA OCTAVIA WRC

16. Petter Solberg - Phil Mills
    FORD FOCUS WRC

17. Toshihiro Araï - Roger Freeman
    SUBARU IMPREZA WRC

18. Frédéric Dor - Didier Breton
    SUBARU IMPREZA WRC

19. Manfred Stohl - Peter Muller
    MITSUBISHI LANCER Evo 6

22. Roberto Sanchez - Jorge Del Buono
    SUBARU IMPREZA WRX

31. Claudio Menzi - Edgardo Galindo
    MITSUBISHI LANCER Evo 6

33. Rudi Stohl - Ilka Petrasko
    MITSUBISHI LANCER

37. Gabriel Pozzo - Rudolfo Ortiz
    MITSUBISHI LANCER Evo 6

51. Michael Plant - Robert Plant
    MINI COOPER

48th SAFARI RALLY - KENYA

3rd leg of the 2000 world rally championships for constructors and drivers
3rd leg of the production car drivers' and team's world cups
Date 25 - 27 february 2000
Route: 2700,44km divided into 3 legs
12 timed sections on dirt roads (1061,00 km.)
1st leg: Friday 25 february: Nairobi - Whistlings Thorns - Nairobi, 4 stages (350,84 km)
2nd leg: Saturday 26 february: Nairobi - Equator Park - Nairobi, 4 stages (359,32km)
3rd leg: Sunday 27 february: Nairobi - Whistlings Thorns - Nairobi, 4 stages (350,84 km)
Starters - Finishers: 51 - 17
Conditions: Good weather, hot, very dusty roads.

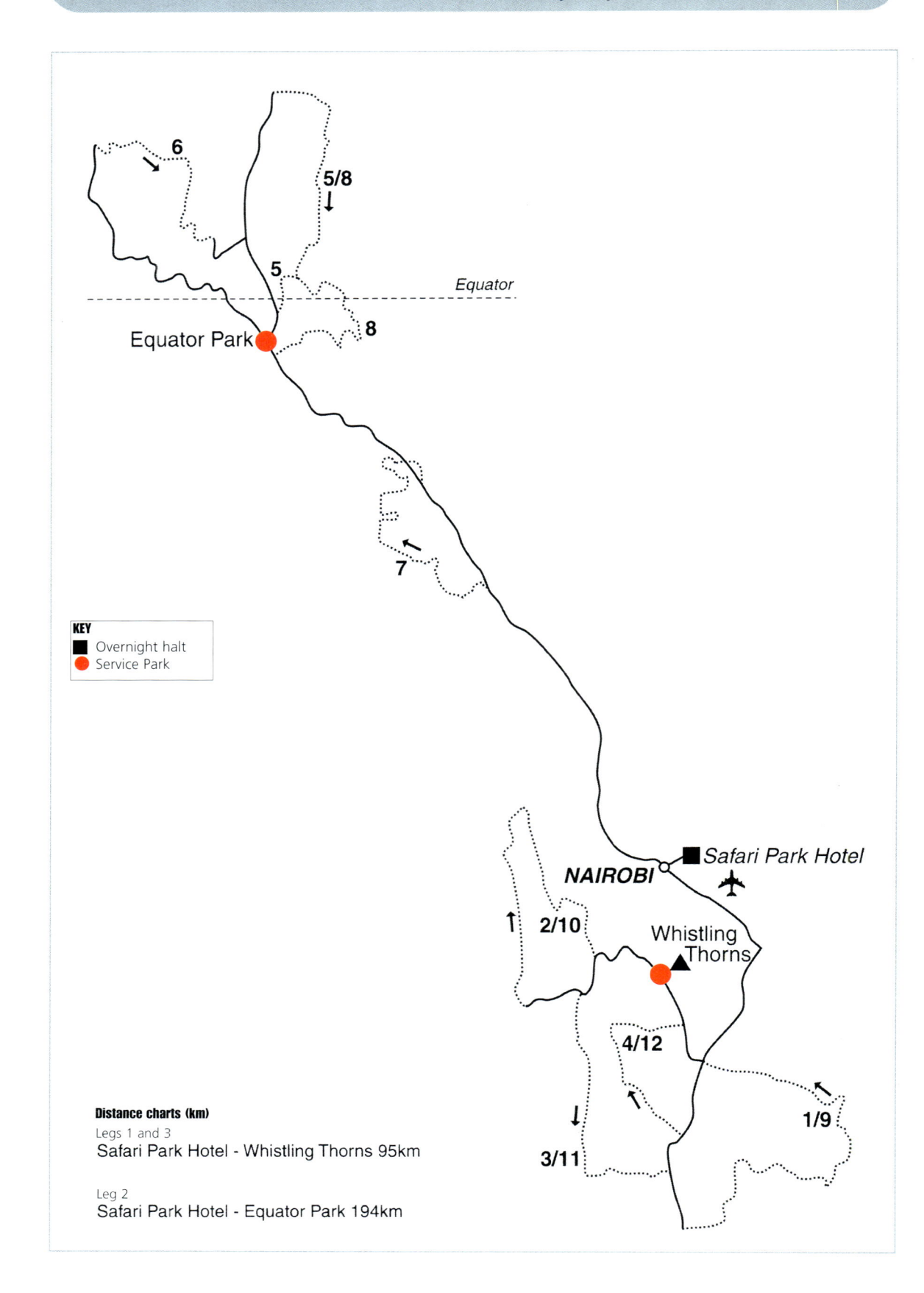

KEY
■ Overnight halt
● Service Park

Distance charts (km)
Legs 1 and 3
Safari Park Hotel - Whistling Thorns 95km

Leg 2
Safari Park Hotel - Equator Park 194km

COMPETITIVES SECTORS TIMES

SC.1 Orien 1 (112,43 km)
1. Auriol 47'13"; 2. Makinen 47'27"; 3. Burns 47'28"; 4. Sainz 48'49"; 5. Gardemeister 49'07"; 6. Kankkunen 49'52"; Gr.N Pozzo 55'07"

SC.2 Oltepesi 1 (116,92 km)
1. Burns 54'06"; 2. Kankkunen 55'04"; 3. McRae 57'32"; 4. Auriol 57'38"; 5. Araï 57'53"; 6. Sainz 58'38"; Gr.N Pozzo 1h05'49"

SC.3 Olorian 1 (71,40 km)
1. Burns 35'04"; 2. Kankkunen 35'39"; 3. Auriol 35'59"; 4. McRae 36'03"; 5. Gronholm 36'15"; 6. Loix 37'07"; Gr.N Pozzo 44'37"

SC.4 Kajiado 1 (50,09 km)
1. Burns 23'44"; 2. Solberg 23'58"; 3. Kankkunen et Gronholm 24'11"; 5. Loix 24'21"; 6. Araï 25'54"; Gr.N Menzi 29'00"

SC.5 Marigat (123,21 km)
1. Burns 1h00'04"; 2. Kankkunen 1h00'41"; 3. McRae 1h00'59"; 4. Sainz 1h01'09"; 5. Araï 1h02'33"; 6. Loix 1h05'05"; Gr.N Stohl et Menzi 1h12'44"

SC.6 Nyaru (68,64 km)
1. Sainz 46'15"; 2. McRae 46'29"; 3. Solberg 47'01"; 4. Auriol 47'13"; 5. Kankkunen 47'22"; 6. Burns 47'37"; Gr.N Menzi 54'47"

SC.7 Morendat (93,81 km)
1. Sainz 46'03"; 2. Burns 47'47"; 3. Auriol 48'05"; 4. Kankkunen 48'45"; 5. McRae 48'56"; 6. Gronholm 48'59"; Gr.N Sanchez 1h02'25"

SC.8 Marigat (59,92 km)
1. Sainz 27'55"; 2. Kankkunen 28'44"; 3. Auriol 29'04"; 4. Solberg 29'28"; 5. Burns 29'33"; 6. Schwarz 31'26"; Gr.N Stohl 35'46"

SC.9 Orien 2 (112,43 km)
1. Auriol 47'54"; 2. Burns 48'54"; 3. Kankkunen 49'37"; 4. Solberg 51'04"; 5. Araï 52'05"; 6. Schwarz 53'53"; Gr.N Menzi 57'42"

SC.10 Oltepesi 2 (116,92 km)
1. Burns 56'11"; 2. Kankkunen 56'43"; 3. Sainz 57'24"; 4. Solberg 58'41"; 5. Araï 59'08"; 6. Climent 1h01'21"; Gr.N Menzi 1h09'57"

SC.11 Olorian 2 (71,40 km)
1. Sainz 34'48"; 2. Solberg 36'22"; 3. Kankkunen 36'47"; 4. Auriol 37'26"; 5. Burns 37'30"; 6. Araï 38'07"; Gr.N Menzi 1h09'57"

SC.12 Kajiado 2 (50,09 km)
1. Sainz 23'18"; 2. Kankkunen 24'25"; 3. Burns 25'15"; 4. Climent 25'52"; 5. Auriol 26'22"; 6. Schwarz 26'35"; Gr.N Stohl 30'34"

RESULTS AND RETIREMENTS

	Driver/Co-Driver	Car	Gr.	Total time
1	Richard Burns - Robert Reid	Subaru Impreza WRC	A	8h33m13s
2	Juha Kankkunen - Juha Repo	Subaru impreza WRC	A	8h37m50s
3	Didier Auriol - Denis Giraudet	Seat Cordoba WRC Evo 2	A	8h55m57s
4	Carlos Sainz - Luis Moya	Ford Focus WRC	A	9h01m31s
5	Petter Solberg - Phil Mills	Ford Focus WRC	A	9h04m40s
6	Toshihiro Araï - Roger Freeman	Subaru Impreza WRC	A	9h18m06s
7	Armin Schwarz - Manfred Hiemer	Skoda Octavia WRC	A	9h32m11s
8	Luis Climent - Alex Romani	Skoda Octavia WRC	A	9h51m13s
9	Claudio Menzi - Edgardo Galindo	Mitsubishi Lancer Evo 6	N	10h39m07s
SC.2	Frederic Dor - Didier Breton	Subaru Impreza WRC	A	Engine
SC.2	Tommi Makinen - Risto Mannisenmaki	Mitsubishi Lancer Evo 6	A	Battery
SC.2	Toni Gardemeister - Paavo Lukander	Seat Cordoba WRC Evo 2	A	Personal decision
SC.4	Gilles Panizzi - Hervé Panizzi	Peugeot 206 WRC	A	Suspension
SC.7	Freddy Loix - Sven Smeets	Mitsubishi Lancer Evo 6	A	Suspension
SC.8	Colin McRae - Nicky Grist	Ford Focus WRC	A	Engine
SC.8	Marcus Gronholm - Timo Rautiainen	Peugeot 206 WRC	A	Embrayage

PREVIOUS WINNERS

1973	Mehta - Drews / Datsun 240 Z		1987	Mikkola - Hertz / Audi 200 Quattro
1974	Singh - Doig / Mitsubishi Colt Lancer		1988	Biasion - Siviero / Lancia Delta Intégrale
1975	Andersson - Hertz / Peugeot 504		1989	Biasion - Siviero / Lancia Delta Integrale
1976	Singh - Doig / Mitsubishi Colt Lancer		1990	Waldegaard - Gallagher / Toyota Celica GT-Four
1977	Waldegaard - Thorszelius / Ford Escort RS		1991	Kankkunen - Piironen / Lancia Delta Integrale
1978	Nicolas - Lefebvre / Peugeot 504 v6 Coupé		1992	Sainz - Moya / Toyota Celica Turbo 4WD
1979	Metha - Doughty / Datsun 160 J		1993	Kankkunen - Piironen / Toyota Celica Turbo 4WD
1980	Metha - Doughty / Datsun 160 J		1994	Duncan - Williamson / Toyota Celica Turbo 4WD
1981	Metha - Doughty / Datsun Violet GT		1995	Fujimoto - Hertz / Toyota Celica Turbo 4WD
1982	Metha - Doughty / Datsun Violet GT		1996	Makinen - Harjanne / Mitsubishi Lancer EV.3
1983	Vatanen - Harryman / Opel Ascona 400		1997	McRae - Grist / Subaru Impreza WRC
1984	Waldegaard - Thorszelius / Toyota Celica Turbo		1998	Burns - Reid / Mitsubishi Carisma GT
1985	Kankkunen - Gallagher / Toyota Celica Turbo		1999	Colin Mc Rae - Nicky Grist / Ford Focus WRC
1986	Waldegaard - Gallagher / Toyota Celica Turbo			

MICHELIN

EVENT LEADERS

SC.1	Auriol
SC.2 > SC.12	Burns

BEST PERFORMANCES

	1	2	3	4	5	6
Burns	5	2	2	-	2	1
Sainz	5	-	1	2	-	1
Auriol	2	-	3	3	1	-
Kankkunen	-	6	3	1	1	1
McRae	-	1	2	1	1	-
Solberg	-	1	1	4	-	-
Makinen	-	1	-	-	-	-
Gronholm	-	-	1	-	1	1
Climent	-	-	-	1	-	1
Araï	-	-	-	-	4	2
Loix	-	-	-	-	1	2
Gardemeister	-	-	-	-	1	-
Schwarz	-	-	-	-	-	3

CHAMPIONSHIP CLASSIFICATIONS

Drivers
1. Tommi Makinen	16
2. Richard Burns	12
3. Juha Kankkunen	11
4. Marcus Gronholm	10
5. Carlos Sainz	9
6. Didier Auriol	4

Constructors
1. Subaru	25
2. Mitsubishi	18
3. Ford	13
4. Peugeot	11
5. Seat	7
6. Skoda	4

Group N
1. Manfred Stohl	17
2. Jani Paasonen	10
2. Claudio Menzi	10

Team's cup
1 Turning Point Racing Team (Holowczyc)	10
1 Spike Subaru Team (Araï)	10
3 Toyota Middle East (Bakashab)	6

While the big cats often stalk the African savannah, the Mitsubishis, like the rest of the herd using Michelin tyres, were seriously lame and easy prey.

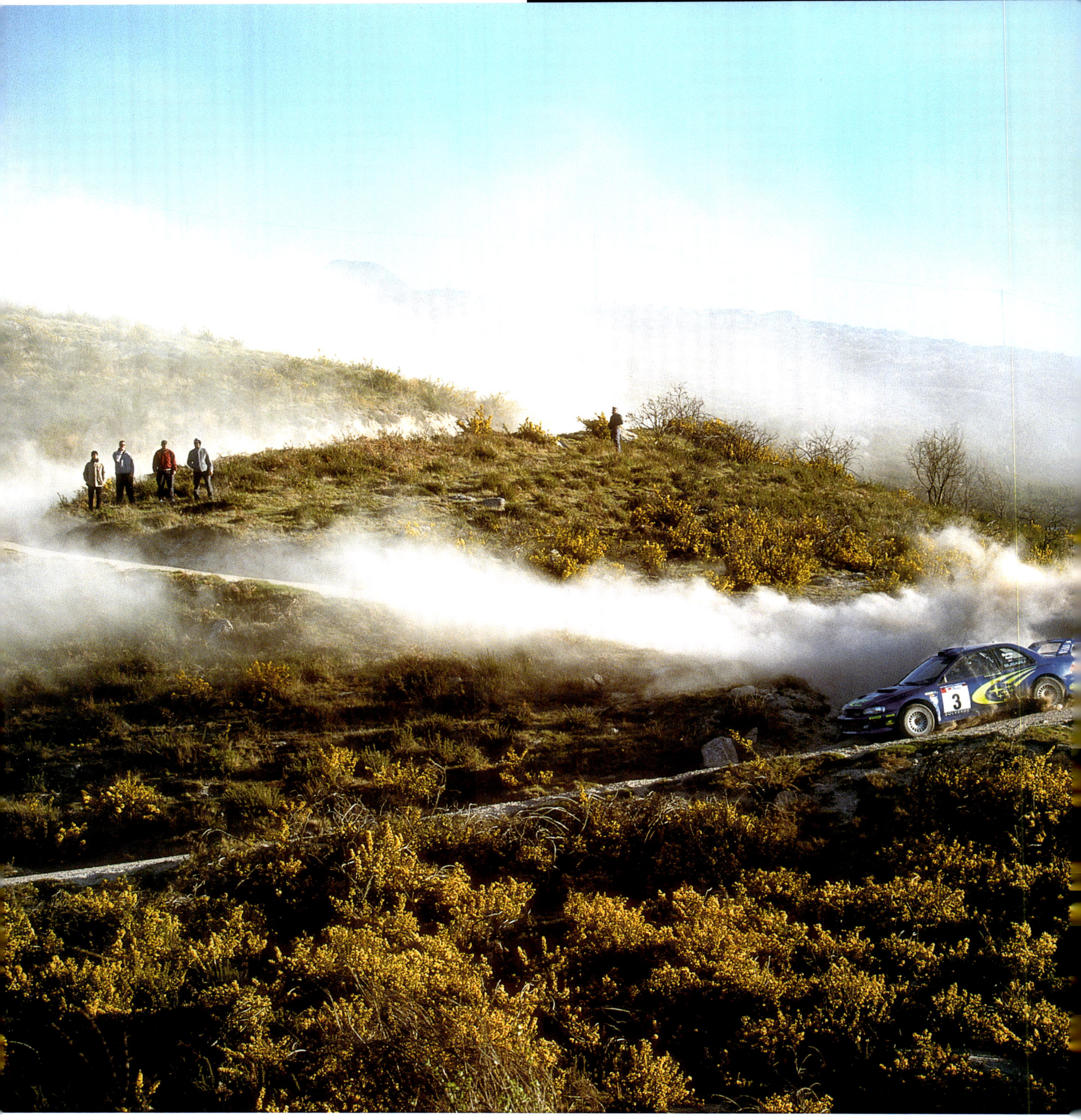

portugal

A new Subaru and another win for a determined Burns, who had to fight off an aggressive Gronholm. Life was looking good for the Englishman.

THE RALLY

In the bank for Burns

The epidemic hit right from the start of one super-special, won with brio by Gronholm, before working its way through the Portuguese Rally field with devastating effect.

There appeared to be no effective vaccine for the disease and only those of robust constitution had any hope of avoiding its insidious attack. The Doctor Mechanics could treat it of course, but once it had taken hold it was difficult to shake off. Power steering failure, broken piston, steering rack going wobbly, bearings failing and oil spewing, the list of symptoms which troubled three of the top stars on the very first stage was indeed a long one, much to the amusement of those who escaped the bug. "Carlos' arms will be getting a good work out," laughed Didier Auriol. "He hasn't been in the peak of physical condition recently!" Sainz, along with McRae and Burns had all been hit by a bad case of the mechanicals and driving a rally car certainly required plenty of sweat and effort on bone dry tracks in boiling heat, exacerbated by forest fires. The poor Porto locals could be forgiven for losing interest in the event as they fought to save their land and homes.

Colin McRae was first on the injured list right from the very first early morning stage. Despite losing his power steering before the end, he still managed to set a more than impressive fastest time to take the lead in his Ford. He was unable to defend this position on the next two stages as there was no service available. The British crew kept adding more and more oil, but the damaged system was leakier than a sieve. Shortly afterwards and by now a long way back, he dropped out with engine failure. Before the start, the Ford engineers had been concerned about the frailty of their new power unit and, sure enough the new baby Cosworth proved to be in need of some strengthening. It was a grateful Richard Burns who found himself in the lead, although it would be wrong to claim he only inherited it, as he was in flamboyant form, setting two then four fastest times. He put on a great display, which proved just how quick was his new Subaru Impreza WRC P2000 on its first outing. His pursuers were soon left trailing in his wake and choking on his dust, which meant we faced the chance of a rather dull couple of days sport. The list of runners was dwindling with every passing stage.

Kankkunen chose to park his Subaru in a tree. Makinen tore his steering apart in a pothole. Sainz was another who found himself without power steering, a fate which also befell the Peugeot drivers:

Burns has reason to smile after taking the revised Impreza WRC to a win on its first event.

Gronholm lost around fifteen seconds trying to restart his engine in the Fafe-Luilhas stage after spinning and stalling. Delecour saw all his hard work come to nothing when the left front damper on his 206 suddenly gave up the ghost over a bump, losing him 1.12.

Unluckily for Burns, but luckily for the sake of adding interest to the event, his power steering also went on the blink, which meant the Scotsman found himself at the wheel of a vehicle which had gone from flying rally car to haulage truck in the space of three stages. "It's really disappointing," was all he could say at the end of the leg, his forearms bandaged in wet towels to relieve the pain. "That's rallying!"

This meant that, despite not having set a single fastest time, the consistent Gronholm found himself in the lead at the end of the first leg, with a 28.6 lead over Sainz and 42.4 ahead of Burns.

It did not take long for the second leg to turn into a duel. The backdrop was certainly special in the beautiful Serra da Estrela, with its deep valleys, steep rock faces peppered with running streams, populated by wolves, deer and other wildlife. It was a fitting stage for the battle between the two youngsters as they raced down the sandy stages under an oppressive sun, the tracks lined by a huge and enthusiastic crowd who had blocked all the roads in the Arganil region, between Lisbon and Porto. If this was a film set, then Richard Burns was impeccably cast as the crack marksman, in the manner of Lee Marvin, a man of few words and a look of permanent concentration - the bounty hunter par excellence. The man he was stalking was the equally lanky, more so in fact, Marcus Gronholm. But the Finn wore a haunted expression, as though bowing to the inevitability of his fate. The others, all of them, were only there to make up the numbers. That even applied to Carlos Sainz, who managed one fastest time and also to Francois Delecour, who was in trouble with his brakes, a slow puncture and dust clouds when he got stuck behind Martin, who was in bother.

As for Didier Auriol, the second leg was nothing less than purgatory, with an erratically handling chassis, no power steering and a broken universal joint. All this meant that the rally had come down to a straight fight between Marcus Gronholm and Richard Burns. It was immediately apparent that the Englishman was quickest, setting five fastest times out of the first six stages. Gronholm was a worthy adversary, but this time he was not in the same league. And while he came up with a few excuses to explain his lack of pace, they lacked conviction. "Is it the car, the driver or the tyres? I don't know."

In the opposing camp, the team appeared to have adopted some of the unfriendly ways of Formula 1, with all the crew decked out with name badges and a special area erected around the cars to stop the spectators getting too close. Everyone was working with their usual quiet and calm efficiency. "When I look at the tyres on the other cars, I can see immediately that my Pirellis have an advantage," claimed Burns. "On top of that, the car's going really well and I can attack without having to worry about it, especially on the quick bits where it really is amazing."

Towards the end of the day, he stole the lead off Gronholm, but then he was slowed a bit by the dark and the dust and eventually finished the leg in second place.

At the wheel of a Team Grifone Toyota, Harri Rovanpera wanted to prove that he was worthy of better than getting the sack from Seat at the end of '99. He finished fourth.

PORTUGAL

That would give him a major advantage on the final leg. He was now following the Finn, who would have the job of brushing the top layer of dust off the track, thus making it quicker. More importantly, it was obvious that Burns and his Subaru was the strongest combination. Any outcome other than a win for the Englishman was illogical and almost unfair.

Of course, Gronholm was still in the lead at the start of the third leg, with a 14.6 advantage. But these infinitesimal moments of eternity were about as much use as a straw house to the little piggy and it only took Burns two stages to blow him away. At the start of the last stage a mere 1.7 separated them; nothing in real terms, maybe a difference of forty metres between the Impreza and the 206, based on the rally's average speed of 86.6 km/h after 387.20 km of stages.

But paradoxically, those 1.7 seconds seemed as solid as a rock for the Englishman and indeed, he went on to win the stage. More importantly, for the first time in his career, he was now leading the world championship.

Year by year, the Portuguese rally has become a model of how to handle the safety side of the sport, although the marshals take the odd risk.

Misfortune for Martin: penalised for servicing illegally, he lost a good sixth place.

THE WINNER

Burns does the double

On cloud nine and amazingly chatty for a lad who has been known to get a tad big headed at times, Richard Burns was flying on the wings of delight once he crossed the finish line. He had put on a perfect demonstration, with 12 fastest times from 23 stages, he was perfectly relaxed at the critical moments and he concentrated hard when he had to deal with pressure from Gronholm. It was a stunning performance. It was all done at the wheel of a much modified Subaru and he never put a foot wrong. He even had to deal with a dark moment, forced to run in the dust of a slowing Sainz on the second stage. "There is no outstanding factor to explain this win," was his post event analysis. "I think it was a combination of the car, tyres and driver, which was perfect. I am in complete harmony with the new Subaru. I am not saying that I could not have won here with the Impreza 99, which I took to the win in the Safari. But it would have been less of a certainty." He went on to pay tribute to his team. "This victory is the result of two months hard work from the team. I am delighted to thank them in this way." The ever media conscious David Richards was feeling so magnanimous, he even found time to praise Marcus Gronholm. "Richard has a good chance of taking the title and Marcus might just be his most serious rival."

Nothing could detract from the fact that Burns had pulled off a major coup. He was now out on his own in the lead of the drivers' classification, six points ahead of Gronholm and Makinen. It was the first time in eighteen months that anyone had managed to get ahead of the Finnish colossus. Didier Auriol had caught up with him in 1999, but never got in front. The lanky lad from Reading had gone one better. Was it the end of an era of total and impressive dominance by Tommi Makinen, who had things all his own way since 1996? "I hope so, I really hope so," joked Burns who did not beat around the bush.

THE TALKING POINT OF THE RALLY

Safety is OK

The Portuguese Rally has always had a bad reputation. The over excited state of its spectators, their uncontrolled passion and madness meant that in the past, they had played the role of toreadors with the passing cars in the role of the bulls. It had often ended in tears on this great event. In 1986, the death of three spectators, hit by Joaquim Santos, had come as a shock to lovers of the sport. Today, the situation has been turned around. This event has almost become a model of what can be done to control crowds at motor sport events. A huge number of police do an incredible job and there were never any concerns about safety in the stages. While the rally itself never had any bother with spectators, the link sections were generally out of bounds to them, which meant that those which were open were very heavily congested. In fact, on the final leg, run not far from the border with Spain, to the north of Porto, most of the roads were quite simply closed to all traffic. With the three day event attracting a massive 950,000 strong crowd, it was obvious that this was the only realistic solution. For the drivers at least, this was a model rally. Carlos Sainz was just one of many drivers to heap praise on the organisation of the Portuguese event. "A few years ago, you could only dream of competing in an event like this. While Portugal used to be the worst in the past, the remarkable job done by the organisers has proved that even here it is possible. That's good news for everyone, although I admit it's really difficult for the spectators."

THE COMEBACK

Hello Harri

The last time we had seen him was at the end of 1999, disgusted and down and out. Shown the door like some common criminal by Seat, just like his Italian colleague Piero Liatti, Harri Rovanpera had made way for Didier Auriol, understandable really, and also for Toni Gardemeister, less so, even though the latter was seen as the future little miracle from Suomi. So Harri hopped home, doing just one rally in Sweden, which was nothing much to write home about, at the wheel of a Seat Cordoba WRC. But there were better things in store than the desperate little Spanish coupe: a nice 1999 factory Toyota Corolla WRC for example.

Immediately, Harri Rovanpera was back on top form in Portugal, driving the same car which Sainz and Auriol had used the previous year. This driver, who easily loses his motivation, finished fourth in the car prepared by the Grifone team, entered thanks to financial backing from his manager, Timo Joukhi. The team planned to do other rallies as well. "As long as he doesn't go to Mitsubishi," claimed Grifone boss Fabrizio Tabaton. There was indeed a strong rumour he would be replacing an off-form Freddy Loix in the factory team. In the end, it did not happen and Rovanpera had to wait for his home event in Finland to make his reappearance on the scene. With the same team and support, he put on a great show, only losing second place to Colin McRae in the closing stages. With two sparkling performances his career appeared to be back on track. ■

PORTUGAL

Using and abusing his 206 WRC, Marcus Gronholm was the only man who really put up any sort of challenge against eventual winner Burns. His second place in Porto was still good enough to put him in second place in the drivers' championship, equal with Makinen, six points behind the Englishman.

PORTUGAL

PORTUGAL

These two cars made their debut in 1999. Compared with the big and bulky Skoda Octavia WRC, the Peugeot 206 is a model of balance and efficiency. It has to be said the two teams do not have the same budgets and with very limited funds, the worthy Czech team sometimes performed miracles.

33rd PORTUGUESE RALLY

4th leg of the 2000 world rally championship for constructors and drivers
4th leg of the production car drivers' and team's world cups

Date 16 - 18 march 2000
Route 1646,96 km divided into 3 legs,
23 special stages on dirt roads (398,35 km.)
Prologue: Thursday 16 march: Matosinhos - Baltar - Matosinhos, 1 stage (3,2 km)
1st leg: Friday 17 march: Matosinhos - Cabeceiras de Basto - Matosinhos, 10 stages (155,60 km)
2nd leg: Saturday 18 march: Matosinhos - Arganil - Matosinhos, 9 stages (179,25 km)
3rd leg: Sunday 19 march: Matosinhos - Ponte de Lima - Matosinhos, 3 stages (60,30 km)
Starters - Finishers: 114 - 48
Conditions: nice warm weather, dusty roads.

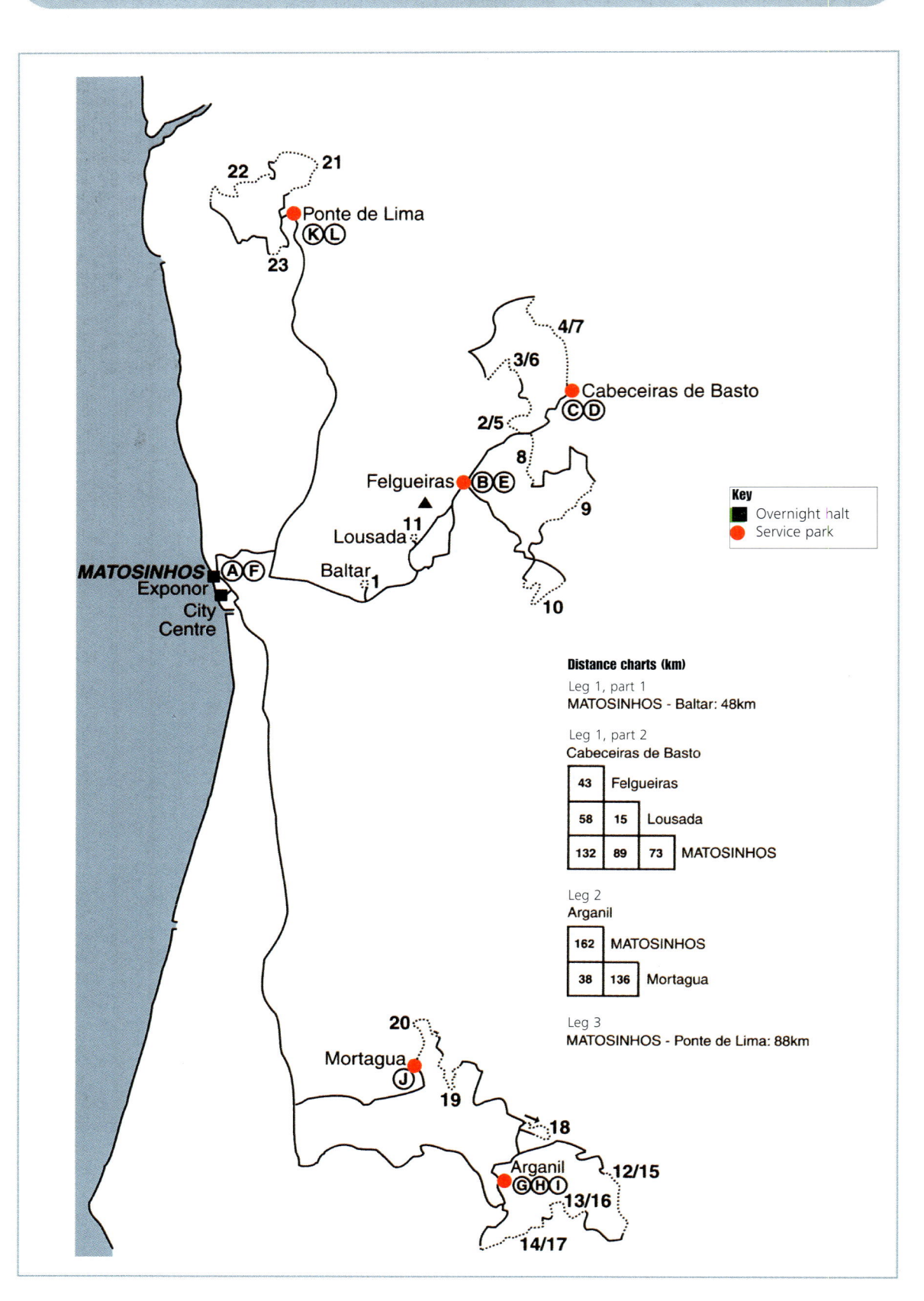

TOP ENTRIES

#	Driver - Co-driver	Car
1	Tommi Makinen - Risto Mannisenmaki	MITSUBISHI LANCER Evo 6
2	Freddy Loix - Sven Smeets	MITSUBISHI CARISMA GT
3	Richard Burns - Robert Reid	SUBARU IMPREZA WRC 2000
4	Juha Kankkunen - Juha Repo	SUBARU IMPREZA WRC 2000
5	Colin McRae - Nicky Grist	FORD FOCUS WRC
6	Carlos Sainz - Luis Moya	FORD FOCUS WRC
7	Didier Auriol - Denis Giraudet	SEAT CORDOBA WRC Evo 2
8	Toni Gardemeister - Paavo Lukander	SEAT CORDOBA WRC Evo 2
9	François Delecour - Daniel Grataloup	PEUGEOT 206 WRC
10	Marcus Gronholm - Timo Rautiainen	PEUGEOT 206 WRC
11	Armin Schwarz - Manfred Hiemer	SKODA OCTAVIA WRC
12	Luis Climent - Alex Romani	SKODA OCTAVIA WRC
14	Kenneth Eriksson - Staffan Parmander	HYUNDAI ACCENT WRC
15	Alister McRae - David Senior	HYUNDAI ACCENT WRC
16	Harri Rovanpera - Risto Pietilainen	TOYOTA COROLLA WRC
17	Gustavo Trelles - Jorge Del Buono	MITSUBISHI LANCER Evo 6
19	Petter Solberg - Phil Mills	FORD FOCUS WRC
20	Thomas Radstrom - Jorgen Skallamn	TOYOTA COROLLA WRC
21	Pedro Matos Chaves - Sergio Paiva	TOYOTA COROLLA WRC
22	Adruzilo Lopez - Luis Liboa	PEUGEOT 206 WRC
23	Rui Madeira - Fernando Prata	SEAT CORDOBA WRC
24	Frederic Dor - Didier Breton	SUBARU IMPREZA WRC
25	Markko Martin - Michael Park	TOYOTA COROLLA WRC
26	Krzysztof Holowczyc - Jean Marc Fortin	SUBARU IMPREZA WRC
27	Pasi Hagstrém - Tero Gardemeister	TOYOTA COROLLA WRC
28	Janne Tuohino - Miikka Anttila	TOYOTA COROLLA WRC
29	Abdullah Bakhashab - Bob Willis	TOYOTA COROLLA WRC
34	Serkan Yazici - Erkan Bodur	TOYOTA COROLLA WRC
35	Michael Guest - David Green	HYUNDAI COUPE Evo 2
36	Kris Princen - Dany Colebunders	RENAUT MEGANE MAXI
37	Miguel Campos - Carlos Magalhaes	MITSUBISHI CARISMA GT
38	Manfred Stohl - Peter Muller	MITSUBISHI LANCER Evo 6
39	Uwe Nittel - Detlef Ruf	MITSUBISHI LANCER Evo 6
40	Roberto Sanchez - Ruben Garcia	SUBARU IMPREZA WRX
41	Gianluigi Galli - Guido Dé Amore	MITSUBISHI LANCER Evo 6
44	Claudio Menzi - Edgardo Galindo	MITSUBISHI LANCER Evo 6
49	Patrick Magaud - Guyléne Brun	FORD PUMA KIT CAR
52	John Buffum - Neil Wilson	MITSUBISHI LANCER Evo 5
55	Gabriele Pozzo - Rodolfo Ortiz	MITSUBISHI LANCER Evo 6

Key
■ Overnight halt
● Service park

Distance charts (km)

Leg 1, part 1
MATOSINHOS - Baltar: 48km

Leg 1, part 2
Cabeceiras de Basto

43	Felgueiras		
58	15	Lousada	
132	89	73	MATOSINHOS

Leg 2
Arganil

162	MATOSINHOS	
38	136	Mortagua

Leg 3
MATOSINHOS - Ponte de Lima: 88km

SPECIAL STAGE TIMES

ES.1 Baltar (3,2 km)
1. Gronholm 3'06"2; 2. Rovanpera 3'06"4; 3. C.McRae 3'06"6; 4. Radstrom 3'08"2; 5. Kankkunen 3'08"6; 6. Burns 3'09"0; Gr.N Stohl 3'19"2

ES.2 Fafe-Lameirinha 1 (15,16 km)
1. C. McRae 9'58"6; 2. Sainz 10'04"1; 3. Burns 10'0"5; 4. Auriol 10'05"6; 5. Delecour 10'09"2; 6. Rovanpera 10'09"5; Gr.N Campos 10'32"7

ES.3 Fafe-Luilhas 1 (11,39 km)
1. Burns 8'29"5; 2. Auriol 8'32"9; 3. Delecour 8'33"5; 4. Sainz 8'33"8; 5. Gronholm 8'34"6; 6. Solberg 8'35 0; Gr.N Ferreyros 8'53"1

ES.4 Cabreira 1 (26,68 km)
1. Burns 17'41"3; 2. Gronholm 17'53 4; 3. Sainz 17'57"5; 4. Rovanpera 17'58"1; 5. Delecour 18'02"0; 6. Auriol 18'06"4; Gr.N Campos 18'41"7

ES.5 Fafe-Lameirinha 2 (15,16 km)
1. C. McRae 9'52"4; 2. Gronholm 9'56"1; 3. Burns et Delecour 9'56"6; 5. Sainz 9'57"1; 6. Makinen 10'00"7; Gr.N Campos 10'32"7

ES.6 Fafe-Luilhas 2 (11,39 km)
1. Burns 8'24"2; 2. Sainz 8'24"8; 3. C. McRae 8'25"0; 4. Delecour 8'28"9; 5. Solberg 8'30"0; 6. Makinen 8'31"4; Gr.N Campos 8'55"5

ES.7 Cabreira 2 (26,68 km)
1. Burns 17'42"5; 2. Gronholm 17'44"7; 3. Makinen 17'50"0; 4. Solberg 17'54"6; 5. Eriksson 17'58"2; 6. Loix 18'01"1; Gr.N Menzi 18'56"5

ES.8 Vizo (11,77 km)
1. Rovanpera 7'31"5; 2. Martin 7'31"6; 3. Gronholm 7'31"7; 4. Makinen 7'33"4; 5. Sainz 7'33"8; 6. Radstrom 7'34"3; Gr.N Stohl 7'50"2

ES.9 Fridao (14,20 km)
1. Sainz 10'25"4; 2. Gronholm 10'28"0; 3. Rovanpera 10'28"7; 4. Auriol 10'32"7; 5. Delecour 10'32"9; 6. Marin 10'34"6; Gr.N Nittel 11'00"8

ES.10 Aboboreira (17,87 km)
1. Sainz 12'18"7; 2. Gronholm 12'20"0; 3. Delecour 12'23"2; 4. Solberg 12'24"5; 5. Loix 12'27"1; 6. Auriol 12'28"1; Gr.N Nittel 12'58"7

ES.11 Lousada (5,30 km)
1. Delecour 3'59"1; 2. Sainz 3'59"4; 3. Lopes 3'59"5; 4. Gronholm et Martin 4'00"1; 6. Hagstrom 4'00"4; Gr.N Leal 4'14"4

ES.12 Piodao 1 (24,78 km)
1. Burns 16'46"0; 2. Gronholm 17'05"0; 3. Sainz 17'05"5; 4. Loix 17'07"9; 5. Delecour 17'10"8; 6. Rovanpera 17'11"0; Gr.N Nittel 18'16"4

ES.13 Arganil 1 (14,27 km)
1. Burns 9'39"6; 2. Gronholm 9'46"9; 3. Sainz 9'50"8; 4. Rovanpera 9'54"7; 5. Solberg 9'57"6; 6. Delecour 10'00"7; Gr.N Campos 10'50"8

ES.14 Gois 1 (19,62 km)
1. Burns 11'24"0; 2. Gronholm 11'28"7; 3. Sainz 11'35"3; 4. Solberg 11'35"5; Delecour 11'36"3; 6. Gardemeister 11'41"9; Gr.N Campos 12'39"3

ES.15 Piodao 2 (24,78 km)
1. Solberg 17'09"6; 2. Burns 19'09"7; 3. Rovanpera 17'14"5; 4. Delecour 17'18"7; 5. Sainz 17'18"2; Gr.N Pozzo 19'20"2

ES.16 Arganil 2 (14,27 km)
1. Burns 9'49"9; 2. Sainz 9'52"5; 3. Gronholm 9'55"3; 4. Loix 9'55"9; 5. Rovanpera 9'57"6; 6. Solberg 10'01"3; Gr.N Stohl 11'07"2

ES.17 Gois 2 (19,62 km)
1. Burns 11'24"0; 2. Felecour 11'30"0; 3. Sainz 11'30"9; 4. Solberg 11'32"5; 5. Gronholm 11'35"2; 6. Rovanpera 11'38"0; Gr.N Stohl 12'45"7

ES.18 Tabua (13,40 km)
1. Sainz 8'35"9; 2. Burns 8'36"9; 3. Gronholm 8'37"9; 4. Delecour 8'38"2; 5. Rovanpera 8'38"6; 6. Loix 8'39"6; Gr.N Campos 9'10"5

ES.19 Agueneira (23,13 km)
1. Gronholm 16'59"6; 2. Sainz 17'04"4; 3. Delecour 17'07"7; 4. Burns 17'14"2; 5. Martin 17'18"8; 6. Rovanpera 17'20"0; Gr.N Campos 18'40"3

ES.20 Mortazel -Mortagua (25,38 km)
1. Gronholm 17'17"7; 2. Burns 17'28"7; 3. Rovanpera 17'42"3; 4. Gardemeister 17'54"2; 5. Delecour 17'59"8; 6. Loix 18'04"4; Gr.N Ferreyros 19'33"7

ES.21 Ponte de Lima Est (23,49km)
1. Burns 15'58"9; 2. Sainz 16'10"3; 3. Gronholm 16'11"4; 4. Martin 16'19"9; 5. Loix 16'25"1; 6. Gardemeister 16'25"6; Gr.N Ferreyros 17'24"6

ES.22 Ponte de Lima Ouest (25,66 km)
1.Burns 19'04"2 ; 2. Gronholm 19'08"0; 3. Sainz 19'23"5; 4. Delecour 19'27"7; 5. Rovanpera et Martin 19'37"1; Gr.N Ferreyros 20'59"3

ES.22 Ponte de Lima Sud (11,15km)
1. Burns 8'12"9; 2. Gronholm 8'17"7; 3. Sainz 8'27"8; 4. Loix 8'30"7; 5. Delecour 8'34"9; 6. Rovanpera 8'36"1; Gr.N Campos 9'24"5

RESULTS AND RETIREMENTS

	Driver/Co-Driver	Car	Gr.	Total time
1	Richard Burns - Robert Reid	Subaru Impreza WRC 2000	A	4h34m00,0s
2	Marcus Gronholm - Timo Rautiainen	Peugeot 206 WRC	A	4h34m06,5s
3	Carlos Sainz - Luis Moya	Ford Focus WRC	A	4h36m09,2s
4	Harri Rovanpera - Risto Pietilainen	Toyota Corolla WRC	A	4h37m18,2s
5	François Delecour - Daniel Grataloup	Peugeot 206 WRC	A	4h38m06,3s
6	Markko Martin - Michael Park	Toyota Corolla WRC	A	4h40m11,6s
7	Freddy Loix - Sven Smeets	Mitsubishi Carisma GT	A	4h41m28,9s
8	Armin Schwarz - Manfred Hiemer	Skoda Octavia WRC	A	4h41m47,4s
9	Tony Gardemeister - Paavo Lukander	Seat Cordoba WRC Evo 2	A	4h42m24,2s
10	Didier Auriol - Denis Giraudet	Seat Cordoba WRC Evo 2	A	4h46m38,0s
15	Miguel Campos - Carlos Magalhaes	Mitsubishi Carisma GT	N	4h58m02,5s
ES.4	Juha Kankkunen - Juha Repo	Subaru Impreza WRC 2000	A	Accident
ES.4	Alister McRae - David Senior	Hyundaï Accent WRC	A	Transmission
ES.7	Krzysztof Holowczyc - Jean Marc Fortin	Subaru Impreza WRC	A	Suspension
ES.7	Tommi Makinen - Risto Manisenmaki	Mitsubishi Lancer Evo 6	A	Accident
ES.7	Colin McRae - Nicky Grist	Ford Focus WRC	A	Engine
ES.10	Thomas Radstrom - Jorgen Skallamn	Toyota Corolla WRC	A	Transmission
ES.14	Kenneth Eriksson - Staffan Parmander	Hyundaï Accent WRC	A	Fire
ES.14	Uwe Nittel - Detlef Ruf	Mitsubishi Lancer Evo 6	N	Turbo
ES.15	Gustavo Trelles - Jorge Del Buono	Mitubishi Lancer Evo 6	N	Electronics
ES.19	Petter Solberg - Phil Mills	Ford Focus WRC	A	Clutch

EVENT LEADERS

ES.1	Gronholm
ES.2 > ES.3	C. McRae
ES.4 > ES.8	Burns
ES.9 > ES.16	Gronholm
ES.17 > ES.18	Burns
ES.19 > ES.21	Gronholm
ES.22 > ES.23	Burns

BEST PERFORMANCES

	1	2	3	4	5	6
Burns	12	3	2	1	-	1
Gronholm	3	10	5	1	2	-
Sainz	3	6	7	1	2	1
Delecour	1	1	3	5	7	1
Rovanpera	1	1	2	3	3	5
Solberg	1	-	-	4	2	2
Martin	-	1	-	2	2	1
Auriol	-	1	-	2	-	2
Makinen	-	-	1	1	-	2
Lopes	-	-	1	-	-	-
Loix	-	-	-	3	2	3
Gardemeister	-	-	-	1	-	2
Radstrom	-	-	-	1	-	1
Kankkunen	-	-	-	-	1	-
Eriksson	-	-	-	-	1	-
Hagstrom	-	-	-	-	-	1

CHAMPIONSHIP CLASSIFICATIONS

Drivers
1. Richard Burns	22
2. Tommi Makinen	16
2. Marcus Gronholm	16
4. Carlos Sainz	13
5. Juha Kankkunen	11
6. Didier Auriol	4

Constructors
1. Subaru	35
2. Mitsubishi	20
2. Peugeot	20
4. Ford	17
5. Seat	7
6. Skoda	5

Group N
1. Manfred Stohl	23
2. Jani Paasonen	10
2. Claudio Menzi	10

Team's cup
1. Turning Point Racing Team (Holowczyc)	10
1. Spike Subaru Team (Araï)	10
1. Frédéric Dor Rally Team (Dor)	10

PREVIOUS WINNERS

1973	Thérier - Jaubert / Alpine Renault A 110
1974	Pinto - Bernacchini / Fiat 124 Abarth
1975	Alen - Kivimäki / Fiat 124 Abarth
1976	Munari - Maiga / Lancia Stratos
1977	Alen - Kivimäki / Fiat 131 Abarth
1978	Alen - Kivimäki / Fiat 131 Abarth
1979	Mikkola - Hertz / Ford Escort RS
1980	Röhrl - Geistdörfer / Fiat 131 Abarth
1981	Alen - Kivimäki / Fiat 131 Abarth
1982	Mouton - Pons / Audi Quattro
1983	Mikkola - Hertz / Audi Quattro
1984	Mikkola - Hertz / Audi Quattro
1985	Salonen - Harjanne / Peugeot 205 T16
1986	Moutinho - Fortes / Renault 5 Turbo
1987	Alen - Kivimäki / Lancia Delta HF 4WD
1988	Biasion - Cassina / Lancia Delta Integrale
1989	Biasion - Siviero / Lancia Delta Integrale
1990	Biasion - Siviero / Lancia Delta Integrale
1991	Sainz - Moya / Toyota Celica GT-Four
1992	Kankkunen - Piironen / Lancia HF Integrale
1993	Delecour - Grataloup / Ford Escort RS Cosworth
1994	Kankkunen - Grist / Toyota Celica Turbo 4WD
1995	Sainz - Moya / Subaru Impreza
1996	Madeira - Da Silva / Toyota Celica GT-Four
1997	Makinen - Harjanne / Mitsubishi Lancer Ev.4
1998	McRae - Grist / Subaru Impreza WRC
1999	McRae - Grist / Ford Focus WRC

www.fordracing.net
Telefonica MoviStar
MARTINI
Valvoline
MICHELIN
Grist
McRae
5

catalunya

A long and unjust barren spell came to an end at last. Colin McRae was back in the winner's circle, while Peugeot's ambitions drowned in a sea of over complication and over reaching.

THE RALLY

McRae, survival of the fittest

A pale and watery sun finally deigned to barge its way through a couple of clouds to send a dull halo of light over the Catalan hills. It was proof that the sun did indeed exist, but not only did it get up late that day, it also went to bed early at nighttime, dead on five o'clock, when it was all over and the leg had come to an end, prayers had been said and the chorus boys were no doubt already in bed.

If indeed prayers were offered up, then they were probably for the tyres; those anthracite-black round objects, which underneath their bland and often tatty exterior and their nine kilos of rubber and steel are, when all is said and done, a monstrous technical achievement. No one doubted their importance on the heights above Lloret del Mar. The little holiday town has its own patron saint, called Cristina, who can be seen on the outside of the Saint Romand church, with a strange black wheel at the end of one arm.

At the end of the first leg, several prayers had been said to Saint Michelin and Saint Pirelli, asking them to look after the impatient drivers who set off full of hope to tackle the Pyrenees. Because it rained and rained throughout the length of this second leg and the storms were as rough as they were unpredictable. Throughout the 100 kilometres of timed sections that day, one had to be inspired by the skies to make exactly the right choice of tyre.

Right from the word go, Burns seemed to have the best advice. For the first three stage loop, the championship leader had opted for intermediate tyres, pretty similar to wets. It was the perfect decision which helped him to claim the fastest times and build up a lead that extended to 23.9 over his nearest rival during the course of the day. "I must admit that running first on the road has been an advantage. I can run very deep into the corners and my Subaru is throwing mud on the track which must be a problem for those behind!" Later, he was to lose some ground through poor tyre choice. Despite this error of judgement, he was still quickest on three of the six stages that day, enough to hang onto the lead, with the pursuing pack desperately trying to stay in touch.

They were led by the Ford boys, Sainz ahead of McRae, with the Scotsman eventually finishing the leg in second place, just 8 seconds down.

Then it was Tommi Makinen's turn to shine. As for the Peugeots, when it came to the game of "Pick The Right Tyre," their crews wore the dunce's cap and a sad expression, given that the 206s were not going well and were generally off the pace.

McRae cannot believe his eyes: after a year without a win, he has finally made it to the top of the podium.

The sun finally came out for the second leg, run through the heights of Tarragona in the south of the region. It is a magnificent setting with the Sierra de Roquerole, Sierra Montsant, Sierra de Gorraptes, Gratallops, La Riba and Coll Roig. All these high craggy hills, covered with olive, pine and chestnut trees, whose branches hang over the run down terraces of sleepy little villages, perched around old churches, were ringing to the sound of screaming engines and the cheers of a huge crowd, thrilling to the skills of the competitors.

The final confrontation was eventually played out in as many acts as there were stages - five in the longest leg of the event. Kicking off proceedings was the daunting Catalan challenge that is the 45.88 km of Gratallops to Escalladei. Colin McRae proved its master, setting an incredible fastest time, 8 seconds under Philippe Bugalski's record time from 1999. This allowed him to threaten Richard Burns right from the start of the day. "As we'll be tackling this stage again in the afternoon, it's a great way to start," bragged the Ford driver. "The others now know what they can expect."

For his part, Burns who had led the first leg, claimed extenuating circumstances. "I'm having gear selection problems. The gearbox has become very slow," he explained at the end of the stage. "On top of that, my brakes are beginning to fade. I don't know how much time all that has cost me. 10, 15, maybe 20 seconds." Never mind, he was still leading from his fellow Brit and the rivalry between the two men was as strong as ever on this rally.

Colin's driving was as tasty as a single malt from the homeland and he was quickest again in the second run through Gratallops. But the gap to second placed Sainz was infinitesimal to say the least, just a tenth of a second separating the two men after 48 furious kilometres. In fact the top four, McRae, Sainz, Panizzi and Makinen were all within 1.2! It would be hard to imagine a more competitive situation. In Catalunya, there was an element of predictability to it all, as once the roads dry out the gaps come down and almost disappear completely.

Finally, having had the roads opened for him, it fell to Carlos Sainz to put on a show at the end of the day, taking the last two stages, once a slight understeer problem on his Focus had been solved. He also made the most of the fact that McRae had eased off a touch. "Apart from the Monte Carlo which is such a specialist event, this is my first all-tarmac rally with the Ford," explained His Eminence King Carlos. "All the work of the past few months has now paid off."

As the rally rested in preparation for the final push, we faced the tantalising prospect of a thrilling fight between the three leaders as McRae, Burns and Sainz were within ten seconds of one another, with four stages and 110 kilometres remaining.

None of these three drivers was able to stamp his authority on the rally as the last day got underway. With two stages remaining, Colin McRae and Richard Burns were separated by just 1.1 and in third place, Carlos Sainz was just 5.5 further back. "I'm not interested in finishing, I just want to win," intoned the Scotsman. "If I finish, then I'll have won. It's an exciting fight and the fact that Burns is a fellow Brit doesn't put me under any extra pressure."

Of course, McRae was also up against the local hero in the shape of Carlos Sainz, whose scowling countenance graced the front pages of all the newspapers. At the end of the day, all Burns' and Sainz's efforts were in vain, even if they both put on a great show in their attempts to shut down McRae. In second place, Burns consolidated his lead in the world championship, nine points ahead of Makinen, who finished fourth. The Englishman was also ten points up on Gronholm and eleven on Sainz. "What is positive about this, is that it's the first tarmac rally where I have been competitive. I honestly didn't expect that Robert and me would be on the pace on this surface. It's something to celebrate. Maybe I no longer have a weak point."

In the constructors' classification, victory for McRae, with Sainz third, meant that the blue oval was back in contention, in second spot behind Subaru. "It's good to be a winner again," concluded a delighted Ford boss Malcolm Wilson.

A low profile for Peugeot, which blew its own trumpet before the event, only to be put in its place once the rally was underway.

THE WINNER

McRae reborn

The joy of winning is that it confers humanity on the victor, even in the case of Colin McRae, often seen as a cross between Terminator and Highlander. It was almost touching to see the smile and emotion on his face. It certainly made him more sympathetic. It was worth watching his arrival in the final service area of the Catalan rally. His usual scowl had evaporated, even under the cloudy skies that

CATALUNYA

hung over the sad little town of Manlleu, not exactly the place one would choose to build castles in the air. He was grinning from ear to ear, evidently happy with the win and maybe even happy with life. There was plenty to smile about, because McRae had become a stranger to victory, his last one was now thirteen months old. It had been followed by a disastrous run of retirements, which had as much to do with the dubious reliability of his Ford Focus as his occasional moments of madness and inattention. He had written himself off with monotonous regularity, the four horsemen of the apocalypse apparently never very far from his side.

This victory had slaked his thirst, especially as it was constructed on a peerless performance at the wheel, producing several fastest stage times, one of them on the final leg. It had not all been plain sailing however. The clutch had to be changed at the first service point on the last morning and as the repair took longer than the time allowed, it cost him a 10s penalty. Nevertheless, the Scotsman managed to put 7 seconds over on Burns and 8.4 on Sainz, by the end of the 37 kilometres of the St. Julia to Arbucies stage. It was a stylish drive, warmly applauded by the large crowd, some of whom had been keen enough to camp overnight in the mountains to get a front row seat.

"This stage was really the turning point," the winner would tell us later. "The surface was mixed, part dry and part greasy and that made life even more complicated. When Nicky and me saw our time, we realised we could win." This was world championship win number nineteen for the Scotsman and he reckoned that after such a tough contest, it was one of his best.

"Not having won for ages, I had forgotten what it feels like," said the delighted driver, before being prompted to think of even greater prizes. "If we can string together one or two more results like this, then maybe we can start thinking about the title again." Winning evidently gives you an appetite.

DELUSIONS
A time of dashed hopes

Peugeot's Vincent Laverne sported a cheerful expression above his immaculate dark blue uniform. But he might have done better to keep his thoughts to himself and his mouth tight shut. "It feels like revenge for the Monte Carlo," he joked the day before the start of the Catalan Rally. The team coordinator had perfectly summed up the mood in the Peugeot Sport camp.

There were at least three good reasons to explain the feelings of optimism. After the disastrous events in Monaco back in January, the grey WRC had shown its true potential and proved reliable. Secondly, tarmac had always been something of a speciality surface for Peugeot, especially when its driving ranks are bursting with specialised talent in this domain, in the form of Delecour and Panizzi and finally, the Sochaux firm had turned up in Spain with the latest evolution of the 206.

The team's chief engineer, Michel Nandan was only too happy to give the guided tour: "The new car is fitted with three controlled differentials, the rear is also hydraulic now, like the front and rear ones. This gives greater flexibility in terms of set up and improves driveability. On top of that, we have an improved engine here, with new inlet and exhaust manifolds and a new turbo. This has given it a wider power band and it has got rid of the hole in the bottom end of the rev range. Finally, the wiring loom is lighter and simpler. Overall, the car is four to five kilos lighter."

Gilles Panizzi can afford to look daft. He was expecting a lot from this rally, but he had to make do with sixth place, having handed fifth to his team leader Gronholm.

Add in a much modified hydraulic system and a redesigned deflector on the bonnet, aimed at improving cooling as well as directing hot air away from the air intake on the roof and you have the full factory tour. But despite the fact that Nikko is one of Peugeot's main sponsors, there is no guarantee that the route to victory is preordained and radio controlled. Quite the contrary in fact as Catalunya proved to be yet another wrong turning for the French company.

Right from the very first stages, it was patently obvious that the 206 was powerless against the Fords and Burns' Subaru. "We are going round in circles," admitted team manager Xavier Carlotti. "There's a glitch somewhere. We expected a lot from the 2000 car."

While Delecour had gearbox problems in the closing stages, the trouble ran deeper than that. It was more insidious and had something to do with the way the improved engine was running. "We have a central electronics system which links the differentials to the way the engine is being used," explained Francois Delecour's engineer, Julien Loisy. "On our evolution car, the interaction between these two elements is not working perfectly and our settings are all wrong." In simple terms, it seemed that the extra power from the engine was causing the bother. The problem had been spotted even before the start and the engineers had decided to err on the side of caution by slightly reducing the power of the tubos. So, it did not really matter that Panizzi had to eventually hand over fifth place to a hard charging Gronholm, who set his first ever fastest stage time on tarmac, as the Finn was better placed in the championship. It was just the final twist in an event that was best forgotten. The disappointment is always stronger when you expect to do well.

"THE WOLF"
Auriol's long night

For its home event, the Seat factory being just down the road from Barcelona, the Spanish team was cursed with bad luck even before the start. The shake down session on the Wednesday prior to the start had shown there was much that needed shaking down on Didier Auriol's car. The front end of his car appeared to be suffering with a severe case of Saint Vitus' dance. It was very hard to explain as there was no trace of the malady on team-mate Toni Gardemeister's car. Less than twenty four hours before the start, team boss Jaime Puig took the decision to build up the spare car for Auriol to use. The mechanics worked all night to get it ready, complete with the big novelty for this event, a "joystick" gear shift. They did a good job, but not long after the start of the rally, the front end handling problem reappeared. "As soon as I accelerate, there is a very strange movement in the drive train," explained Auriol, who improved a bit by the middle of the event. He was finally posting times worthy of a former world champion, before it all fell apart again. A winner here in 98, second the year after, he dropped to thirteenth place this time. "It's hard to deal with, when you are used to fighting up at the front end." ■

On home turf, the Seat team was expecting to do well here. But Auriol had a miserable time, finishing thirteenth.

CATALUNYA

A more than successful outing for Richard Burns. The Englishman finished an impressive second on the Catalan tarmac, a surface which is not his strong point. It was just what was needed to maintain his lead in the championship.

Tommi Makkinen did manage to pick up two fastest times and finish a worthy fourth, but he was powerless in terms of the World Championship. It was starting to bother him as it seemed the Lancer was past its sell-by date.

CATALUNYA

The Catalunya rally might well be run over roads which the drivers are not very keen on - wide, with few corners and not technically challenging, but the event itself is hugely popular. Run through spectacular scenery, the Spanish leg of the world championship is very well organised and has become a cornerstone of the series.

CATALUNYA

TOP ENTRIES

1. Tommi Makinen - Risto Mannisenmaki
   MITSUBISHI LANCER Evo 6
2. Freddy Loix - Sven Smeets
   MITSUBISHI CARISMA GT
3. Richard Burns - Robert Reid
   SUBARU IMPREZA WRC 2000
4. Juha Kankkunen - Juha Repo
   SUBARU IMPREZA WRC 2000
5. Colin McRae - Nicky Grist
   FORD FOCUS WRC
6. Carlos Sainz - Luis Moya
   FORD FOCUS WRC
7. Didier Auriol - Denis Giraudet
   SEAT CORDOBA WRC Evo 2
8. Toni Gardemeister - Paavo Lukander
   SEAT CORDOBA WRC Evo 2
9. François Delecour - Daniel Grataloup
   PEUGEOT 206 WRC
10. Gilles Panizzi - Hervé Panizzi
    PEUGEOT 206 WRC
11. Armin Schwarz - Manfred Hiemer
    SKODA OCTAVIA WRC
12. Luis Climent - Alex Romani
    SKODA OCTAVIA WRC
14. Kenneth Eriksson - Staffan Parmander
    HYUNDAI ACCENT WRC
15. Alister McRae - David Senior
    HYUNDAI ACCENT WRC
16. Marcus Gronholm - Timo Rautiainen
    PEUGEOT 206 WRC
17. Jesus Puras - Marc Marti
    CITROEN XSARA KIT CAR
18. Henrik Lundgaard - Jens Christian Anker
    TOYOTA COROLLA WRC
19. Adruzilo Lopez - Luis Liboa
    PEUGEOT 206 WRC
20. Andrea Navarra - Simona Fedeli
    TOYOTA COROLLA WRC
21. Andrea Dallavilla - Danilo Fappani
    SUBARU IMPREZA WRC
22. Salvador Canellas - Carlos Del Barrio
    SEAT CORDOBA WRC
23. Markko Martin - Michael Park
    TOYOTA COROLLA WRC
24. Abdullah Bakhashab - Bob Willis
    TOYOTA COROLLA WRC
25. Toshihiro Araï - Roger Freeman
    SUBARU IMPREZA WRC
26. Serkan Yazici - Erkan Bodur
    TOYOTA COROLLA WRC
28. Michael Guest - David Green
    HYUNDAI COUPE Evo 2
29. Kris Princen - Dany Colebunders
    RENAUT MEGANE MAXI KIT CAR
30. Gustavo Trelles - Jorge Del Buono
    MITSUBISHI LANCER Evo 6
31. Manfred Stohl - Peter Muller
    MITSUBISHI LANCER Evo 6
32. Uwe Nittel - Detlef Ruf
    MITSUBISHI LANCER Evo 6
33. Roberto Sanchez - Ruben Garcia
    SUBARU IMPREZA WRX
34. Ramon Ferreyros - Gonzalo Saenz
    MITSUBISHI LANCER Evo 6
36. Miguel Campos - Carlos Magalhaes
    MITSUBISHI CARISMA GT
38. Pernilla Walfridsson - Ulrika Mattsson
    MITSUBISHI LANCER Evo 6
41. Fabrice Morel - Philippe Guellerin
    PEUGEOT 206 WRC
54. Patrick Magaud - Guylène Brun
    FORD PUMA KIT CAR
63. Gabriele Pozzo - Rodolfo Ortiz
    MITSUBISHI LANCER Evo 6
64. Claudio Menzi - Edgardo Galindo
    MITSUBISHI LANCER Evo 6

36th SPANISH RALLY

5th leg of the 2000 world rally championship for constructors and drivers
5th leg of the production car drivers' and team's world cupam's cup" 2000
Date 31 march - 02 april 2000
Route 1874,70 km divided into 3 legs,
15 special stages on tarmac roads (383,09 km.)
1st leg: Friday 31 march: Lhoret de Mare - Manlleu - Lhoret de Mare, 6 stages (91,06 km)
2nd leg: Saturday 1st april: Lhoret de Mare - Reus - Lhoret de Mare, 5 stages (181,65 km)
3rd leg: Sunday 02 april: Lhoret de Mare - Manlleu - Lhoret de Mare, 4 stages (110,38 km)
Starters - Finishers: 91 - 55
Conditions: rain then sun, damp roads then dry for the last two legs.

Skoda finally entered the record books thanks to Schwarz (here we see Climent) who scored the Czech marque's first ever fastest stage time.

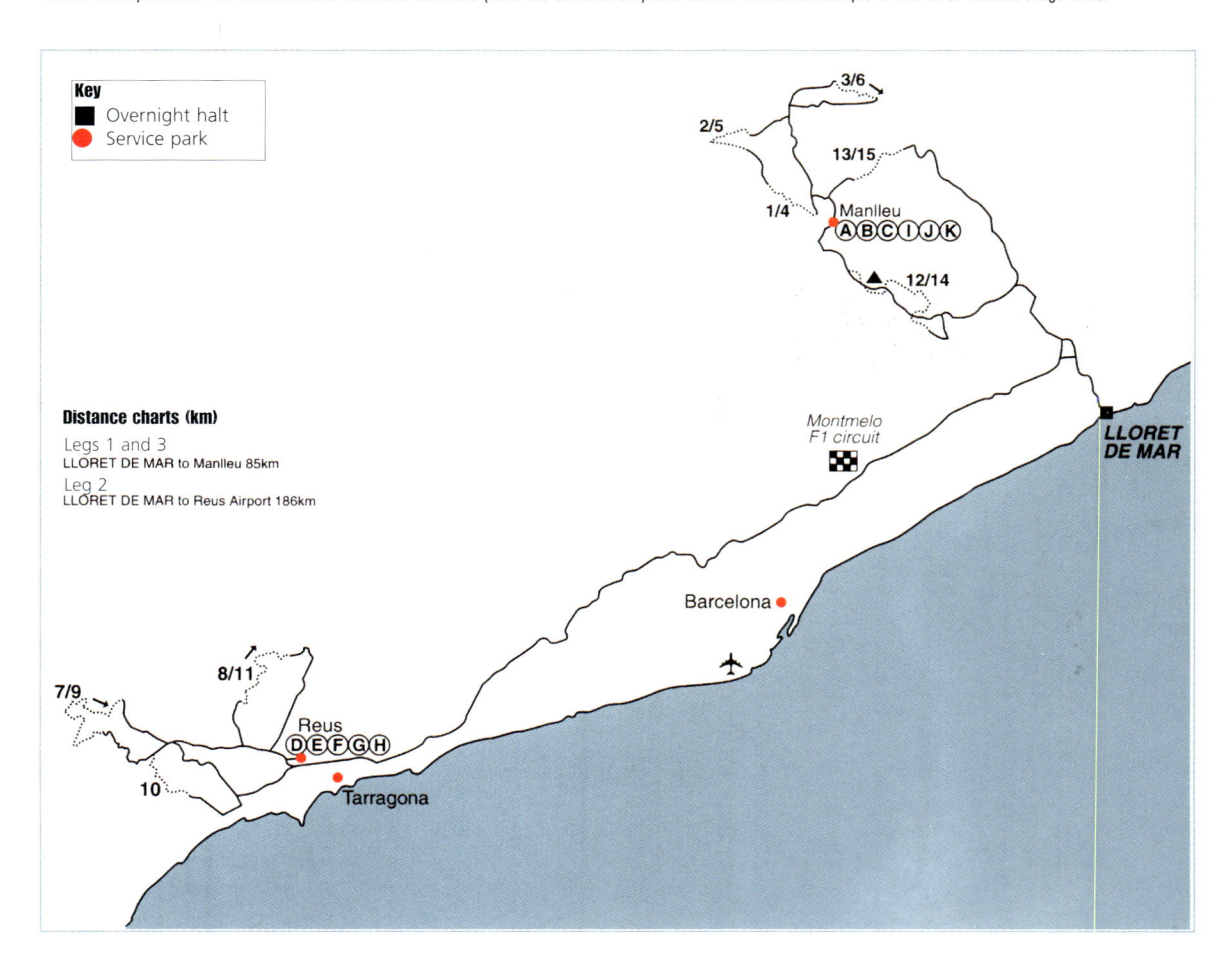

Key
- ■ Overnight halt
- ● Service park

Distance charts (km)
Legs 1 and 3
LLORET DE MAR to Manlleu 85km
Leg 2
LLORET DE MAR to Reus Airport 186km

SPECIAL STAGE TIMES

ES.1 La Trona 1 (12,88 km)
1. Burns 9'07"3; 2.Delecour 9'11"4; 3. C. McRae 9'13"6; 4. Gronholm 9'14"1; 5. Panizzi 9'16"6; 6. Martin 9'19"3; Gr.N Stohl 9'50"9

ES.2 Alpens - Les Lloses 1 (21,99 km)
1. Burns 14'30"3; 2. C. McRae et Sainz 14'35"5; 4. Makinen 14'41"1; 5. Delecour 14'44"1; 6. Martin 14'49"3; Gr.NNittel 15'40"2

ES.3 Coll de Santigosa 1 (10,66 km)
1. Sainz 7'07"6; 2. C. McRae 7'09"0; 3. Burnsz 7'09"3; 4. Makinen 7'11"2; 5. Delecour 7'13"4; 6. Gronholm 7'15"0; Gr.N Stohl 7'39"2

ES.4 La Trona 2 (12,88 km)
1. Burns 9'31"5; 2. C. McRae 9'44"2; 3. Makinen 9'44"4; 4. Sainz 9'45"0; 5. Gardemeister 9'46"6; 6. Gronholm 9'50"0; Gr.N Stohl 10'20"4

ES.5 Alpens - Les Lloses 2 (21,99 km)
1. Schwarz 15'00"8; 2. Makinen 15'03"1; 3. C. McRae 15'05"2; 4. Panizzi 15'06"0; 5. Navarra 15'07"5; 6. Sainz 15'10"7; Gr.N Nittel 15'49"1

ES.6 Coll de Santigosa 2 (10,66 km)
1. C. McRae 7'08"6; 2. Panizzi 7'10"2; 3. Sainz 7'11"0; 4. Makinen 7'11"2; 5. Gronholm 7'14"1; 6. Burns 7'14"4; Gr.N Trelles 7'44"5

ES.7 Gratallops - Escaladei 1 (45,88 km)
1. C. McRae 29'00"2; 2. Delecour 29'01"5; 3. Panizzi 29'02"5; 4. Sainz 29'04"9; 5. Makinen 29'15"8; 6. Burns 29'18"9; Gr.N Nittel 31'12"7

ES.8 La Riba 1 (36,16 km)
1. Makinen 22'36"4; 2. Burns 22'37"8; 3. Sainz 22'43"1; 4. Loix 22'44"1; 5. C. McRae 22'45"2; 6.Panizzi 22'46"1; Gr.N Nittel 24'16"2

ES.9 Gratallops - Escaladei 2 (45,88 km)
1. C. McRae 29'04"1; 2. Sainz 29'04"2; 3. Panizzi 29'04"7; 4. Makinen 29'05"3; 5. Burns 29'11"6; 6. Gronholm 29'13"7; Gr.N Trelles 31'14"5

ES.10 Coll Roig (17,57 km)
1. Sainz 10'41"3; 2. Burns 10'42"4; 3. Panizzi 10'43"0; 4. Delecour 10'43"7; 5. Makinen 10'45"9; 6. C. McRae 10'46"5; Gr.N Nittel 11'25"9

ES.11 La Riba 2 (36,16 km)
1. Sainz 22'41"0; 2. Burns 22'43"0; 3. C. McRae 22'45"4; 4. Panizzi 22'47"6; 5. Gronholm 22'49"6; 6. Delecour 22'50"9; Gr.N Nittel 24'18"1

ES.12 St Julia - Arbucies 1 (36,85km)
1. C. McRae 22'46"0; 2. Panizzi 22'52"1; 3. Burns 22'53"0; 4. Delecour 22'53"6; 5. Sainz 22'54"4; 6. Makinen 22'52"2; Gr.N Nittel 24'53"2

ES.13 Coll de Bracons 1 (18,34 km)
1. Makinen 12'03"7; 2. Sainz 12'04"4; 3. Panizzi 12'05"9; 4. Burns 12'06"4; 5. C. McRae 12'06"6; 6. Gronholm 12'08"1; Gr.N Trelles 13'05"9

ES.14 St Julia - Arbucies 2 (36,85km)
1. C. McRae 22'43"1; 2. Burns 22'47"9; 3. Sainz 22'48"6; 4. Makinen 22'50"1; 5.Panizzi 22'53"3; 6. Gronholm 22'56"4; Gr.N Nittel 24' 39"5

ES.15 Coll de Bracons 2 (18,34 km)
1. Gronholm 12'09"3; 2. Burns et C. McRae 12'09"8; 4. Sainz 12'10"5; 5. Makinen 12'11"3; 6. Loix 12'16"3; Gr.N Trelles 13'09"3

RESULTS AND RETIREMENTS

	Driver/Co-Driver	Car	Gr.	Total time
1	Colin McRae - Nicky Grist	Ford Focus WRC	A	4h07m13,0s
2	Richard Burns - Robert Reid	Subaru Impreza WRC 2000	A	4h07m18,9s
3	Carlos Sainz - Luis Moya	Ford Focus WRC	A	4h07m24,7s
4	Tommi Makinen - Risto Manisenmaki	Mitsubishi Lancer Evo 6	A	4h07m53,2s
5	Marcus Gronholm - Timo Rautiainen	Peugeot 206 WRC	A	4h09m04,7s
6	Gilles Panizzi - Hervé Panizzi	Peugeot 206 WRC	A	4h09m23,9s
7	François Delecour - Daniel Grataloup	Peugeot 206 WRC	A	4h10m49,4s
8	Freddy Loix - Sven Smeets	Mitsubishi Carisma GT	A	4h11m25,5s
9	Andrea Navarra - Simona Fedeli	Toyota Corolla WRC	A	4h12m18,4s
10	Markko Martin - Michael Park	Toyota Corolla WRC	A	4h12m42,0s
17	Uwe Nittel - Detlef Ruf	Mitsubishi Lancer Evo 6	N	4h26m10,7s
ES.1	Adruzilo Lopes - Luis Lisboa	Peugeot 206 WRC	A	Accident
ES.4	Kris Princen - Dany Colebunders	Renaut Megane Maxi	A	Clutch
ES.6	Michael Guest - David Green	Hyundaï coupé Evo 2	A	Accident
ES.7	Jesus Puras - Marc Marti	Citroën Xsara Kit Car	A	Engine
ES.9	Alister McRae - David Senior	Hyundaï Accent WRC	A	Engine
ES.11	Tony Gardemeister - Paavo Lukander	Seat Cordoba WRC Evo 2	A	Lost a wheel
ES.11	Juha Kankkunen - Juha Repo	Subaru Impreza WRC 2000	A	Withdraw
ES.14	Luis Climent - Alex Romani	Skoda Octavia WRC	A	Lost a wheel
ES.14	Fabrice Morel - Philippe Guellerin	Peugeot 206 WRC	A	Transmission shaft

EVENT LEADERS

ES.1 > ES.6   Burns
ES.7 > ES.15 C. McRae

BEST PERFORMANCES

	1	2	3	4	5	6
C. McRae	5	4	3	-	2	1
Burns	3	5	2	1	1	2
Sainz	3	3	3	3	1	1
Makinen	2	1	1	5	3	1
Gronholm	1	-	-	1	2	5
Schwarz	1	-	-	-	-	-
Panizzi	-	2	4	2	2	1
Delecour	-	2	-	2	2	1
Loix	-	-	-	1	-	-
Navarra	-	-	-	-	1	1
Gardemeister	-	-	-	-	1	-
Martin	-	-	-	-	-	2

CHAMPIONSHIP CLASSIFICATIONS

Drivers
1. Richard Burns — 28
2. Tommi Makinen — 19
3. Marcus Gronholm — 18
4. Carlos Sainz — 17
5. Colin McRae — 14
6. Juha Kankkunen — 11

Constructors
1. Subaru — 41
2. Ford — 31
3. Mitsubishi — 23
3. Peugeot — 23
5. Seat — 7
6. Skoda — 5

Group N
1. Manfred Stohl — 27
2. Miguel Campos — 13
2. Gustavo Trelles — 12

Team's cup
1. Toyota Team Saudi Arabia (Bakhashab) — 16
1. Spike Subaru Team (Araï) — 16
3. Turning Point Racing Team (Holowczyc) — 10

PREVIOUS WINNERS

1991 Schwarz - Hertz
     Toyota Celica GT-Four
1992 Sainz - Moya
     Toyota Celica Turbo 4WD
1993 Delecour - Grataloup
     Ford Escort RS Cosworth
1994 Bertone - Chiapponi
     Toyota Celica Turbo 4WD
1995 Sainz - Moya
     Subaru Impreza
1996 McRae - Ringer
     Subaru Impreza
1997 Makinen - Harjanne
     Mitsubishi Lancer Ev.4
1998 Auriol - Giraudet
     Toyota Corolla WRC
1999 Bugalski - Chiaroni
     Citroën Xsara Kit Car

Carlos Sainz harvested more points for Malcolm Wilson's team.

HYUNDAI
Castrol
Hella
V7 MSD
MICHELIN
Castrol
Castrol
MICHELIN
Hella

argentina

Run in difficult conditions, Burns emerged victorious to tighten his grip on the title. On a rally he hardly knew, Gronholm was once again very impressive.

THE RALLY

Burns soars like a Condor

Argentina is a harsh country, populated by tough men. It is a land that offers no concessions, shows little pity and has few airs and graces. There is a beautiful savagery to the valley which winds through the centre of the Sierra Chica, with its hills covered in clouds, which thankfully never shed their load before the start of the rally. This is a land where you must be brave and give your all.

"Argentinidad" is the name given to this country's very own brand of machismo, mixing pride, courage and a sense of honour and freedom. It is best exemplified by the gauchos and for this event the rally drivers must also adopt the argentinidad mentality and this year more than ever. Why? Because they appear to have attacked this event from the very first moment, a look of determination on their faces. They were at one another's throats as soon as the amusing little overture that is the super-special was over. It had been held the night before, in front of a large crowd, whose passion for the spectacle was much warmer than the cool autumnal evening.

Burns played the role of showman that night, but once the rally proper was underway, he found obstacles in his path, starting with the engine of his Subaru, which was overheating.

First to take up the baton was Marcus Gronholm, who was soon into his stride and eating up the miles in his 206 to take the lead. "Yes, I have to admit, I am a bit surprised," he admitted. "But we have only just started," he added, before rounding off his comments with his catch phrase that always seems to hint at an impatient streak - " we will see." It was a pretty good showing from a lad who had only been here once before.

Actually, the big Finn was only the first of many to enjoy a moment of glory on this first leg. After Gronholm, it was Burns' turn, followed by Sainz to set the fastest times, so that we had first a Peugeot, then a Subaru and then a Ford. Listening to the local radio station, LV3, it was obvious that the commentator was finding it all too exciting, giving the rally the sort of treatment he usually reserved for a soccer match featuring the famous Boca Junior team.

During the first leg, there were those for whom there was no glory, but only despair. Among those was Francois Delecour, whose engine caught fire. At least Didier Auriol's woes had an element of humour about them. As he emerged from the stage, having set an excellent time, the Seat driver found himself lying in some animal excreta as he changed a puncture. "Could someone get some soap and water ready," laughed co-driver Denis Giraudet as he warned the team by radio. "Mr. Auriol has covered himself in dog mess!"

There's nothing like a good bath to sort out a problem of this sort and luckily for Auriol, he found a stream on the next stage in which to bathe. Sadly his car was stuck there, it might still be there today. The same applied to Gardemeister, in exactly the same spot, minus the dog mess.

Keeping out of all trouble was none other than Carlos Sainz, who finished on a rush to take the lead at the end of the first day. It would not last. He might have been spared ill fortune, but a driving error would do the job instead. It happened in a left hand corner with a bump that led into a right hander, or not in the case of Sainz. The Spaniard planted his Focus into a barrier which made papier mache of his radiator. "I am really sorry for the team," was his contrite comment over the radio as he admitted his error. Richard Burns did not miss the opportunity to have a little dig at the Spaniard. "Carlos must have turned the wheel while the car was in the air. It doesn't always work," he said in an acerbic tone.

He could afford to adopt a superior attitude, as he had been on great form, quickest on six out of the seven stages. This great drive meant he was eating up the gap to Gronholm which had stood at 35.4 at the start of the leg. He deposed the Finn at the end of the day, finishing a good 9.3 ahead, apart from one nasty moment with a ditch. "There are several reasons why he is quicker," explained a surprisingly calm Gronholm. "His car is going well here, the Pirelli tyres might be a little bit better than the Michelins on these damp roads and he also knows the stages better than me."

That still left the toughest leg of the rally to go and Burns would have not only Gronholm to contend with, as McRae was just 12 behind. It would all be played out on the high stages of the rally, with the runs through El Condor and Giulio Cesar.

Up there, in the grandiose Sierra Grande, the scene was set to await the arrival of the brave troops who were still on the battlefield. After a night of heavy rain which had turned to a storm at times, the mountain did not look welcoming, with its summit shrouded in mist. The vertiginous roads were running with torrents of water and mud, between the weird rocks which seemed to have been left on the ground by some giant hand in an earlier and anarchic act of creation. It was chaos. The day God worked on the Cumbre de Achala, he must have been in a particularly foul mood.

In these conditions, on these roads, bravery is not enough. You need madness and no sense of self preservation. While he might give the appearance of being a nice sensible young man, these conditions and mental requirements were right up Richard Burns' street. So before a pallid light of day had completely brushed away the night time, he was already flat chat at work with no sign of hesitation or even trepidation. Just to make sure everyone realised he was the boss, he set fastest time on the first three stages. It did not seem to matter that his Subaru engine was yet again showing signs of overheating, nor that cattle and horses strayed across his rapid path. The mud splattered Subaru driver confirmed his domination, while the opposition was left to choke on the mud flying behind him. McRae's Focus came to a dead halt in the village of Luran on the first stage. As for Kankkunen, he was unable to match the pace of his young team mate. As it turned out, the only one who seemed capable of putting up any sort of fight was Gronholm. Once again, the Peugeot driver was impeccable. But for him, the rally would have become very boring. To start with, he managed to escape almost undamaged from a huge moment. "I got a really big fright. I very nearly rolled, but in the end my car hit a mud bank." It was indeed fortunate, because the rear axle was only twisted, but it would surely have broken on contact with anything harder. On top of that the front bumper had bought it, on a day when most of the cars had the odd battle scar to show off. Gronholm being Gronholm, he showed no sign of taking it easy after that. He set off on the offensive, even more determined than before, setting fastest time in the apocalypse that was the misty La Posta. But it was all in vain.

Having been on first name terms with the Condors in the mountains, Burns rammed home his advantage in the drivers' championship, extending his lead over Gronholm to 14 points, thanks to this, his third win of the season.

This year, in the Argentinian autumn, Burns was really out on his own as he scored his third win of 2000.

Colin McRae, the first British world champion, no longer has anything to teach Richard Burns, who takes the title lead.

THE UNEXPECTED

Hyundai in the history books

Hyundai had never scored points in the World Rally Championship. But now, ever since the 2000 Argentinian Rally, they can hold their heads up high. Seventh place for Alistair McRae allowed the Korean manufacturer to feature in the record books. The points were actually those available for sixth spot, as that place was occupied by Petter Solberg in the Ford, who was ineligible for points, the Norwegian not having been entered for that privilege by his team.

Scoring points in only its fourth rally with the Accent WRC was already something of a victory for Hyundai. It was true that the Korean company, whose cars are prepared by the English firm MSD, benefited from the misfortune of many other cars which had been running higher up the order, but both its cars had made it to the finish, despite a few troubles along the way. Alister McRae had to deal with an overheating engine on the first day and then he had transmission worries on the second, followed by gearbox gremlins on the final leg.

His team mate, Kenneth Eriksson was eighth, despite power steering and differential problems, as well as radiator bothers and problems fording a stream, an overheating engine, a broken windscreen and a cockpit that insisted on misting up all the time. It was a long list!

When the Hyundais were trouble free, the Accent displayed a certain amount of potential. "We had hoped to score our first points around the mid season," rejoiced team boss David Whitehead. "To have done just that is fantastic. Now it is up to us to get to the end of the remaining rallies."

THE THUNDERBOLT
Cyprus at the heart of the conflict

The weather was glorious on the shake-down day, well organised on the hills of Villa Carlos Paz. It was a splendid day and it looked as though we were in for a great rally. Then suddenly, a thunderbolt hit the mountain and it had come all the way across the seas from Europe, from Cyprus to be precise. The FIA had pulled an event out of its hat. It decided that the Cyprus Rally, already a counter for the European Rally Championship, would now replace the Chinese round, which had pulled out of the series at the end of March, because of a lack of sponsors. The rumour had been doing the rounds for some weeks and now it was confirmed with a laconic press release. Due to run from 7th to 10th September, the reappearance of this once famous event did not please everyone; far from it in fact. Most opposed were the constructors, who were unanimous in their objection. "They tell us four months in advance," said an apoplectic Mitsubishi boss Andrew Cowan. "How can the FIA take such a decision? In the past, we the constructors have shown our support for them and this is how they repay that support. It's not a question of money, but its a logistical nightmare." Peugeot team manager Xavier Carlotti added weight to the argument. "China was an overseas rally with everything freighted out. With this one in Europe, we will have to rush back to the factory from Finland, set off again for Cyprus and then to make matters worse, we will be back to the factory and straight off to Corsica, a tarmac event not a loose surface once. Logistically, it is very tough." As far as Jaime Puig of Seat was concerned, FIA was moving too quickly. "A 14 rally calendar with two in reserve is one thing. We would have taken measures to turn the thing around. But not like this! Cyprus? Why not, but in 2001."

The next morning, the teams held a meeting and there was a talk of a mass boycott of the rally. But this sort of decision requires unanimity, which they could not reach; notably because of the British teams who like to abide by the letter of the law and avoid any confrontation with FIA. The drivers on the other hand were unanimous. "Cyprus is a well organised event," explained Carlos Sainz's co-driver Luis Moya. "But this decision makes no economic or sporting sense." As for Didier Auriol, he admitted he could not understand the decision. "The fact the rally is not that interesting from a sporting point of view is one thing, but when none of the teams want to do it, then why not listen to what they say?" The answer is simple. On the rallies commission, the constructors have three votes out of twenty eight and the drivers none. They had adopted this idea before putting it to the FIA World Council, which approved it by a fax vote! It goes without saying that in a situation like this, there was not a lot the teams could do about it. Shekhar Mehta, president of the FIA Rallies Commission gave a halfhearted explanation. "The Cypriots put themselves forward from the moment the Chinese event was cancelled. They have been on the list to stage a world championship event for 18 years and it is important to show that the club of world rally organisers is not a members only one."

In more general terms, the Cyprus affair raised the old spectre of the calendar and the possible future increase in the number of rallies counting towards the championship. The FIA was working on it flat out. Known for his diplomacy, Mehta is also a dab hand at the politics, which meant it was necessary to read between the lines of what he had to say. "For the moment we are looking at what is happening. We are asking questions. Are there some worthwhile rallies that are not on the calendar? Is the current 14 the right number? When television will generate more revenue thanks to the job taken on by David Richards, will we be under more pressure to extend the championship? There are many questions." Mehta himself would soon be off to supervise rallies in Turkey and the Lebanon, the second of these in the company of the aforementioned Mr. Richards. Both events had strong financial backing from Marlboro and they would not look out of place on the world stage. Nor would the Ypres Rally in Belgium, another rally which had declared its candidacy. There was also a lot of talk about events in Canada and South Africa, as well as the USA and Japan. It would be the work of a moment to turn the world rally championship into the 18 round series which is exactly what some factions within FIA had in mind for 2002.

THE THREAT
Gronholm has a close call

Cordoba was the scene of more than one spat. The end of the rally was marred by the threat of a penalty hanging over Marcus Gronholm.

With panache and pace, Marcus Gronholm took second place, which came under threat from the stewards at the end of the rally. He escaped punishment.

What had gone on in the refuelling zone in the Mina Clavero service area? The driver had indeed opened the bonnet of his 206 WRC, when it is strictly forbidden to do any work on the cars in the refuelling zone. The Peugeot clan was more than a bit worried, as it brought back bad memories of the penalty inflicted on the Estonian Martin in Portugal, when his co-driver had done some work on the car, picking up a 1.30s penalty. The FIA stewards decided to hear the driver out, accompanied by his co-driver Timo Rautiainen and a member of the Peugeot team. They had little choice but to agree that the driver had acted in the interests of safety, as he had noticed some smoke coming from the engine bay and he just wanted to check there was no risk of fire. It had been a close call and Gronholm almost lost a great second place. ∎

ARGENTINA

ARGENTINA

Freddy Loix had good cause to be pleased. This was his best event in 2000. Although he was fifth, the likeable Belgian struggled. Whose fault was that? The team's according to the driver and the driver's according to the team. Whatever the cause, yet again Mitsubishi was pretty much a one car team this year.

The Ford drivers put their heart and soul into it, but it was not enough. McRae and Sainz left South America with zero points. The Spaniard went off the road and the Scotsman's engine broke. It was a bad result. Of the three works Focus, only Petter Solberg got to the finish of this tough event, in sixth place.

ARGENTINA

ARGENTINA

But for Marcus Gronholm, the Argentinian rally could have been a bore. After giving himself a huge fright on the third leg, he set a great fastest time, just as appalling weather turned the event into a real struggle. Thanks to the efforts of the Peugeot man, Burns could not let up for a moment on the way to victory.

Tackling this bump in the middle of the third leg, produced some stylish action. Here we see the world champion, who managed to haul his ageing Mitsubishi up to third spot.

ARGENTINA

TOP ENTRIES

1 Tommi Makinen - Risto Mannisenmaki
   MITSUBISHI LANCER Evo 6

2 Freddy Loix - Sven Smeets
   MITSUBISHI CARISMA GT

3 Richard Burns - Robert Reid
   SUBARU IMPREZA WRC 2000

4 Juha Kankkunen - Juha Repo
   SUBARU IMPREZA WRC 2000

5 Colin McRae - Nicky Grist
   FORD FOCUS WRC

6 Carlos Sainz - Luis Moya
   FORD FOCUS WRC

7 Didier Auriol - Denis Giraudet
   SEAT CORDOBA WRC Evo 2

8 Toni Gardemeister - Paavo Lukander
   SEAT CORDOBA WRC Evo 2

9 François Delecour - Daniel Grataloup
   PEUGEOT 206 WRC

10 Marcus Gronholm - Timo Rautiainen
   PEUGEOT 206 WRC

14 Kenneth Eriksson - Staffan Parmander
   HYUNDAI ACCENT WRC

15 Alister McRae - David Senior
   HYUNDAI ACCENT WRC

16 Petter Solberg - Philip Mills
   FORD FOCUS WRC

17 Frederic Dor - Kevin Gormley
   SUBARU IMPREZA WRC

18 Krzytof Holowczyc - Jean Marc Fortin
   SUBARU IMPREZA WRC

19 John Papadimitriou - Petropoulos
   SUBARU IMPREZA WRC

20 Serkan Yazici - Erkan Bodur
   TOYOTA COROLLA WRC

21 Jorge Raul Recalde - Diego Curletto
   FORD ESCORT COSWORTH

22 Gustavo Trelles - Jorge Del Buono
   MITSUBISHI LANCER Evo 6

23 Manfred Stohl - Peter Muller
   MITSUBISHI LANCER Evo 6

24 Roberto Sanchez - Ruben Garcia
   SUBARU IMPREZA WRX

25 Claudio Menzi - Edgardo Galindo
   MITSUBISHI LANCER Evo 6

28 Andrea Aghini - Loris Roggia
   MITSUBISHI CARISMA GT

29 Ramon Ferreyros - Gonzalo Saenz
   MITSUBISHI LANCER Evo 6

34 Gabriele Pozzo - Rodolfo Ortiz
   MITSUBISHI LANCER Evo 6

20th RALLY OF ARGENTINA

6ème leg of the 2000 world rally championship for constructors and drivers
6ème leg of the production car drivers' and team's world cupam's cup" 2000
Date 11 - 14 may 2000
Route: 1558,84 km divided into 3 legs,
22 special stages on dirt roads (391.40 km) with one stage cancelled (370,33 km.)
Prologue: Thursday 11 may: Villa Carlos Paz - Villa Carlos Paz, 2 stages (6,88 km)
1st leg: Friday 12 may: Villa Carlos Paz - La Cumbre - Cordoba, 7 stages (126,92 km)
2nd leg: Saturday 13 may: Cordoba - Santa Rosa de Calamuchita - Cordoba, 7 stages (131,53km)
3rd leg: Sunday 14 may: Cordoba - Mina Clavero - Cordoba, 6 stages (121,07 km)
Starters - Finishers: 78 - 35
Conditions: cloudy with rain, muddy roads with several fords.

Both Seats drowned out in the same ford on the same stage. A nice one-two!

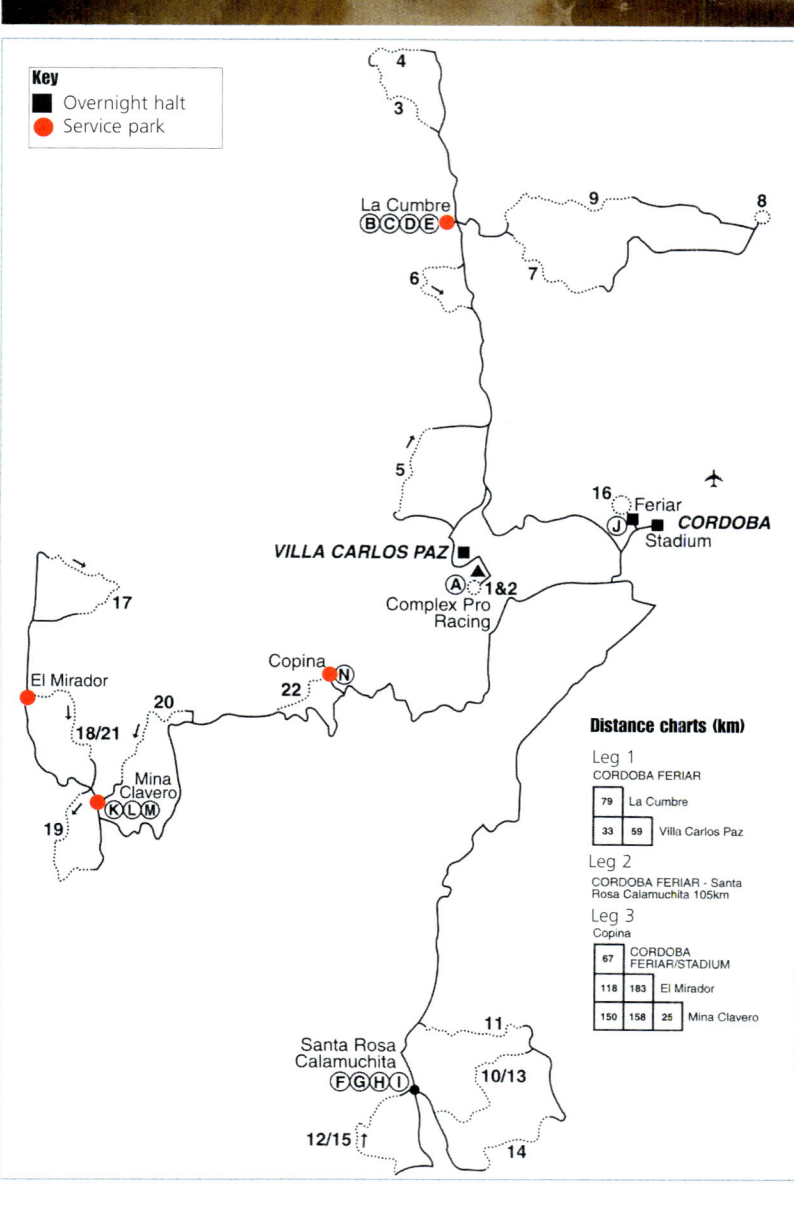

Key
■ Overnight halt
● Service park

Distance charts (km)

Leg 1
CORDOBA FERIAR
| 79 | La Cumbre |
| 33 | 59 | Villa Carlos Paz |

Leg 2
CORDOBA FERIAR - Santa Rosa Calamuchita 105km

Leg 3
Copina
67	CORDOBA FERIAR/STADIUM
118	183	El Mirador
150	158	25	Mina Clavero

SPECIAL STAGE TIMES

ES.1 Complejo Pro-Racing 1 (3,44 km)
1. Burns 2'29"2; 2. Gronholm 2'29"4; 3. Sainz 2'29"6; 4. C. McRae 2'30"7; 5. Delecour 2'30"9; 6. Kankkunen 2'31"3; Gr.N Pozzo 2'37"2

ES.2 Complejo Pro-Racing 2 (3,44 km)
1. Burns 2'26"5; 2. Gronholm 2'26"7; 3. Sainz 2'27"3; 4. Delecour 2'28"4; 5. Auriol 2'28"9; 6. Kankkunen 2'29"2; Gr.N Pozzo 2'35"8

ES.3 Capilla del Monte - San Marcos Sierras (23,02km)
1. Gronholm 17'37"2; 2. C. McRae 17'41"7; 3. Sainz 17'47"0; 4. Makinen 17'47"5; 5. Auriol 17'48"3; 6. Burns17'48"8; Gr.N Trelles 18'27"6

ES.4 San Marcos Sierras - Charbonier (9,61 km)
1. Burns 6'41"2; 2. Gronholm 6'43"5; 3. Makinen 6'44"0; 4. C. McRae 6'45"8; 5. Sainz 6'46"3; 6. Kankkunen 6'49"4; Gr.N Sanchez 7'13"2

ES.5 Tanti (16 km)
Annulée, spectateurs trop nombreux

ES.6 Villa Giardino - La Falda (22,53 km)
1. Sainz 16'16"0; 2. C. McRae 16'18"2; 3. Kankkunen 16'23"0; 4. Makinen 16'25"7; 5. Gronholm 16'28"8; 6. Burns 16'31"7; Gr.N Ligato 17'35"5

ES.7 La Cumbre - Agua de Oro (23,46 km)
1. Sainz 20'19"8; 2. Gronholm 20'22"9; 3. C. McRae 20'24"6; 4. Kankkunen 20'27"7; 5. Makinen 20'32"3; 6. Burns 20'39"7; Gr.N Trelles 21'43"8

ES.8 Super especial Colonia Caroya (3,40 km)
1. Gronholm 2'29"8; 2. Makinen 2'29"9; 3. C. McRae 2'30"0; 4. Sainz 2'30"2; 5. Solberg 2'30"4; 6. Loix 2'30"5; Gr.N Trelles 2'34"0

ES.9 Ascochinga - La Cumbre (28,83 km)
1. Sainz 19'06"1; 2. Gronholm 19'08"2; 3. Delecour 19'11"2; 4. Kankkunen 19'12"4; 5. Burns 19'13"7; 6. Makinen 19'13"8; Gr.N Pozzo 19'54"6

ES.10 Santa Rosa de Calamuchita - San Agustin 1 (26,10 km)
1. Burns 15'24"9; 2. C; McRae 15'32"2; 3. Gronholm 15'34"9; 4. Makinen 15'36"5; 5. Sainz 15'39"5; 6. Kankkunen 15'40"2; Gr.N Pozzo 16'31"1

ES.11 San Agustin - Villa Gral. Belgrano (12,46 km)
1. C. McRae 9'47"9; 2. Burns 9'52"4; 3. Gronholm 9'54"4; 4. Kankkunen 10'00"6; 5. Makinen 10'04"3; 6. Delecour 10'05"3; Gr.N Pozzo 10'31"1

ES.12 Amboy - Santa Rosa de Calamuchita 1 (21,48 km)
1. Burns 11'19"1; 2. C. McRae 11'21"1; 3. Makinen 11'22"5; 4. Kankkunen 11'24"8; 5. Gronholm 11'27"9; 6. Delecour 11'33"1; Gr.NStohl 12'20"6

ES.13 Santa Rosa de Calamuchita - San Agustin 2 (26,10 km)
1. Burns 15'29"1; 2. Makinen 15'30"1; 3. Kankkunen 15'33"0; 4. Gronholm 15'33"6; 5. C. McRae 15'34"6; 6. Delecour 15'45"7; Gr.N Trelles 16'35"2

ES.14 Las Bajadas - Villa Del Dique (18,67 km)
1. Burns 10'04"3; 2. Kankkunen 10'06"6; 3. Gronholm 10'10"8; 4. Makinen 10'11"7; 5. C; McRae 10'13"3; 6. Delecour 10'15"1; Gr.N Trelles 10'54"2

ES.15 Amboy - Santa Rosa de Calamuchita 2 (21,48 km)
1. Burns 11'14"4; 2. Kankkunen 11'18"1; 3. Makinen 11'20"7; 4. C. McRae 11'20"8; 5. Gronholm 11'24"1; 6. Delecour 11'26"2; Gr.N Pozzo 12'21"4

ES.16 Camping General San Martin (4,90 km)
1. Burns 4'13"0; 2. Kankkunen 4'13"9; 3. C. McRae 4'14"8; 4. Makinen et Gronholm 4'16"2; 6. Delecour 4'16"6; Gr.N Pozzo 4'34"0

ES.17 Chamico - Ambul (26,60 km)
1. Burns 18'06"4; 2. Gronholm 18'28"4; 3. Makinen 18'38"0; 4.Kankkunen 18'51"9; 5. Loix 19'17"5; 6. Solberg 19'21"8; Gr.N Trelles 20'06"7

ES.18 El Mirador - San Lorenzo 1 (20,65 km)
1. Burns 12'02"1; 2. Makinen 12'05"9; 3. Gronholm 12'10"6; 4. Kankkunen 12'16"4; 5. Delecour 12'39"7; 6. A. McRae 12'49"4; Gr.N Pozzo 13'19"9

ES.19 Cura Brochero - Nono (19,31 km)
1. Burns 9'44"7; 2. Kankkunen 9'45"6; 3. Gronholm 9'46"5; 4. Makinen 9'48"2; 5. Solberg 10'00"6; 6. Delecour 10'05"2; Gr.N Pozzo 10'37"8

ES.20 La Posta - Mina Clavero (24,04 km)
1. Gronholm 16'45"7; 2. Burns 16'49"6; 3. Kankkunen 17'01"9; 4. Makinen 17'03"6; 5. Solberg 17'19"0; 6. Eriksson 17'39"7; Gr.N Pozzo 18'26"2

ES.21 El Mirador - San Lorenzo 2 (20,65 km)
1. Makinen 12'12"0; 2. Gronholm 12'21"8; 3. Kankkunen 12'23"0; 4. Burns 12'26"2; 5. Solberg 12'36"9; 6. Eriksson 12'47"2; Gr.N Sanchez 13'31"0

ES.22 El Condor - Copina (16,77 km)
1. Burns 15'12"6; 2. Makinen 15'26"3; 3. Gronholm 15'46"7; 4. Kankkunen 15'53"6; 5. Eriksson 16'31"2; 6. Loix 16'34"1; Gr.N Sanchez 17'40"7

RESULTS AND RETIREMENTS

	Driver/Co-Driver	Car	Gr.	Total time
1	Richard Burns - Robert Reid	Subaru Impreza WRC 2000	A	4h10m20,7s
2	Marcus Gronholm - Timo Rautiainen	Peugeot 206 WRC	A	4h11m28,1s
3	Tommi Makinen - Risto Manisenmaki	Mitsubishi Lancer Evo 6	A	4h11m52,3s
4	Juha Kankkunen - Juha Repo	Subaru Impreza WRC 2000	A	4h12m43,5s
5	Freddy Loix - Sven Smeets	Mitsubishi Carisma GT	A	4h18m54,3s
6	Petter Solberg - Philip Mills	Ford Focus WRC	A	4h21m20,3s
7	Alister McRae - David Senior	Hyundaï Accent WRC	A	4h23m38,5s
8	Kenneth Eriksson - Staffan Parmander	Hyundaï Accent WRC	A	4h30m55,8s
9	Gustavo Trelles - Jorge Del Buono	Mitsubishi Lancer Evo 6	N	4h32m00,2s
10	Gabriel Pozzo - R. Ortiz	Mitsubishi Lancer Evo 6	N	4h33m01,1s

ES.6	Tony Gardemeister - Paavo Lukander	Seat Cordoba WRC Evo 2	A	Clutch
ES.6	Didier Auriol - Denis Giraudet	Seat Cordoba WRC Evo 2	A	Clutch
ES.7	Jorge Raul Recalde - Diego Curletto	Ford Escort Cosworth	A	Brakes
ES.9	Andrea Aghini - Loris Roggia	Mitsubishi Carisma GT	N	Accident
ES.11	Carlos Sainz - Luis Moya	Ford Focus WRC	A	Accident
ES.13	Manfred Stohl - Peter Muller	Mitsubishi Lancer Evo 6	N	Engine
ES.17	Colin McRae - Nicky Grist	Ford Focus WRC	A	Engine

EVENT LEADERS

ES.1 et ES.2	Burns
ES.3 > ES.6	Gronholm
ES.7 > ES.9	Sainz
ES.10 > ES.14	Gronholm
ES.15 > ES.22	Burns

BEST PERFORMANCES

	1	2	3	4	5	6
Burns	13	2	-	1	1	3
Gronholm	3	7	6	2	3	-
Sainz	3	-	3	1	2	-
Makinen	1	4	4	7	2	1
C. McRae	1	4	3	3	2	-
Kankkunen	-	4	4	7	-	4
Delecour	-	-	1	1	2	7
Solberg	-	-	-	-	4	1
Auriol	-	-	-	-	2	-
Eriksson	-	-	-	-	1	2
Loix	-	-	-	-	1	2
A. McRae	-	-	-	-	-	1

CHAMPIONSHIP CLASSIFICATIONS

Drivers
1.	Richard Burns	38
2.	Marcus Gronholm	24
3.	Tommi Makinen	23
4.	Carlos Sainz	17
5.	Colin McRae	14
6.	Juha Kankkunen	14

Constructors
1.	Subaru	54
2.	Ford	31
3.	Mitsubishi	29
3.	Peugeot	29
5.	Seat	7
6.	Skoda	5

Group N
1.	Manfred Stohl	27
2.	Gustavo Trelles	22
3.	Miguel Campos	13

Team's cup
1.	Toyota Team Saudi Arabia (Bakhashab)	16
1.	Spike Subaru Team (Araï)	16
1.	Frédéric Dor Rally Team (Dor)	16

PREVIOUS WINNERS

1980	Rohrl - Geistdorfer	Fiat 131 Abarth
1981	Fréquelin - Todt	Talbot Sunbeam Lotus
1983	Mikkola - Hertz	Audi Quattro
1984	Blomqvist - Cederberg	Audi Quattro
1985	Salonen - Harjanne	Peugeot 205 T16
1986	Biasion - Siviero	Lancia Delta S4
1987	Biasion - Siviero	Lancia Delta HF Turbo
1988	Recalde - Del Buono	Lancia Delta Integrale
1989	Ericsson - Billstam	Lancia Delta Integrale
1990	Biasion - Siviero	Lancia Delta Integrale 16v
1991	Sainz - Moya	Toyota Celica GT4
1992	Auriol - Occelli	Lancia Delta HF Integrale
1993	Kankkunen - Grist	Toyota Celica Turbo 4WD
1994	Auriol - Occelli	Toyota Celica Turbo 4WD
1995	Recalde - Christie	Lancia Delta HF Integrale
1996	Makinen - Harjanne	Mitsubishi Lancer Ev.3
1997	Makinen - Harjanne	Mitsubishi Lancer Ev.4
1998	Makinen - Mannisenmaki	Mitsubishi Lancer Ev.5
1999	Kankkunen - Repo	Subaru Impreza WRC

www.fordracing.net
Telefonica MoviStar
MARTINI
Valvoline
Telefonica MoviStar
MARTINI
V6 FMC

acropolis

Solid and speedy, the Ford Focus scored a dominant one-two finish, but it was not without controversy. Sainz would take a long time to get over the team orders in favour of McRae.

THE RALLY

McRae wins despite Sainz

If there is one country where you can count on tradition being important, its Greece. You don't mess around with its history and habits. So when the national rally in your country is called the Acropolis, there is a very good chance that as the cars come in, one by one at the end of the event, their appearance will be a pretty close approximation to the ancient monument that bears its name. In other words, tatty, scraped and dented.

The 2000 edition of this event, the 47th in its history would do nothing to change this venerable tradition and of course, in keeping with the rules of engagement, the destruction would kick in right from the start. We will concentrate on the factory entries, because if we had to look at the decimation throughout the entire field, the "Rally Yearbook" would be as long as the Iliad and the Odyssey put together.

Problems kicked off right from stage one, the 20.02 km Skourta. One can usually count on dear old Freddy Loix to run into bother and this was no exception and the Belgian did not disappoint, getting no further than this stage thanks to a broken rear suspension link. He put on a great display of three wheeled driving in his Mitsubishi but it was all in vain. Still on Skourta and it was Gardemeister's turn next. As usual, dare one say as always, the power steering on his Cordoba gave up the ghost in the stage. Do the Spanish engineers feel their drivers' arms need muscling up and therefore refuse to find a solution to the problem? The Finn is pretty tough and it's lucky for his Iberian crew that he never vented his anger on them. Seat just cannot get the hang of power steering, be it on the Acropolis or any other event this season and they just keep spewing out oil.

Delecour was Skourta's final victim, as he started behind the two previous unfortunates and was therefore held up by them for quite some distance, thus losing around thirty seconds in all.

Klidi was the next stage, shorter than the first and for its 15.48 km, the carnage abated. The only unfortunate was Gardemeister who continued to struggle with a car that had all the flying ability of a lead weight, but at least he kept going to the next stage, Thiva. This time it was Marcus Gronholm, the current leader since setting fastest time on the first stage, who encountered his own personal demons in the shape of spins and rolls combined. It is what you would expect from a man sponsored by a brewery.

"I cut a corner a bit too much," he explained without trying to pass the blame, "and I hit a lump of concrete. That pulled out the front right wheel and launched the car into a roll." Luckily for him, his support crew set to with a vengeance, building him an almost new 206, changing the damaged suspension, the front sub-frame, the gearbox, the power steering, the four dampers and the windows! The excellent Peugeot Express service understandably took slightly longer than the permitted twenty minutes and it cost Gronholm 1m 20. But at least he was able to keep going. The mechanics were deeply touched by the spontaneous applause for their efforts which came from the assembled mulititudes.

Thiva had not finished with the field just yet. Apart from the giant in the 206, his fellow countryman and world champion was also running on three wheels, after a contretemps with a wall. Having continued after that incident, he then retired at the end of the stage with broken rear suspension. Two Mitsubishis were out with the same problem and the boys in red were scratching their heads.

Just for good measure and to make sure his team-mate did not suffer on his own, Didier Auriol found himself at the wheel of a Cordoba minus power steering. Thanks a lot Seat!

Thiva also found Solberg having a shunt, while Climent went off and Burns had problems with his front suspension. Although the championship leader was delighted to see the avalanche of misfortune fall on his main rivals, his joy did not last long, as the rear brakes on his Impreza gave up the ghost on the final descent towards Mavrolimni during the Agii Theodori stage, the final one of the day.

At the end of this leg, the best positions belonged to those who had escaped the pitfalls of the merciless roads. That turned out to be the Fords: McRae had set two fastest times, the two others being down to Gronholm, including one where he was equalled by Solberg. When they arrived in Itea, McRae had a 38.5s lead over Sainz, who had been briefly slowed by anti-roll bar worries, with Delecour 1.12.9 behind in a great third place, despite giving away time at the start of the event.

Yes, the gaps were big, but no one was in a position to stake their claim on the Acropolis.

Nevertheless, the second leg went off once again like a dream for the Focus WRC. A slight oil leak from the power steering slowed the leader a touch, while team-mate Sainz had benign bothers with the rear brakes. In simple terms, even though Burns racked up four scratch times on the second leg, the Ford tandem emerged on top once again, without any bother.

The M-Sport cars proved to be far tougher than the rest, who one by one ran into bother again, thanks mainly to the tough Greek roads rather than any element of competition. On that Saturday, it was Didier Auriol who kicked off the new list of those retiring on the first stage; in his case a broken front suspension dashing his hopes. During the day, Gardemeister also threw in the towel with incurable steering woes. No more Seats, Mitsubishis or Hyundais and there were very nearly no more Peugeots either. Having survived a puncture, Marcus Gronholm had to call it a day with turbo failure, within sight of the end of this leg. As for Delecour, he had to sit and watch as his 206 bust into flames! "On a quick bit, something broke at the front," explained the Frenchman, "and the car immediately went sideways. It was a miracle that we managed to stop with the wheels hanging over the edge. We tried to edge it back slowly, but then the back end caught fire. We couldn't see anything. Daniel (Grataloup) let off the automatic fire extinguishers but it was not enough. Finally, we had to throw earth on the fire to put it out." Third place had naturally melted in the heat of the incident and now belonged to Burns, who was either very quick or very slow at times when his dampers gave up the ghost. In the other Subaru, Kankkunen was not finding life any easier, twice breaking his Impreza's front suspension.

McRae had a substantial 48.1 advantage over Sainz and was 3 minutes ahead of Burns, which could have led him to believe he would be tackling the final leg with victory already in his grasp. Especially as Sainz was under team orders not to attack him in anyway

Carlos Sainz's mechanical worries did not last long, unlike his anger with his team, which festered for ever.

Ninth attempt at the Acropolis for Auriol who, at the wheel of an ever recalcitrant Seat, retired with broken front suspension.

ACROPOLIS

and the Englishman never even got to start the second stage as the Impreza engine had given up the ghost. As expected the Scotsman was taking things easy, but the Spaniard was giving it welly. It took a strong dose of team manager intervention to keep to the right running order (see separate story) This splendid Ford one-two, the first of the season, ahead of Subaru survivor Kankkunen, was spoilt by this internal strife. The incident would end up having repercussions for the remainder of the season.

THE RAGE IN SPAIN
Hard Iberian

When he signed up Carlos Sainz at the end of the previous season on a two year deal to partner Colin McRae, M-Sport boss Malcolm Wilson knew he would have to deal with two very strong personalities, who would take some dominating. The two men had not got on for a long time now, ever since the Spaniard was on the favourable end of some Subaru team orders in the Catalunya Rally. It still rankled with McRae. At the time he was David Richards' little pet and the Highlander felt betrayed and relations were strained between the two men as they continued to drive

Sitting on his Mitsubishi, Makinen contemplates the extent of the damage on Gronholm's 206, which broke its front suspension early in the rally.

Although he would retire towards the end of the event with a broken engine, Burns had cause for optimism, as he had finished the first part of the season with a commanding lead.

under the same banner. This time it was Sainz's turn to be reined in. It was a logical call for McRae to win, a call given by Ford motor sport boss Martin Whitaker no less.
This did not go down well with the Spaniard who attacked like a mad thing on the final leg. After four stages, he had snuck into the lead. "All I was asked to do was bring the car to the finish," he said in justification. "I've been running at the same pace since the start. If I catch up, well what's wrong with that? It's my job to win!"

Malcolm Wilson was furious and jumped out of his Mondeo to go and sort it out, by intercepting Sainz on a road section before the last two stages. No one knows what was said, but strong and serious words were exchanged. The matter was settled before the end of the event was tackled, despite the Spaniard's evident irritation. "I can understand that you give team orders at the end of the championship when the title is up for grabs. But it's not acceptable halfway through the season. The team decided to take on two top drivers and it should learn to live with that."
McRae was understandably edgy. "We had been asked to cool it and we did. Carlos prefers to keep on pushing. That's his problem. We were quickest for two thirds of the rally and we have nothing more to prove. But we could break the car, because, it's not like in New Zealand or Corsica here. In the Acropolis, you can go out without making a mistake, just because it is so tough. You therefore have to take into account what it would mean to Ford to pick up sixteen points in the Constructors' championship."
But Sainz will always be Sainz. In the penultimate stage, he was still on the offensive and consolidated his lead, just to keep the suspense going and to build up the pressure on his bosses. Finally, 50 metres from the stop point at Stromi-Inohori, which marked the end of the event, he parked up for the two minutes needed to let McRae pass him and take the win.
The matter was not yet over. At the time, the Scotsman was in negotiation with Peugeot and the Spaniard was also talking to the French company for 2001, even if it meant breaking his Ford contract. Once the event was over, Whitaker and Wilson had to travel to Madrid to have it out with Carlos. It had caused a stir and confidence was frittered away. As for the two drivers, they never spoke to one another again and even the word hello appeared to be off-limits, even if we would later learn they would still be locked in together for 2001.

BURNS ON CLOUD NINE...
...at the halfway point of the season

Seven rallies in six months and the same number again in the next five. The 2000 season had reached its mid-point, marked by civil war in the Ford camp.
The "springtime champion" was undoubtedly Richard Burns. The Englishman and his Subaru had stamped his authority with three convincing wins (Kenya, Portugal and Argentina.) He had also shown

crushing form in Monaco, until the engine in his Subaru refused to fire up at Gap and he was again second in Catalunya on the tarmac surface which was not reckoned to be the strongest weapon in his armoury. Monaco and this Acropolis had been the two low points, but they were nothing to worry about. Burns now had no less than a 24 point advantage over McRae and Gronholm who were equal second on 14.
For his part, the Scotsman had been delighted to return to the winner's circle after a never ending hiatus which had lasted over a year until he won again in Catalunya. He was convinced things were looking good and was apparently not in the least bit convinced that Marcus Gronholm would be a threat. The Finn had impressed onlookers, thanks to one win and four points finishes, but not many expected the good form to last for long. Lack of experience and foolhardiness, linked to the fact the 206 was such a new car were cited as reasons for the Swedish winner to slip quietly back into the pack.
Makinen's situation looked far more serious. After a fantastic win in Monaco, followed by a well earned second spot in Sweden, the World Champion saw his chances slip away, mainly due to the geriatric nature of his Mitsubishi. The man himself also appeared to have lost some of the gritty determination which had characterised his four previous championships. A page of history was being turned. Makinen was 15 points down on Burns, as was Carlos Sainz, who despite the bitter taste left by the Acropolis debacle, had a great start to the season with two second places and the same number of thirds. But he had been dominated by his team mate at Ford, just as he had been by Auriol at Toyota. It was pretty difficult to see how the Spaniard could turn the situation around. As for the others, Kankkunen appeared to have slept through the past couple of months. Auriol was fighting a miserable Seat, while Delecour and Gardemeister could only hope and pray for a better second half to the season.
In the constructors' championship, Subaru was in command thanks to Burns and was the only team to have scored points in all seven events. The Anglo-Japanese outfit was on a flying 58 points, against 47 for Ford, who had this Greek one-two to thank, 31 for Peugeot and 29 for Mitsubishi. The future looked good for Subaru as forthcoming events had always proved propitious for it and its drivers.
In fact, only the Group N Championship battle between Manfred Stohl (27 points) and four times world champion, Gustavo Trelles (22) seemed to carry any doubt about it. Drivers, constructors, production cars were all creating a false impression. ■

ACROPOLIS

Tommi Makinen's charge did not last long. On the third stage, the Finn hit a wall, ripping off his Mitsubishi's right rear wheel. The mechanics managed to fix it, but on the next stage, a rear suspension pivot broke, forcing his retirement. The same cause and effect also put paid to Loix's hopes just a few kilometres into the rally.

Just like this 206 suspension, the Peugeot team was on the deck at the mid-season, dropping behind in the Constructors' championship at the end of this event. The Acropolis was a disaster for them, with a breakage epidemic, which forced Gronholm to retire, while Delecour could do no better than ninth.

ACROPOLIS

Trusting in fate, Delecour put his all into this tough event. The ninth place he secured with the help of co-driver Daniel Grataloup brought Peugeot the meagre consolation of two championship points.

Colin McRae was impeccable. It did require some intervention from Ford management to calm down Sainz, so that the Scotsman could win, but his performance on the first two legs proved that he deserved this win. He was not the best Ford performer though. With six fastest times to his name, Solberg had made a good impression before retiring near the end of the rally.

47th ACROPOLIS RALLY

7th leg of the 2000 world rally championship for constructors and drivers
7th leg of the production car drivers' and team's world cups
Date 09 - 11 june 2000
Route: 1407,56 km divided into 3 legs,
19 special stages on dirt roads (403,71 km.)
1st leg: Friday 9 june: Athènes - Inoi - Itéa, 5 stages (102,25 km)
2nd leg: Saturday 10 june: Itéa - Parnassos - Itéa, 7 stages (159,57 km)
3rd leg: Sunday 11 june: Itéa - Parnassos - Itéa, 7 stages (141,89 km)
Starters - Finishers: 117 - 45
Conditions: good weather, very hot, dusty and rough dirt roads.

TOP ENTRIES

1. Tommi Makinen - Risto Mannisenmaki
   MITSUBISHI LANCER Evo 6
2. Freddy Loix - Sven Smeets
   MITSUBISHI CARISMA GT
3. Richard Burns - Robert Reid
   SUBARU IMPREZA WRC 2000
4. Juha Kankkunen - Juha Repo
   SUBARU IMPREZA WRC 2000
5. Colin McRae - Nicky Grist
   FORD FOCUS WRC
6. Carlos Sainz - Luis Moya
   FORD FOCUS WRC
7. Didier Auriol - Denis Giraudet
   SEAT CORDOBA WRC Evo 2
8. Toni Gardemeister - Paavo Lukander
   SEAT CORDOBA WRC Evo 2
9. François Delecour - Daniel Grataloup
   PEUGEOT 206 WRC
10. Marcus Gronholm - Timo Rautiainen
    PEUGEOT 206 WRC
11. Armin Schwarz - Manfred Hiemer
    SKODA OCTAVIA WRC
12. Luis Climent - Alex Romani
    SKODA OCTAVIA WRC
14. Kenneth Eriksson - Staffan Parmander
    HYUNDAI ACCENT WRC
15. Alister McRae - David Senior
    HYUNDAI ACCENT WRC
16. Petter Solberg - Phil Mills
    FORD FOCUS WRC
17. Markko Martin - Michael Park
    TOYOTA COROLLA WRC
18. John Papadimitriou - Nikos Petropoulos
    SUBARU IMPREZA WRC
19. Leonidas Kirkos - George Polyzois
    FORD ESCORT WRC
20. Krzysztof Holowczyc - Jean Marc Fortin
    SUBARU IMPREZA WRC
21. Aris Vovos - Spyros Koltsidas
    TOYOTA COROLLA WRC
22. Jean Pierre Richelmi - Thierry Barjou
    SUBARU IMPREZA WRC
23. Toshihiro Araï - Roger Freeman
    SUBARU IMPREZA WRC
24. Hamed Al-Wahaibi - Tony Sircombe
    SUBARU IMPREZA WRC
25. Abdullah Bakhashab - Bob Willis
    TOYOTA COROLLA WRC
26. Frédéric Dor - Didier Breton
    SUBARU IMPREZA WRC
27. Serkan Yazici - Erkan Bodur
    TOYOTA COROLLA WRC
28. Gustavo Trelles - Jorge Del Buono
    MITSUBISHI LANCER Evo 6
29. Manfred Stohl - Peter Muller
    MITSUBISHI LANCER Evo 6
30. Uwe Nittel - Detlef Ruf
    MITSUBISHI LANCER Evo 6
34. Claudio Menzi - Edgardo Galindo
    MITSUBISHI LANCER Evo 6
35. Gabriele Pozzo - Rodolfo Ortiz
    MITSUBISHI LANCER Evo 6
36. Michael Guest - David Green
    HYUNDAI COUPE Evo 2
37. Kris Princen - Dany Colebunders
    RENAULT MEGANE MAXI KIT CAR
38. Philippe Bugalski - Jean Paul Chiaroni
    CITROEN SAXO KIT CAR
42. "Leonidas" - Maria Pavli
    RENAULT MEGANE MAXI KIT CAR

Consistent and reliable, Juha Kankkunen finished third without setting a single fastest time.

The indestructible Leonidas was in action again, at the wheel of his Maxi Megane.

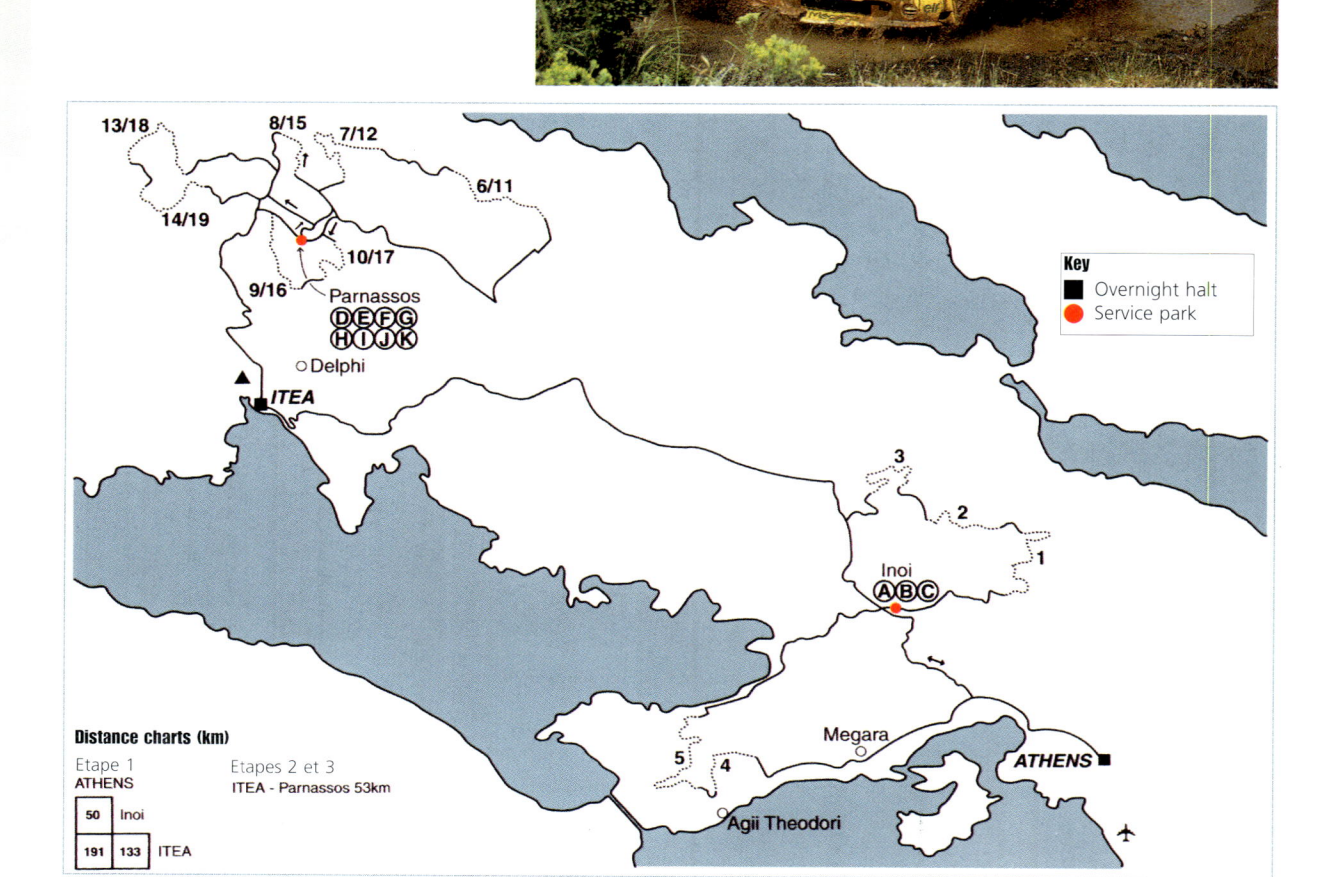

Key
■ Overnight halt
● Service park

Distance charts (km)
Etape 1
ATHENS
50 Inoi
191 133 ITEA

Etapes 2 et 3
ITEA - Parnassos 53km

SPECIAL STAGE TIMES

ES.1 Skourta (20,02 km)
1. Gronholm 1'54"6; 2. Solberg 11'55"5; 3. C. McRae 11'56"7; 4. Eriksson 12'01"8; 5. Burns 12'07"4; 6. Sainz 12'07"5; Gr.N Menzi 13'05"5

ES.2 Klidi (8,09 km)
1. C. McRae 5'50"1; 2. Sainz 5'40"5; 3. Gronholm 5'40"7; 4. Solberg 5'42"0; 5. Makinen 5'43"1; 6. Martin 5'44"0; Gr.N Stohl 6'06"0

ES.3 Thiva (20,12 km)
1. C. McRae 16'23"1; 2. Sainz 16'27"6; 3. Burns 16'36"7; 4. Kankkunen et Delecour 16'37"2; 6. Auriol 16'40"3; Gr.N Stohl 17'43"9

ES.4 Kineta (9,47 km)
1. Gronholm et Solberg 5'20"7; 3. C. McRae 5'22"1; 4. Delecour 5'22"9; 5. Sainz 5'24"8; 6. A. McRae 5'26"0; Gr.N Pozzo 5'52"6

ES.5 Agii Theodori (15,16 km)
1. C.McRae 24'47"6; 2. Gronholm 24'53"1; 3. Sainz 25'07"7; 4. Delecour 25'07"8; 5. Solberg 25'24"1; 6. Gardemeister 25'31"1; Gr.N Menzi 26'49"5

ES.6 Zeli 1 (28,32 km)
1. Burns 20'44"9; 2. Sainz 20'52"1; 3. Solberg 21'00"9; 4. Gronholm 21'04"6; 5. C. McRae 21'06"3; 6. Delecour 21'09"7; Gr.N Pozzo 22'24"5

ES.7 Mendenista 1 (28,05 km)
1. C. McRae 19'58"5; 2. Gronholm 20'02"6; 3. Sainz 20'08"4; 4. Solberg 20'26"5; 5. Burns 20'35"8; 6. Gardemeister 20'41"1; Gr.N Pozzo 22'20"4

ES.8 Paleohori 1 (10,71 km)
1. Burns 7'46"0; 2. Sainz 7'47"0; 3. Gronholm 7'47"1; 4. Delecour 7'51"4; 5. C. McRae 7'51"7; 6. Vovos 7'53"4; Gr.N Pozzo 8'24"3

ES.9 Gravia 1 (25,56 km)
1. Sainz 18'18"6; 2. C. McRae 18'18"9; 3. Burns 18'24"5; 4. Delecour 18'35"1; 5. Vovos 18'37"8; 6. Schwarz 18'50"1; Gr.N Trelles 19'51"6

ES.10 Elatos 1 (10,56 km)
1. Burns 8'40"3; 2. C. McRae 8'40"6; 3. Sainz 8'43"9; 4. Delecour 8'51"5; 5. Schwarz 8'53"6; 6. Araï 8'56"4; Gr.N Menzi 9'12"6

ES.11 Zeli 2 (28,32 km)
1. Burns 20'48"8; 2. Sainz 20'57"9; 3. C. McRae 20'59"3; 4. Delecour 21'01"6; 5. Kankkunen 21'06"8; 6. Solberg 21'20"2; Gr.N Pozzo 22'28"4

ES.12 Mendenista 2 (28,05 km)
1. C. McRae 20'04"1; 2. Sainz 20'21"1; 3. Solberg 20'37"1; 4. Kankkunen 20'42"3; 5. Araï 20'46"6; 6. Burns 20'50"3; Gr.N Pozzo 22'39"8

ES.13 Pavliani 1 (24,71 km)
1. Sainz 20'23"2; 2. Solberg 20'25"3; 3. C. McRae 20'32"2; 4. Delecour 20'35"3; 5. Kankkunen 20'46"1; 6. Schwarz 20'53"4; Gr.N Nittel 21'30"9

ES.14 Stromi 1 (22,82 km)
1. Solberg 18'02"9; 2. Sainz 18'12"0; 3. Delecour 18'17"7; 4. C. McRae 18'22"4; 5. Kankkunen 18'32"2; 6. Schwarz 18'38"7; Gr.N Nittel 19'21"3

ES.15 Paleohori 2 (10,71 km)
1. Solberg 7'45"9; 2. Delecour et Sainz 7'46"7; 4. Kankkunen 7'52"1; 5. Araï 7'58"1; 6. Dor 8'04"4; Gr.N Nittel 8'18"2

ES.16 Gravia 2 (25,56 km)
1. Sainz 18'28"0; 2. Solberg 18'29"4; 3. Delecour 18'33"6; 4. Kankkunen 18'38"4; 5. Araï 18'47"3; 6. Schwarz 18'47"3; Gr.N Trelles 19'33"4

ES.17 Elatos 2 (10,56 km)
1. Solberg 8'46"5; 2. Sainz 8'47"8; 3. Delecour 8'52"1; 4. Yazici 8'56"7; 5. Kankkunen 8'58"7; 6. Richelmi 9'00"4; Gr.N Nittel 9'09"8

ES.18 Pavliani 2 (24,71 km)
1. Solberg 20'16"2; 2. Sainz 20'28"9; 3. Sainz 20'30"4; 4. Araï 20'45"5; 5. Kankkunen 20'52"6; 6. Bakhashab 21'02"1; Gr.N Stohl 21'39"5

ES.19 Stromi 2 (22,82 km)
1. Solberg 18'15"0; 2. Araï 18'38"0; 3. Richelmi 18'41"9; 4. Kankkunen 18'42"2; 5. Delecour 18'44"9; 6. Bakhashab 18'55"7; Gr.N Trelles 19'18"9

RESULTS AND RETIREMENTS

	Driver/Co-Driver	Car	Gr.	Total time
1	Colin McRae - Nicky Grist	Ford Focus WRC	A	4h56m54,8s
2	Carlos Sainz - Luis Moya	Ford Focus WRC	A	4h57m17,9s
3	Juha Kankkunen - Juha Repo	Subaru Impreza WRC 2000	A	5h03m33,1s
4	Toshihiro Araï - Roger Freeman	Subaru Impreza WRC	A	5h04m35,6s
5	Armin Schwarz - Manfred Hiemer	Skoda Octavia WRC	A	5h06m05,8s
6	Abdullah Bakhashab - Bobby Willis	Toyota Corolla WRC	A	5h09m49,7s
7	Jean Pierre Richelmi - Thierry Barjou	Subaru Impreza WRC	A	5h10m28,1s
8	Frederic Dor - Didier Breton	Subaru Impreza WRC	A	5h10m 54,6s
9	François Delecour - Daniel Grataloup	Peugeot 206 WRC	A	5h12m07,1s
10	John Papadimitriou - Nikos Petropoulos	Subaru Impreza WRC	A	5h13m16,4s
11	Gabriel Pozzo - Amelio Rodolfo Ortiz	Mitsubishi Lancer Evo.6	N	5h18m51,8s
ES.1	Freddy Loix - Sven Smeets	Mitsubishi Carisma GT	A	Suspension
ES.1	Kenneth Eriksson - Staffan Parmander	Hyundaï Accent WRC	A	Engine
ES.3	Luis Climent - Alex Romani	Skoda Octavia WRC	A	Accident
ES.3	Tommi Makinen - Risto Mannisenmaki	Mitsubishi Lancer Evo.6	A	Suspension
ES.3	Markko Martin - Michael Park	Toyota Corolla WRC	A	Carter broken
ES.3	Krzysztof Holowczyc - Jean Marc Fortin	Subaru Impreza WRC	A	Steering
ES.4	Hamed Al Wahaibi - Tony Sircombe	Toyota Corolla WRC	A	Engine
ES.5	Alister McRae - David Senior	Hyundaï Accent WRC	A	Suspension
ES.5	Didier Auriol - Denis Giraudet	Seat Cordoba WRC Evo 2	A	Suspension
ES.6	Tony Gardemeister - Paavo Lukander	Seat Cordoba WRC Evo 2	A	Steering
ES.9	Marcus Gronholm - Timo Rautainen	Peugeot 206 WRC	A	Engine
ES.9	Richard Burns - Robert Reid	Subaru Impreza WRC 2000	A	Engine
ES.19	Petter Solberg - Phil Mills	Ford Focus WRC	A	Transmission

EVENT LEADERS

ES.1 > ES.2	Gronholm
ES.3 > ES.15	C. McRae
ES.16 > ES.18	Sainz
ES.19	C. McRae

BEST PERFORMANCES

	1	2	3	4	5	6
Solberg	6	3	2	2	1	9
C. McRae	5	2	4	1	2	-
Burns	4	-	2	-	2	1
Sainz	3	9	4	-	2	1
Gronholm	2	2	2	1	-	-
Delecour	-	1	4	7	2	1
Araï	-	1	-	1	3	1
Richelmi	-	-	1	-	-	1
Kankkunen	-	-	-	-	5	5
Eriksson	-	-	-	1	-	-
Yazici	-	-	-	1	-	-
Vovos	-	-	-	-	1	1
Makinen	-	-	-	-	1	-
Schwarz	-	-	-	-	-	4
Gardemeister	-	-	-	-	-	2
Bakhashab	-	-	-	-	-	2
Martin	-	-	-	-	-	1
A.McRae	-	-	-	-	-	1

CHAMPIONSHIP CLASSIFICATIONS

Drivers
1. Richard Burns — 38
2. Marcus Gronholm — 24
2. Colin McRae — 24
4. Tommi Makinen — 23
4. Carlos Sainz — 23
6. Juha Kankkunen — 18

Constructeurs
1. Subaru — 58
2. Ford — 47
3. Peugeot — 31
4. Mitsubishi — 29
5. Skoda — 8
6. Seat — 7

Groupe N
1. Manfred Stohl — 31
2. Gustavo Trelles — 28
3. Gabriel Pozzo — 16

Team's cup
1. Spike Subaru Team (Araï) — 26
2. Toyota Team Saudi Arabia (Bakhashab) — 22
3. Frédéric Dor Rally Team (Dor) — 20

PREVIOUS WINNERS

1973	Thérier - Delferrier — Alpine Renault A110
1975	Rohrl - Berger — Opel Ascona
1976	Kallstrom - Andersson — Datsun 160J
1977	Waldegaard - Thorszelius — Ford Escort RS
1978	Rohrl - Geistdorfer — Fiat 131 Abarth
1979	Waldegaard - Thorszelius — Ford escort RS
1980	Vatanen - Richards — Ford Escort RS
1981	Vatanen - Richards — Ford Escort RS
1982	Mouton - Pons — Audi Quattro
1983	Rohrl - Geistdorfer — Lancia Rally 037
1984	Blomqvist - Cederberg — Audi Quattro
1985	Salonen - Harjanne — Peugeot 205 T16
1986	Kankkunen - Piironen — Peugeot 205 T16
1987	Alen - Kivimaki — Lancia Delta HF Turbo
1988	Biasion - Siviero — Lanca Delta Integrale
1989	Biasion - Siviero — Lanca Delta Integrale
1990	Sainz - Moya — Toyota Celica GT4
1991	Kankkunen - Piironen — Lancia Delta Integrale 16v
1992	Auriol - Occelli — Lancia Delta Integrale
1993	Biasion - Siviero — Fort Escort RS Cosworth
1994	Sainz - Moya — Subaru Impreza
1995	Vovos - Stefanis — Lancia Delta Integrale
1996	McRae - Ringer — Subaru Impreza
1997	Sainz - Moya — Ford Escort WRC
1998	McRae - Grist — Subaru Impreza WRC
1999	Burns - Reid — Subaru Impreza WRC

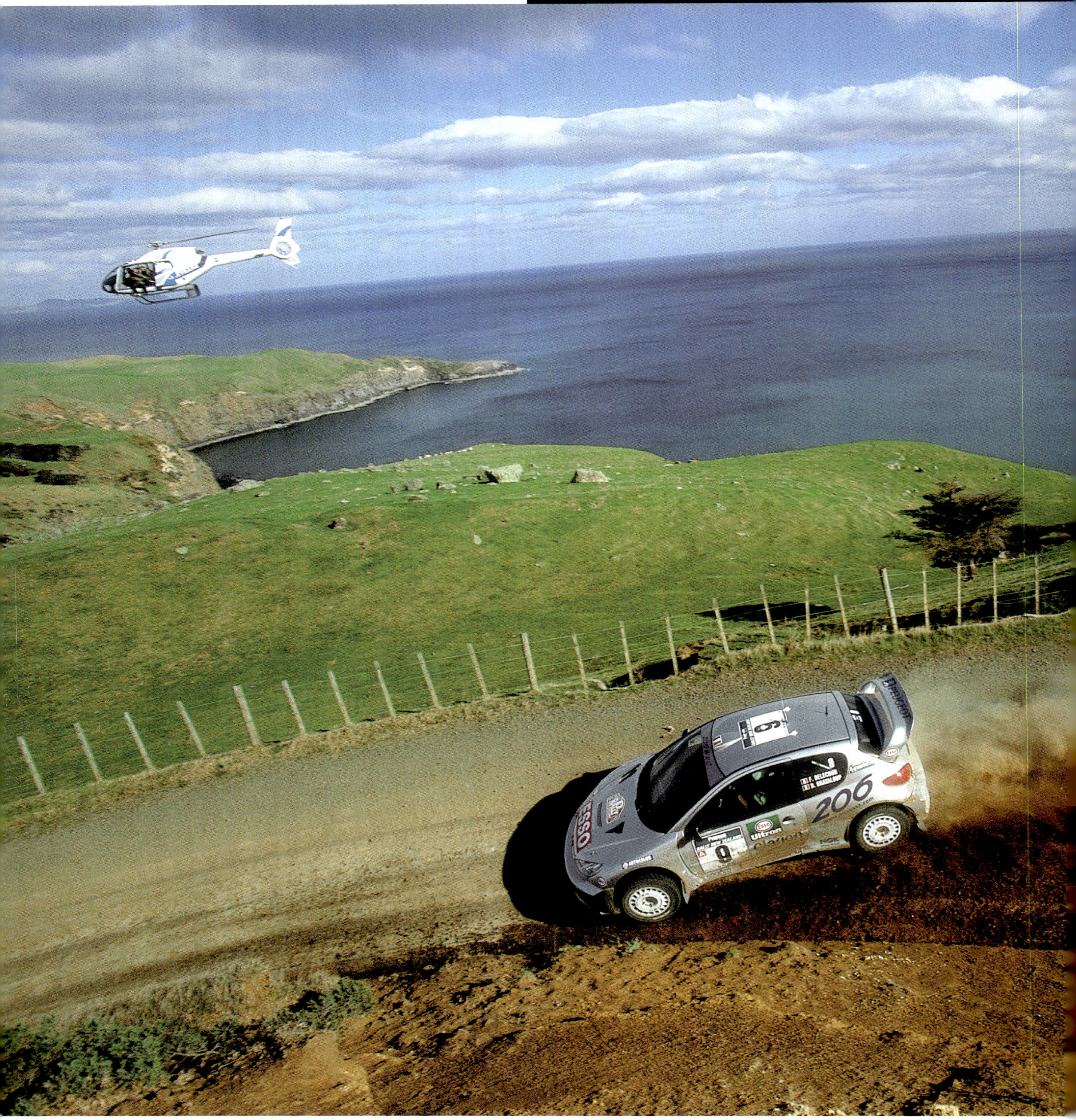

ESSO
Ultron
206

new zealand

He hardly knew the terrain, but Gronholm was in scintillating form as he took the win. Adding to his delight, Burns, his main championship rival, retired in the last few kilometres of the rally.

THE RALLY
Gronholm the boss

Sunrise in the Waikorea valley is a wonderful sight as the sun appears over the lush green hills, burning away the mist and throwing a bright orange light over the land. Toni Gardemeister saw it in a different light as the dazzling rays no doubt contributed to his fate. He took a bump quicker than reason would advise and faster than his Seat could cope with and it catapulted him skywards before the Finn landed in the sort of heap one usually only comes across in a disaster movie.

His car barrel-rolled for about 300 metres, with bits of it flying off like pieces in a jigsaw puzzle. The engine landed here, the gearbox over there and bit further on was the fuel tank and the driver's safety cell, from which he emerged, shocked but largely unscathed. Once they arrived on the scene, the Seat mechanics had to ask by radio if they really had to pick up every single broken little bit of it!

Gardemeister and Lukander would do well to light a few candles to whatever gods are available, because this was their third terrifying crash of the season and there were many who asked themselves how they were still capable and lucky enough to feel the wind blowing in from Auckland, rather than breathing their last.

Unlike the Finn, Francois Delecour had sussed the possible danger of dawn on this stage, during the recce. The stage was well known, except that this year it was run in the opposite direction to usual. Competitors had only been allowed to recce the stage twice and the Seat driver evidently hadn't spotted the trap. The Peugeot driver however had noted it was worth lifting off a tad to slow the flying 206.

It was probably the one and only occasion that day when he did slow. For the rest of the first leg, he was on fantastic form. "Mr. Latebrake" was back and it was good to watch his flamboyant style in action. For once, he was spared all mechanical bothers, allowing him to display his skills in all their glory. He set three fastest times and one of them was really extraordinary. It occurred on the marvellous Whaanga Coast section, with its views of the Pacific. He was the only leader on this leg. "I feel so comfortable with the car that I can try just about anything," he beamed. "I'm taking a lot of risks, because I don't know the route as well as the others. Daniel and me have scared ourselves at least four or five times on each stage. I am very vulnerable!"

It has to be said that their start position on the stages was a big plus. He and his right hand man Daniel Grataloup were running tenth on the road. That meant their tyres could grip a track surface which had been scrupulously cleaned and where all the top layers of dirt and dust had been swept away. There were a few surprises, like the good times being set by the Hyundais of Eriksson and Alister McRae, with the latter going on to set the first ever fastest stage time for the Korean manufacturer. Solberg also made up this trio, as it set about chasing Delecour, proving that a late start position was definitely the way to go. It was all down to the weather, because strangely enough and contrary to what is expected of a kiwi winter, there had been no recent rain to soak the roads and damp down the dust. As championship leader, it fell to Richard Burns to lead the field all day and he suffered accordingly. "I am giving it my best shot, but it's not enough. The roads are very slippery and I'm having problems on the corners and under braking. All I can do is try and keep the gap down to a reasonable level." The same complaint applied to Sainz and McRae, who were also in trouble with engine worries, while Kankkunen was also struggling. As for Makinen, it was the inconsistency of his antique Mitsubishi which was causing him problems. The world champion had been expecting a lot from the new differentials, which had rejuvenated his ancient mount during pre-event practice.

While this Finn was struggling, another, Marcus Gronholm was delighted with his Peugeot. He was running third on the road behind Burns and McRae, but it did not seem to bother him as much as the others and he was just about able to hang onto the Delecour tornado. Gronholm ended the day third, 3.5 behind Norway's Solberg and 13.2 down on leader Delecour, who had put on a very appropriate firework display, given that he is French and that it was July 14th as the cars headed into Auckland.

Sadly, the second leg got off to a terrible start for Delecour. His gearbox started to play up on the second stage and gave up the ghost on the next one. "I never have any luck. I just feel numb. But on the positive side, at least I was having fun with a car that was great to drive." The same fate befell his rival and fellow countryman Didier Auriol. He was tackling the rally at the wheel of a Seat that refused to rise from its slumbers. Didier tried to wake it up by rolling it no less than five times. The day after Bastille Day and he was a prisoner of his own misfortune.

With Delecour out of the way, Gronholm gratefully accepted the lead. But despite putting up some extraordinary stage times, considering he was running second on the road, he was powerless against the British duo of Burns and McRae who were both on frightening form.

A storm was on the way and the wind was swirling around the lush green hills of Ararua and accelerating towards the summit. It was so strong it threatened to blow away the few hardy souls who had ventured out to watch the action. It was howling strong enough to blow the feathers off a kiwi. But, for the time being, as the competitors tackled the longest stage of the rally, the skies had not quite decided to deliver a typically New Zealand style winter downpour.

On the top of the mountain, the only steam poured off the Finn's 206 and the man himself looked close to tears. His emaciated face was running with sweat, his haggard expression reflecting fatigue as well as unhappiness. "I was too slow. It's so slippery. The others will be quick, much quicker. 30 seconds. It'll cost me 30 seconds!" He was still pumped up on a rush of adrenalin and his thoughts were oscillating between madness and despair. Sometimes, even a wind as strong as this is not enough to blow away self doubt.

As Gronholm went on his way, Sainz and Kankkunen hoved into view; both men having a lacklustre event. Then came McRae. As usual, the Scotsman had nothing to say, keeping his eyes glued to the board where everyone's times were posted. Fifth on the road, he was entitled to hope for a miracle. He had made up 15.5 on the Peugeot driver. Nice! But his face betrayed no emotion as he went on his way.

Burns had bettered the Highlander on his way to claiming the fastest time. He had stabbed Gronholm in the back with a blade measuring 22.2 seconds and he was now just 18.8 behind. "There's nothing special about my time. It's just down to running seventh on the road, which has worked in my favour. If you look at the road, you can realise how much gravel is swept away by those ahead of you. I had the same handicap yesterday." Gronholm's fate seemed inevitable, but the weather had a wet surprise in store, much to the delight of the French team. A mass cry of "yes!" went up from the Peugeot mechanics as the heavens finally opened. It would turn the rest of the leg on its head, if one can mix one's anatomical metaphors. McRae went on to set two more fastest times, but Gronholm was having fun in the mud and was flying at the end. The rain had dealt out a new hand of cards and the Finn stole the best ones from the deck to lead this leg with 22.9 and 37.4 on McRae and Burns respectively.

Gronholm's appetite had been whetted now and the giant went on to eat the final miles like an ogre, chewing up his opponents in the process. His feat was on a par with the local Maoris, who had turned French explorer Marion du Fresnes into a culinary event, as the first European to be eaten in this far off land.

The outcome of this rally never looked in doubt on the final leg, run to the south of Auckland, although there was an element of suspense and the odd change of fortune.

Of the seven stages on the menu for this last day, the first of them would play the greatest part in deciding

Gronholm's road to victory nearly ended towards the end of the rally. But his well behaved 206 preferred to stay on its wheels rather than roll.

NEW ZEALAND

THE WINNER
The dreams of Mr. Gronholm

"Vive La France!" was the enthusiastic headline in the New Zealand Herald. The Peugeot crack troops had proved that French flair is not only a rugby union phenomenon and French status had been partially restored in these parts, after the unfortunate Rainbow Warrior sinking in Auckland harbour.

But rather than wallow in the pleasure of recognition, Marcus Gronholm was beginning to dream of greater prizes. His was a bold challenge, but suddenly it looked on the cards after this win. He had now come to within four points of Burns. Could he really become the 2000 world champion? Peugeot would certainly have no complaints, because just as in Formula 1 these days, the drivers' title carried far more public opprobrium than that awarded to the winning team. Burns versus Gronholm, McRae or Sainz had far more spice to it than the Lion versus the Blue Oval or the Subaru crew.

Gronholm's squad did not want to think about it too much. "Remember this is only our first full season," said Timo Rautiainen, not only his co-driver, but also his brother in law. "We will see come November, but the title is something we are thinking of in terms of 2001." Nevertheless, the Finnish pairing's chances looked good, especially as the brand new 206 looked well up to the job in hand. One fact was emerging: Gronholm was so talented, that even on events he hardly knew, he managed the odd miracle. Furthermore, ever since his stupid accident in the 1999 RAC Rally, Gronholm had realised that an attacking approach needs to be tempered with common sense and caution. Further cause for optimism stemmed from the fact that of the six rallies remaining, at least three of them, Finland, Cyprus and the RAC, should suit him very well indeed. Those rallies which would not favour him that much were the tarmac stages of San Remo and Corsica and he knew he would have tread carefully on these events. So there were plenty of reasons to be optimistic. Would the Finn be able to bring the title home to Peugeot, just as Salonen and Kankkunen had done in 1985 and 1986? The final part of the season looked like being a thriller with everything to play for. ■

With winners Rautiainen and Gronholm on either side of him, Peugeot Sport boss Corrado Provera could thank the Kiwi stars.

the final result. The drivers played out their drama against a backdrop which could have come out of the pages of a fairytale: beautifully rounded hills and green fields interspersed with streams where even the sheep and cows looked extra clean, as though they were toys on a kiddies farm set. All that was missing from fantasy land was Snow White and the Seven Dwarves in HO scale.

The stopwatch added a more realistic touch to the setting and the Finn kept the lead - 15 and 10 seconds ahead of the two Brits. It was a comfortable enough margin as the field set off to tackle the remaining six, fairly short stages.

In the next one, the Ford driver looked to be on a charge, but he had a spin. "That mistake cost me any chance of winning," admitted the honest Scot.

The kiwi rally ended very badly for the Subaru team. There were still four stages to go, when both Impreza engines cried enough, at exactly the same time. Leading the championship, Burns left New Zealand with a no-score and Gronholm closing in on him. Bad news, especially as the next rally would be the home event for the Peugeot colossus.

Makinen had suffered similar problems and the inevitable lack of speed had seen him run no higher than eighth. More seriously, it left him without any points in the championship. One wondered why Mitsubishi had pulled the Finn out of the event. His car was repairable and if he had stayed in the rally, he might have picked up one or two points. Admittedly, the Subarus had not yet retired at this point, but this retirement smacked of despair.

The fact that Tommi Makinen had not visited the winner's enclosure for some time now certainly made life easier for those who had to contend with the Finn over the past four years. With every passing rally, one of the top men in the sport appeared to be drifting out of contention. Carlos Sainz's co-driver, Luis Moya had an opinion on the situation. "I don't know if it's good for the level of competition in the sport, but I do know it's a vast improvement for us."

A SLAP IN THE FACE
M for Mitsubishi, Makinen and malediction

A winner here last year, Tommi Makinen did not even finish the 2000 edition of the rally. At the start of the third leg, just as he was attempting to crawl back into the points, the world champion suddenly found himself without brakes in the first stage. Try as he might, the best driver in the world was unable to avoid the ensuing accident. He limped into the next service area with the right front corner hanging off his car. It was hopeless and Makinen decided to throw in the towel, rather than struggle along at the back of the field.

This voluntary retirement was the second of the event for the Japanese team. The day before, Belgium's Freddy Loix had encountered gearbox, electronic and differential troubles which had badly affected the handling of his car, making it unpredictable and dangerous. Unable to work out what to do to the car's electronic brain, the team bosses decided to retire Loix. It had been yet another nondescript performance, but at least he had a good excuse this time.

Things went from bad to worse for Mitsubishi. The winner here in 1999, Makinen retired towards the end of the event.

NEW ZEALAND

Against a backdrop of green hills and white sheep, Hyundai was showing signs of improvement. Not only did Alister McRae set a fastest stage time for the Korean team, but on top of that, Kenneth Erikkson finished fifth in his Accent WRC. On roads that were kind on the cars, the little coupes proved they were getting better.

NEW ZEALAND

It was a delightful setting, but it brought yet more disappointment for Seat. Toni Gardemeister had a truly frightening roll on the very first stage. Luckily, he and co-driver Paavo Lukander escaped injury. Towards the end of the event, Auriol did the same thing, destroying yet another Cordoba. It had been a disastrous event for them.

It had been exactly two years since Carlos Sainz had last won a rally and this time he had to settle for third place behind Gronholm and McRae, on an event where he was never really on top form.

NEW ZEALAND

TOP ENTRIES

1 Tommi Makinen - Risto Mannisenmaki
   MITSUBISHI LANCER Evo 6

2 Freddy Loix - Sven Smeets
   MITSUBISHI CARISMA GT

3 Richard Burns - Robert Reid
   SUBARU IMPREZA WRC 2000

4 Juha Kankkunen - Juha Repo
   SUBARU IMPREZA WRC 2000

5 Colin McRae - Nicky Grist
   FORD FOCUS WRC

6 Carlos Sainz - Luis Moya
   FORD FOCUS WRC

7 Didier Auriol - Denis Giraudet
   SEAT CORDOBA WRC Evo 2

8 Toni Gardemeister - Paavo Lukander
   SEAT CORDOBA WRC Evo 2

9 François Delecour - Daniel Grataloup
   PEUGEOT 206 WRC

10 Marcus Gronholm - Timo Rautiainen
   PEUGEOT 206 WRC

14 Kenneth Eriksson - Staffan Parmander
   HYUNDAI ACCENT WRC

15 Alister McRae - David Senior
   HYUNDAI ACCENT WRC

16 Petter Solberg - Phil Mills
   FORD FOCUS WRC

17 Possum Bourne - Craig Vincent
   SUBARU IMPREZA WRC

18 Toshihiro Araï - Roger Freeman
   SUBARU IMPREZA WRC

20 Gustavo Trelles - Jorge Del Buono
   MITSUBISHI LANCER Evo 6

21 Manfred Stohl - Peter Muller
   MITSUBISHI LANCER Evo 6

22 Hamed Al-Wahaibi - Tony Sircombe
   SUBARU IMPREZA WRC

23 John Papadimitriou - Nikos Petropoulos
   SUBARU IMPREZA WRC

24 Claudio Menzi - Edgardo Galindo
   MITSUBISHI LANCER Evo 6

25 Gabriele Pozzo - Rodolfo Ortiz
   MITSUBISHI LANCER Evo 6

30th NEW ZEALAND RALLY

8th leg of the 2000 world rally championship for constructors and drivers
8th leg of the production car drivers' and team's world cupsam's cup" 2000
Date 13 - 16 july 2000
Route: 1618,76 km divided into 3 legs,
24 special stages on dirt roads (373,37 km.)
Start: Thursday 13th july: Auckland - Auckland, 0 stage
1st leg: Friday 14 july: Auckland- Raglan - Auckland, 8 stages (117,43 km)
2nd leg: Saturday 15 july: Auckland - Maungaturauto Auckland, 9 stages (176,76 km)
3rd leg: Sunday 16 july: Auckland - Te Kauwhata - Auckland, 7 stages (79,18 km)
Starters - Finishers: 70 - 43
Conditions: nice weather for the first leg, overcast and rain for the second and third legs. Dusty dirt roads, later becoming muddy.

Japanese driver Arai is known for his attacking nature. He proved it again in the Antipodes.

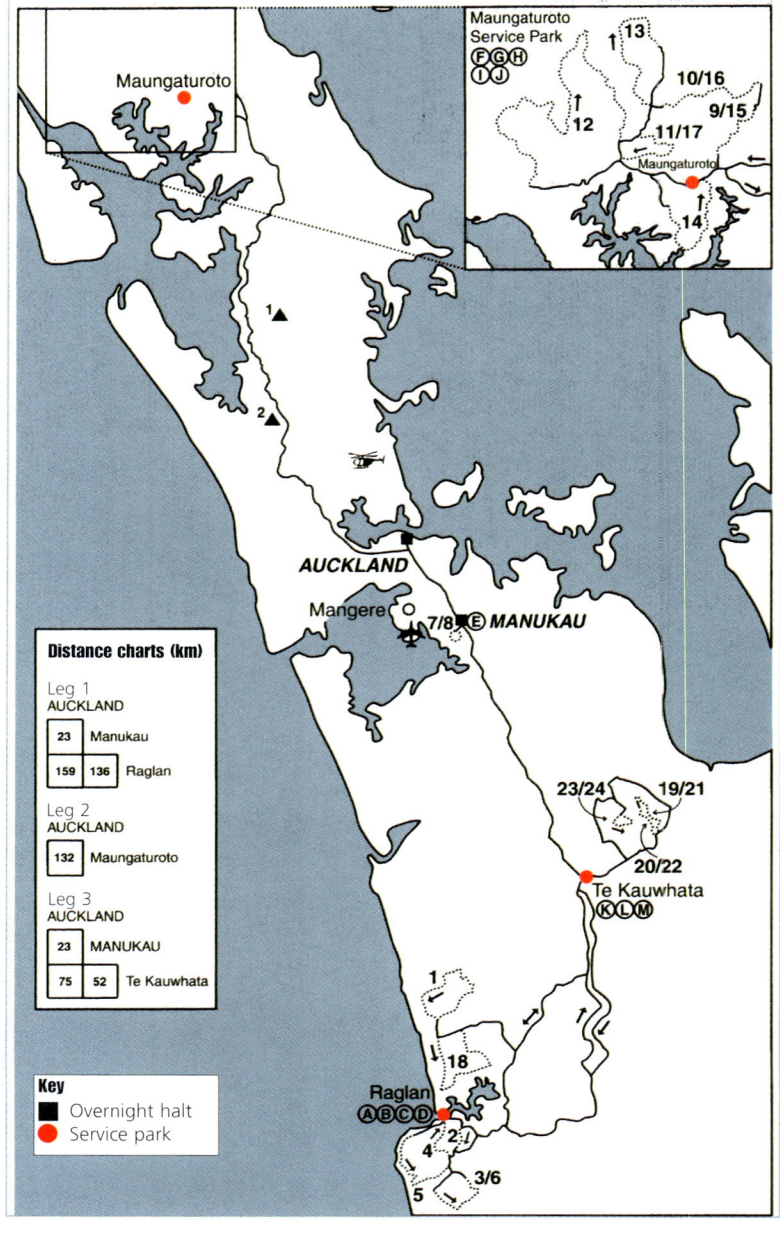

Distance charts (km)

Leg 1
AUCKLAND
23 Manukau
159 136 Raglan

Leg 2
AUCKLAND
132 Maungaturoto

Leg 3
AUCKLAND
23 MANUKAU
75 52 Te Kauwhata

Key
■ Overnight halt
● Service park

SPECIAL STAGE TIMES

ES.1 Te Akau North (32,37 km)
1. Delecour 18'08"1; 2. Gronholm 18'10"6; 3. C. McRae 18'16"5; 4. Sainz 18'17"9; 5. Solberg 18'19"1; 6. Burns 18'22"5; Gr.N Crocker 18'41"5

ES.2 Maungatawhiri (6,52 km)
1. Solberg 3'41"7; 2. Gronholm 3'42"6; 3. Gronholm 3'43"1; 4. Delecour 3'43"9; 5. A. McRae 3'44"9; 6. Kankkunen 3'54"0; Gr.N Jones 3'50"5

ES.3 Te Papatapu 1 (16,75 km)
1. Gronholm 11'13"6; 2. Delecour 11'13"9; 3. Solberg 11'15"3; 4. Eriksson 11'15"4; 5. Sainz 11'16"0; 6. A. McRae 1'20"5; Gr.N Crocker 11'34"0

ES.4 Te Hutewai (11,32 km)
1. Solberg 8'06"3; 2. Eriksson 8'11"4; 3. A. McRae 8'12"9; 4. Kankkunen 8'13"3; 5. Gronholm 8'13"9; 6. Delecour 8'14"7; Gr.N Crocker 8'19"1

ES.5 Whaanga Coast (29,52 km)
1. Delecour 21'23"7; 2. Solberg 21'29"0; 3. Gronholm 21'34"9; 4. Sainz 21'36"0; 5. Eriksson 21'36"3; 6. A. McRae 21'42"4; Gr.N Crocker 22'00"9

ES.6 Te Papatapu 2 (16,75 km)
1. Delecour 11'04"2; 2. Burns 11'05"4; 3. Gronholm 11'05"5; 4. Kankkunen 11'05"9; 5. Solberg 11'08"1; 6. Sainz 11'12"7; Gr.N Al Wahaibi 11'22"7

ES.7 Manukau Super 1 (2,10 km)
1. C. McRae 1'22"3; 2. Sainz 1'22"6; 3. Burns 1'23"4; 4. Kankkunen et Solberg 1'23"8; 6. Gronholm 1'24"1; Gr.N Crocker 1'28"7

ES.8 Manukau Super 2 (2,10 km)
1. C. McRae 1'20"5; 2. Solberg 1'22"6; 3. Burns, Kankkunen et Sainz 1'22"8; 6. Loix, Delecour et Arai 1'23"5; Gr.N Nutahara 1'27"3

ES.9 Waipu Gorge 1 (11,24 km)
1. Burns 6'32"8; 2. C. McRae 6'35"1; 3. Gronholm 6'35"2; 4. Sainz 6'38"2; 5. Kankkunen 6'39"8; 6. Makinen 6'41"6; Gr.N Stohl 6'59"6

ES.10 Brooks 1 (16,03 km)
1. Burns 9'49"9; 2. C. McRae 9'52"7; 3. Gronholm 9'56"8; 4. Kankkunen 9'59"8; 5. Sainz 10'00"4; 6. Makinen 10'00"7; Gr.N Trelles 10'25"2

ES.11 Paparoa Station 1 (11,64 km)
1. Burns 6'18"5; 2. C. McRae 6'20"1; 3. Gronholm 6'21"7; 4. Kankkunen 6'22"7; 5. Sainz 6'25"0; 6. A. McRae 6'27"6; Gr.N Jones 6'40"9

ES.12 Parahi - Ararua (59,00 km)
1. Burns 34'04"5; 2. C. McRae 34'11"2; 3. Gronholm 34'26"7; 4. Kankkunen 34'42"9; 5. Sainz 34'43"1; 6. Makinen 34'44"0; Gr.N Stohl 36'09"7

ES.13 Cassidy (20,12 km)
1. C. McRae 11'35"9; 2. Gronholm 11'40"2; 3. Kankkunen 11'47"5; 4. Sainz 11'48"8; 5. Burns 11'53"9; 6. Solberg 11'55"1; Gr.N Stohl 12'36"3

ES.14 Batley (19,82 km)
1. C. McRae 11'09"0; 2. Burns 11'12"0; 3. Gronholm 11'13"4; 4. Sainz 11'17"2; 5. Kankkunen 11'23"7; 6. C. McRae 11'23"7; Gr.N Al Wahaibi 11'52"7

ES.15 Waipu Gorge 2 (11,24 km)
1. Gronholm 6'33"9; 2. Burns 6'36"2; 3. C. McRae 6'37"0; 4. Kankkunen 6'37"6; 5. Sainz 6'39"5; 6. Solberg 6'42"9; Gr.N Stohl 7'05"2

ES.16 Brooks 2 (16,03 km)
1. Gronholm 9'56"8; 2. Burns 9'58"3; 3. C. McRae 9'59"5; 4. Sainz 10'02"8; 5. Kankkunen 10'05"4; 6. Solberg 10'08"1; Gr.N Trelles 10'47"0

ES.17 Paparoa Station 2 (11,64 km)
1. Gronholm 6'25"5; 2. C; McRae 6'25"2; 3. Burns 6'27"0; 4. Sainz 6'27"5; 5. Kankkunen et Solberg 6'30"7; Gr.N Stohl 7'00"7

ES.18 Te Akau South (31,24 km)
1. A. McRae 18'46"3; 2. Solberg 18'51"9; 3. Eriksson 18'52"1; 4. C. McRae 18'53"6; 5. Sainz 18'57"5; 6. Burns 18'58"2; Gr.N Crocker 19'20'3

ES.19 Ridge 1 (8,53 km)
1. Burns 4'46"3; 2. Gronholm 4'50"7; 3. Kankkunen 4'52"7; 4. Sainz 4'53"8; 5. Eriksson 4'57"3; 6. Solberg 4'57"8; Gr.N Stohl 5'08"4

ES.20 Campbell 1 (7,44 km)
1. C. McRae 3'55"9; 2. Burns 3'58"0; 3. Gronholm 3'59"1; 4. Sainz 3'59"6; 5. Eriksson 4'02"1; 6. Bourne 4'05"8; Gr.N Crocker 4'13"1

ES.21 Ridge 2 (8,53 km)
1. C. McRae 4'45"4; 2.Gronholm 4'46"2; 3. Eriksson 4'49"1; 4. Sainz 4'49"8; 5. Solberg 4'51"1; 6. Bourne 4'53"3; Gr.N Stohl 5'05"1

ES.22 Campbell 2 (7,44 km)
1. C. McRae 3'51"8; 2. Gronholm 3'54"7; 3. Sainz 3'56"6; 4. Solberg 3'57"3; 5. Eriksson 3'57"4; 6. Bourne 4'00"3; Gr.N Stohl 4'08"9

ES.23 Fyfe 1 (8,00 km)
1. C. McRae 4'21"8; 2. Gronholm 4'22"9; 3. Solberg 4'23"4; 4. Eriksson 4'23"6; 5. Sainz 4'25"4; 6. Bourne 4'28"2; Gr.N Crocker 4'34"3

ES.24 Fyfe 2 (8,00 km)
1. Solberg 4'17"7; 2. C. McRae 4'18"6; 3. Eriksson 4'19"1; 4. Gronholm 4'19"7; 5. Sainz 4'20"3; 6. Bourne 4'23"2; Gr.N Stohl 4'31"6

RESULTS AND RETIREMENTS

	Driver/Co-Driver	Car	Gr.	Total time
1	Marcus Gronholm - Timo Rautainen	Peugeot 206 WRC	A	3h45m13,4s
2	Colin McRae - Nicky Grist	Ford Focus WRC	A	3h45m27,9s
3	Carlos Sainz - Luis Moya	Ford Focus WRC	A	3h46m31,8s
4	Petter Solberg - Phil Mills	Ford Focus WRC	A	3h48m14,1s
5	Kenneth Eriksson - Staffan Parmander	Hyundaï Accent WRC	A	3h48m26,1s
6	Possum Bourne - Craig Vincent	Subaru Impreza WRC	A	3h52m08,0s
7	Manfred Stohl - Peter Muller	Mitsubishi Lancer Evo.6	N	3h57m05,4s
8	Geof Argyle - Paul Fallon	Mitsubishi Lancer Evo.6	A	3h58m00,8s
9	Gustavo Trelles - Jorge Del Buono	Mitsubishi Lancer Evo.6	N	3h58m51,7s
10	Reece Jones - Leo Bult	Mitsubishi Lancer Evo.5	N	3h59m26,3s
ES.1	Tony Gardemeister - Paavo Lukander	Seat Cordoba WRC Evo 2	A	Accident
ES.11	François Delecour - Daniel Grataloup	Peugeot 206 WRC	A	Gearbox
ES.14	Toshihiro Araï - Roger Freeman	Subaru Impreza WRC	A	Accident
ES.14	Freddy Loix - Sven Smeets	Mitsubishi Carisma GT	A	Withdraw
ES.16	Didier Auriol - Denis Giraudet	Seat Cordoba WRC Evo 2	A	Accident
ES.18	Tommi Makinen - Risto Mannisenmaki	Mitsubishi Lancer Evo.6	A	Accident
ES.18	Alister McRae - David Senior	Hyundaï Accent WRC	A	Transmission
ES.20	Juha Kankkunen - Juha Repo	Subaru Impreza WRC 2000	A	Electronics
ES.20	Richard Burns - Robert Reid	Subaru Impreza WRC 2000	A	Electronics

EVENT LEADERS

ES.1 > ES.9   Delecour
ES.10 > ES.24 Gronholm

BEST PERFORMANCES

	1	2	3	4	5	6
C. McRae	8	6	3	-	-	-
Burns	5	5	3	-	1	2
Gronholm	4	6	9	1	1	1
Solberg	3	3	2	1	5	4
Delecour	3	1	-	1	-	2
A.McRae	1	-	1	-	1	4
Sainz	-	2	1	11	8	1
Eriksson	-	1	4	2	3	-
Kankkunen	-	-	3	7	4	1
Bourne	-	-	-	-	-	5
Makinen	-	-	-	-	-	3
Loix	-	-	-	-	-	1
Araï	-	-	-	-	-	1

CHAMPIONSHIP CLASSIFICATIONS

Drivers
1. Richard Burns — 38
2. Marcus Gronholm — 34
3. Colin McRae — 30
4. Carlos Sainz — 27
5. Tommi Makinen — 23
6. Juha Kankkunen — 18

Constructors
1. Subaru — 58
2. Ford — 57
3. Peugeot — 41
4. Mitsubishi — 29
5. Skoda — 8
6. Seat — 7

Group N
1. Manfred Stohl — 41
2. Gustavo Trelles — 34
3. Gabriel Pozzo — 16

Team's Cup
1. Spike Subaru Team (Araï) — 26
2. Toyota Team Saudi Arabia (Bakhashab) — 22
3. Frédéric Dor Rally Team (Dor) — 20

PREVIOUS WINNERS

1977	Bacchelli - Rosetti — Fiat 131 Abarth
1978	Brookes - Porter — Ford Escort RS
1979	Mikkola - Hertz — Ford Escort RS
1980	Salonen - Harjanne — Datsun 160J
1982	Waldegaard - Thorzelius — Toyota Celica GT
1983	Rohrl - Geistdorfer — Opel Ascona 400
1984	Blomqvist - Cederberg — Audi Quattro A2
1985	Salonen - Harjanne — Peugeot 205 T16
1986	Kankkunen - Piironen — Peugeot 205 T16
1987	Wittmann - Patermann — Lancia Delta HF 4WD
1988	Haider - Hinterleitner — Opel Kadett GSI
1989	Carlsson - Carlsson — Mazda 323 Turbo
1990	Sainz - Moya — Toyota Celica GT-Four
1991	Sainz - Moya — Toyota Celica GT-Four
1992	Sainz - Moya — Toyota Celica Turbo 4WD
1993	McRae - Ringer — Subaru Legacy RS
1994	McRae - Ringer — Subaru Impreza
1995	McRae - Ringer — Subaru Impreza
1996	Burns - Reid — Mitsubishi Lancer Ev.3
1997	Eriksson - Parmander — Subaru Impreza WRC
1998	Sainz - Moya — Toyota Corolla WRC
1999	Makinen - Mannisenmaki — Mitsubishi Lancer Evo 6

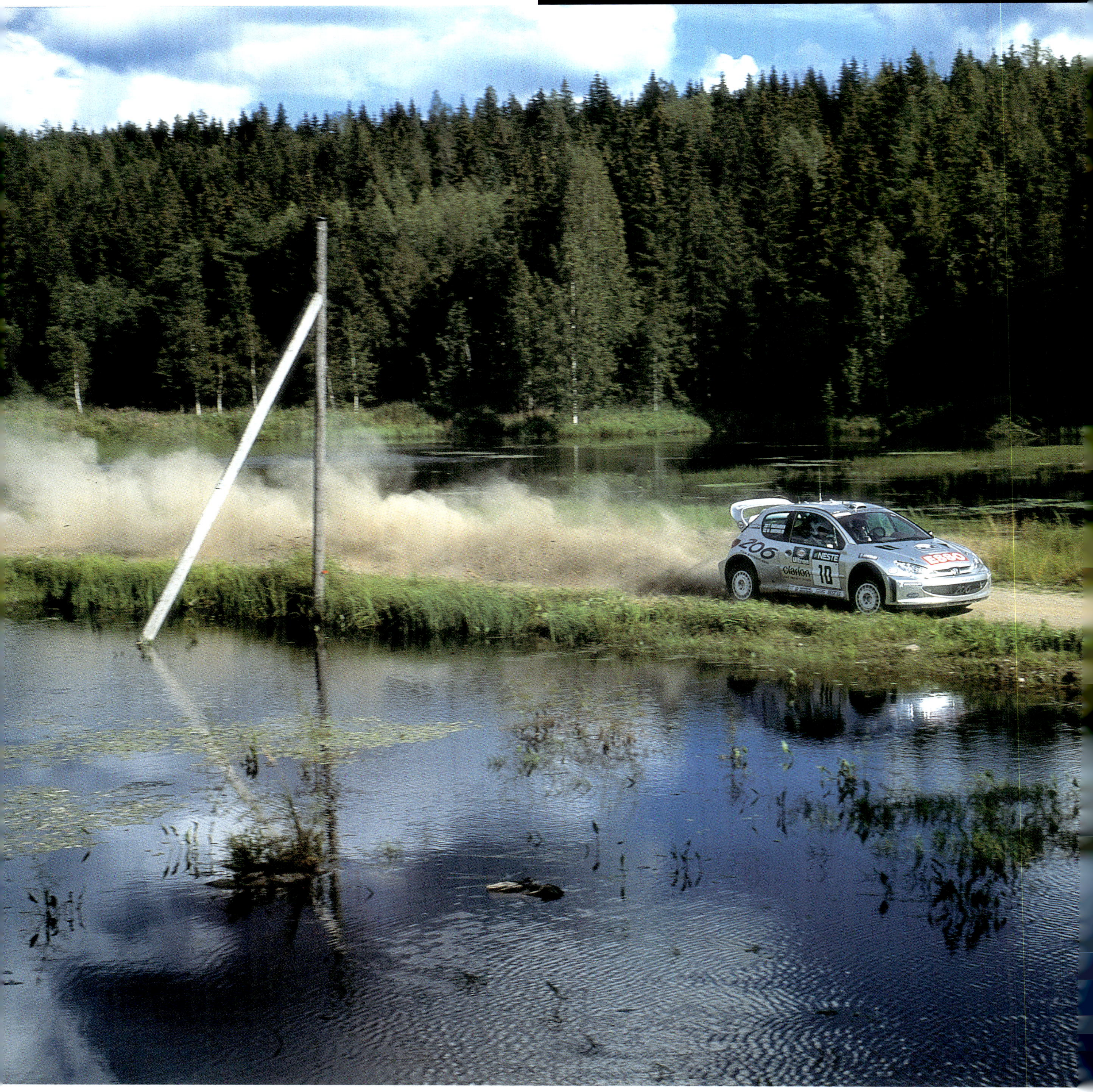

206
NESTE
Clarion
10

finland

It was probably madness for Burns to try and challenge Gronholm, given that all Finns have to win at home. The Englishman paid the price with a major off, but his was a stylish performance never the less.

THE RALLY
Gronholm in a world of his own

The bump in question is well known. It sticks out on the Jokiha stage, before Rantakyla, just at the point where the track leaves the shore of Lake Yla-Kintaus and plunges deep into the forest of pine trees and rocks which protrude from their bed of mulch and mould and mushrooms buried in tree roots. But this is not a time for mushroom picking, far from it. The only thing that matters is the stopwatch and the subsidiary sport of car long-jumping, something of a national pastime in Finland.

O f all the drivers, it was the classy Spaniard, Carlos Sainz, who well and truly pinned the tail on the donkey, with a jump that found him looking down on the tops of the fir trees. It has to be said, the Spaniard no longer had anything to lose. In the first stage, his electronic control unit was on the blink, costing him over five minutes, as well as any chance of victory.

While one valiant competitor was out of the running, there were plenty more to ensure the event lost none of its spectacle. One only had to watch the precise way in which Richard Burns and Marcus Gronholm, running in that order on the road, were tackling the stages to realise that these two were not only head and shoulders above the rest in terms of height, but also in terms of performance levels. This duo could also thank the remarkably effective handling of their cars, on an event where suspension systems have to endure the worst form of torture. On landing after a yump, it was noticeable how the wheels of the Peugeot and Subaru seemed to immediately dig in and find grip, so that the drivers could give it maximum throttle with the minimum loss of time. By comparison, many of the other works cars, most notably the poor Seats, appeared to have all the road holding of a ping-pong ball.

You only had to stand at the roadside on any of the stages, and then confirm the visual impression with a glance at the stopwatch, to see that first place on this event would be played out between the two men who topped the classification in the world championship. The rally would follow a pattern established over time in this historic Finnish rally, that of a duel between the best local up against the quickest challenge from an outsider. A case of once upon a time in the North and all that...

The Peugeot driver's performance confirmed that the only sort of pressure he understood was the one he applied to the throttle pedal and he immediately picked up the first five fastest stage times. But the lead this gave him was only of the slimmest as the Englishman seemed capable of matching his pace with a stylish and often scary performance. A minor excursion into a ditch, without any serious consequences, attested to that fact. As did four fastest stage times.

Third on the road, Colin McRae adopted the role of Indian tracker, as he studied the tyre tracks of the two men ahead. "I can't believe the lines they're taking. They are really cutting the corners. They aren't leaving any room for error." Coming from him, that was indeed a compliment.

The battle had been so heated that Gronholm led Burns into Jyvaskyla at nightfall, with just 4.9 seconds separating them. The biggest surprise came from the fact that the two past masters of these roads, Juha Kankkunen and Tommi Makinen seemed totally incapable of doing anything about it. The former was fifth, 42.8 down and the latter was sixth at 45.2. For the first time in living memory, fastest time in the Laukaa stage was not attributed to either of these two, going instead to England and Richard Burns. Kankkunen's mum, who always watches this rally from her front garden was probably not very impressed.

Once the second leg was underway, the duel fizzled out almost immediately. Burns and Gronholm were straight back at one another's throats. But, the Englishman fell foul of the fact that he did not know the second leg so well with its long and classic stages. Arriving in the tiny village of Juupasilta, at the end of Saturday's first stage, he lost control of his Subaru at the precise moment that he crossed the timing beam. The Impreza, travelling at 192 km/h, took off in a terrifying series of rolls. The driver could do little but admit it had been his fault, having underestimated this tricky right hand corner. "When you are out to win, you have to take risks," he concluded, the damage he suffered being more psychological than physical, despite a few pains in his neck. "As for the championship, the important thing is not to panic." Burns' retirement immediately put his rival in an enviable if slightly delicate situation. "It's true that it takes some of the pressure off," admitted the rally leader. "We were having one hell of a fight. I really frightened myself in Paijala. We came up to a corner really quickly. Phew! The hardest thing for now will be to maintain my concentration. I have a good lead over Harri (Rovanpera, who was now second, 37.1 behind in a private Toyota) but I have to be careful." For the rest of the day, the big blonde drove as though the surface was made of eggshells, all the better to ensure he did not scramble his chances.

There was a mad scramble to make the most of the leader's new found caution and a few fastest times were now up for grabs. His Peugeot team-mate Lindholm set one, Kankkunen did it twice and McRae picked up no less than four fastest times.

There was a spirited fight going on as the Scotsman's third place was threatened by a trio of crazy Finns, Lindholm Kankkunen and Makinen. Everyone was desperate to finish in the points and the crews and cars all showed signs of the strain. There were bumpers hanging off, wings missing, suspensions were unnaturally modified and even the co-drivers were suffering. Both Grist and Mannisenmaki had to be treated by their physios, their backs having taken a terrible pounding from all the heavy landings. The blue Subaru, the red Mitsubishi and the grey Peugeot were all just a bit black and blue. Of the three of them, Mr. K was the worse off, losing four minutes with a puncture.

However, none of these three brave lads were even on the same planet as Gronholm. He comfortably led the field home to end the second leg with an advantage of around a minute over his pursuers.

To be honest, the only point of interest during the final leg centred on who would pick up the minor placings. Gronholm and his little 206 trundled home untroubled for the Finn to record his first win on home turf. Having led from start to finish, he was quickest on eleven of the twenty three stages. Not bad!

The remaining places on the podium were hard fought with poor Harri Rovanpera folding under an assault from McRae with Makinen, Lindholm and Delecour following on behind. As for the winner, this victory had elevated him to the lead in the championship, ahead of Richard Burns and Colin McRae.

"It's a surprise, a nice surprise," said a seriously happy Finn. "I had not expected this result at all, back in January at the start of the Monte. I can't believe it." Not many seemed to share his surprise at this turn of events.

This was no ordinary win for Gronholm, but a victory on home turf, which represents a rite of passage for all Finnish drivers.

Once again, the Seats were off the pace. At the end of this event, it was announced that the unhappy Spanish outfit would quit the sport at the end of the year.

FINLAND

THE WINNER
Gronholm leaps into the lead

Winning gives you an appetite for more and Marcus Gronholm had certainly developed a taste for victory which remained unsated. Driving for a French team, he had learned to like champagne and for the third time in six months, the second time in a row after New-Zealand, the tallest man on the tracks and co-driver Timo Rautiainen had grown used to popping the cork on the magnums. The one they opened in Finland had an extra special flavour.

Winning what will always be known as the Thousand Lakes, in its fiftieth year, was the realisation of a boyhood dream and a major achievement. "The first win is always the best," commented the delighted victor. "But I have to admit that what I feel now is the same as I did the first time in Sweden in February, because this time I did it at home." And Rautiainen had his own thoughts to add: "When you look at the list of past winners of this event, putting our name on the trophy for the fiftieth edition is very special indeed."

They had indeed conquered a monument; one of the most prestigious and demanding events and they had done it in style. With Burns prematurely out of the running, Gronholm found himself alone in the lead, alone in his world, driving quickly but without taking undue risks. There were a few and the Peugeot driver did damage his steering on the last leg. The performance evoked admiration from his team-mate, Francois Delecour. "Look at the big lad!" he laughed. "He's in the lead and he bends the steering. I'm amazed." A Finn never doubts himself. He just gets on with it, plays the game with panache and wins.

It seems like a simple enough task to win in Finland, but the opposite is true. The event forces drivers to defy the laws of physics and gravity, while putting fear to one side. These are the qualities that champions are made of, the skills which allowed Gronholm to overtake Burns in the title race.

Just like the Englishman, he had reached round nine of fourteen, having won three rallies. But unlike his English rival, he had been much more consistent, having finished either first or second in five of the nine events. This solid record was not enough to make him dream of greater glory. "The title is possible, but we must wait and see. There are still five rallies to go, two of them on tarmac, including Corsica, which I do not know."

Nevertheless, the Finn's performance, along with Lindholm's fifth place, meant that his team, while still third, had made up much of the deficit to Ford, who led the field. It was enough to prolong the love affair between Peugeot and Gronholm as they announced in Finland that their contract was now extended to the end of 2002. A perfect end to a perfect rally.

THE START
Seat gets it wrong and quits

In Finland, the Spanish constructor celebrated its fiftieth birthday with the rally debut of the Cordoba WRC E3, the E3 standing for evolution three, which was unveiled by technical director Benoit Bagur before the start of the event. "The main changes concern the engine management and its ancillaries. It now has more torque, improved response time and a broader power band. The wiring loom has been revised and the electronic control unit too. Finally, the front bumper is a bit different and we have worked hard to save weight from a variety of elements." Didier Auriol was only halfhearted in his appreciation of their efforts. "Overall, it's not too bad, but I don't think it will be enough to make up the difference in the long run." If he had had time, Auriol would have been blowing out 42 candles on his birthday cake in Finland. But he had neither the time nor the inclination, faced with several technical problems. At the start, he posted three perfectly respectable times, but from then on the handling of his car inexplicably and inexorably went downhill. "It's a complete catastrophe," he explained over the radio. "I'm going flat out and missing all the apexes. It's serious and dangerous." Watching the Cordoba go down the straights was terrifying, as it seemed incapable of travelling in a straight line. "It's a shame, because I had a good feeling," was his final analysis at the end of the first leg. "Yes, the engine has more torque, even if it lacked response on the climbs, but it wasn't bad. From the fourth stage onwards, I seemed to be at the wheel of a crazy car. It was so bad I went off on the next one. What happened was that, when you braked all the braking went to the rear. I could not stop it spinning. Then the central diff started to play up. Then, when the rain came, I was running on tyres that were much too hard. So even when the car was almost back to normal, there was nothing I could do." While he closed up a bit on the second day, the end of the rally saw him finish a disappointed eleventh, eight minutes behind the winner. "Evolution 3 is a step forward compared with Evolution 2." It would never really get the chance to prove it, because at the next round of the world championship, Seat announced it was pulling out of the series. Of course they claimed this had nothing to do with the lack of results. Of course not! The official reason was that the company wished to concentrate its resources on its road cars. What's the Spanish for "little white lies?"

For years he had been invincible on his home event, but this time Makinen had to give best to Gronholm.

To score points in the constructors' championship, Peugeot had called on the services of Sebastian Lindholm as second driver to Marcus Gronholm. Appropriate as they are cousins!

THE DEFEATED MAN
Makinen loses big time

The four times world champion was counting a lot on Finland to relaunch his championship aspirations. The hopes raised by pre-rally testing, designed to try out modifications to the Lancer, came to nought. He might have finished fourth, but he was hoping for better, hoping to fight for the win. He was never capable of doing so. "Unfortunately, the damping never worked the way we wanted," he explained with contrition. "It was too hard a challenge." Lacking motivation, his driving suffered more than usual, which is not his normal style. On top of that, a very heavy landing after a yump, left his co-driver Mannisenmaki with very bad back pains. In certain sections, he was unable to speak and could not read the pace notes. Now eighteen points behind Gronholm in the championship, Makinen's chances of picking up a fifth consecutive title were tenuous, especially as his car was clearly not on a par with the opposition. He had hoped it would all come good on home turf but it did not. ∎

FINLAND

The Rally of Finland is still referred to as the Rally of the 1000 Lakes. The spectators find some strange ways to enjoy the action. Some were not afraid to get wet to watch the Estonian Markko Martin. Others preferred to go by boat. Each to his own!

FINLAND

FINLAND

Tommi Makinen was really counting on this event to relaunch his assault on the title. Sadly the reigning champion had to deal with a less than perfect Mitsubishi and had to settle for an unfamiliar fourth place on home turf.

A winner here in 1999, Juha Kankkunen once again gave his all and rediscovered some of his old style. He was fighting for third place when he lost four minutes changing a puncture on the second leg. That was the end of it for Mr. K.

TOP ENTRIES

1. Tommi Makinen - Risto Mannisenmaki
   MITSUBISHI LANCER Evo 6
2. Freddy Loix - Sven Smeets
   MITSUBISHI CARISMA GT
3. Richard Burns - Robert Reid
   SUBARU IMPREZA WRC 2000
4. Juha Kankkunen - Juha Repo
   SUBARU IMPREZA WRC 2000
5. Colin McRae - Nicky Grist
   FORD FOCUS WRC
6. Carlos Sainz - Luis Moya
   FORD FOCUS WRC
7. Didier Auriol - Denis Giraudet
   SEAT CORDOBA WRC Evo 3
8. Toni Gardemeister - Paavo Lukander
   SEAT CORDOBA WRC Evo 3
9. Sebastian Lindholm - Jukka Aho
   PEUGEOT 206 WRC
10. Marcus Gronholm - Timo Rautiainen
    PEUGEOT 206 WRC
14. Kenneth Eriksson - Staffan Parmander
    HYUNDAI ACCENT WRC
15. Alister McRae - David Senior
    HYUNDAI ACCENT WRC
16. Petter Solberg - Phil Mills
    FORD FOCUS WRC
17. Harri Rovanpera - Risto Pietilainen
    TOYOTA COROLLA WRC
18. François Delecour - Daniel Grataloup
    PEUGEOT 206 WRC
19. Tapio Laukkanen - Kaj Lindstrom
    FORD FOCUS WRC
20. Markko Martin - Michael Park
    TOYOTA COROLLA WRC
21. Pasi Hagstrom - Tero Gardemeister
    TOYOTA COROLLA WRC
22. Jane Tuohino - Miikka Anttila
    TOYOTA COROLLA WRC
24. Abdullah Bakhashab - Bob Willis
    TOYOTA COROLLA WRC
25. Jouko Puhakka - Tomi Tuominen
    MITSUBISHI CARISMA GT
26. Manfred Stohl - Peter Muller
    MITSUBISHI LANCER Evo 6
27. Juuso Pykalisto - Esko Mertsalmi
    MITSUBISHI CARISMA GT
28. Jani Paasonen - Jakke Honkanen
    MITSUBISHI LANCER Evo 6
29. Gustavo Trelles - Jorge Del Buono
    MITSUBISHI LANCER Evo 6
30. Raphael Sperrer - Per Carlsson
    SEAT CORDOBA WRC Evo 2
33. Jarmo Kytolehto - Arto Kapanen
    HYUNDAI COUPE Evo 2
34. Michael Guest - David Green
    HYUNDAI ACCENT WRC
35. Kenneth Backlund - Tord Andersson
    MITSUBISHI LANCER Evo 6
36. Hamed Al-Wahaibi - Tony Sircombe
    SUBARU IMPREZA WRX
38. Frédéric Dor - Didier Breton
    SUBARU IMPREZA WRC
40. Claudio Menzi - Edgardo Galindo
    MITSUBISHI LANCER Evo 6
43. Gabriele Pozzo - Fabian Cretu
    MITSUBISHI LANCER Evo 6
84. Sebastien Loeb - Daniel Elena
    CITROEN SAXO

50th RALLY OF FINLAND

9th leg of the 2000 world rally championship for constructors and drivers
9th leg of the production car drivers' and team's world cups
Date 18 - 20 august 2000
Route: 1680,14 km divided into 3 legs,
23 special stages on dirt roads (410,18 km.)
1st leg: Friday 18 august: Jyvaskyla - Tikkakoski - Jyvaskyla, 10 stages (128,10 km)
2nd leg: Saturday 19 august: Jyvaskyla - Halli - Jyvaskyla, 8 stages (165,11 km)
3rd leg: Sunday 20 august: Jyvaskyla - Halli - Jyvaskyla, 5 stages (116,97 km)
Starters - Finishers: 122 - 55
Conditions: good weather with the odd shower, dirt roads with a gravel surface.

As in Portugal, Rovanpera drove a great rally, but had to settle for third after handing second to McRae in the steward's room.

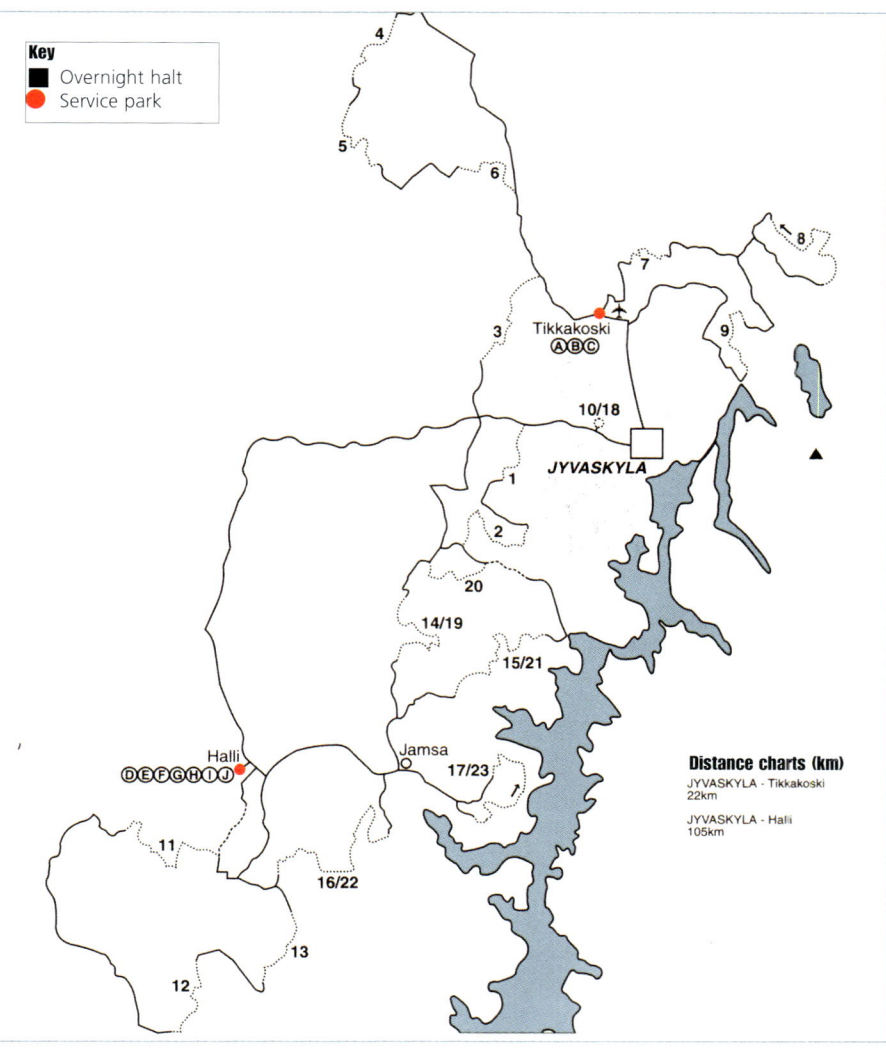

Distance charts (km)
JYVASKYLA - Tikkakoski
22km
JYVASKYLA - Halli
105km

SPECIAL STAGE TIMES

ES.1 Kuohu (7,67 km)
1. Gronholm 3'44"8; 2. Burns 3'45"7; 3. Rovanpera 3'45"8; 4. Lindholm 3'45"9; 5. Makinen 3'46"8; 6. Hagstrom 3'47"6; Gr.N Pykalisto 3'58"3

ES.2 Parkkola (20,11 km)
1. Gronholm 10'06"7; 2. Burns 10'07"9; 3. Rovanpera 10'11"4; 4. Solberg 10'13"2; 5. Auriol 10'13"7; 6. C. McRae 10'14"9; Gr.N Puhakka 10'46"5

ES.3 Mokkipera (13,39 km)
1. Gronholm 6'32"2; 2. Burns 6'33"8; 3. Rovanpera 6'35"7; 4. Makinen 6'36"4; 5. Solberg 6'36"7; 6. Kankkunen et Sainz 6'36"9; Gr.N Pykalisto 6'58"0

ES.4 Muittari (13,51 km)
1. Gronholm 6'05"6; 2. Burns et Delecour 6'09"0; 4. Rovanpera 6'09"2; 5. C. McRae 6'09"8; 6. Lindholm 6'10"2; Gr.N Paasonen 6'27"0

ES.5 Konttimaki (13,08 km)
1. Gronholm 5'40"7; 2. Sainz 5'41"6; 3. Burns et Kankkunen 5'42"4; 5. Rovanpera 5'43"2; 6. C. McRae 5'43"8; Gr.N Pykalisto 6'03"5

ES.6 Palsankyla (13,90 km)
1. Burns 7'28"6; 2. C. McRae 7'28"9; 3. Gronholm 7'31"1; 4. Solberg 7'31"2; 5. Sainz 7'33"6; 6. Rovanpera 7'35"0; Gr.N Paasonen 8'04"1

ES.7 Valkola (8,40 km)
1. Burns 4'30"2; 2. Rovanpera et Solberg 4'30"6; 4. Gronholm 4'30"8; 5. C. McRae 4'31"0; 6. Lindholm 4'31"3; Gr.N Pykalisto 4'45"5

ES.8 Lankamaa (23,44 km)
1. Gronholm 11'47"3; 2. Burns 11'48"8; 3. Kankkunen 11'49"2; 4. Sainz 11'51"8; 5. Rovanpera 11'52"0; 6. C. McRae 11'52"6; Gr.N Paasonen 12'28"0

ES.9 Laukaa (12,37 km)
1. Burns 6'13"0; 2. Gronholm 6'14"1; 3. Rovanpera 6'15"6; 4. Martin 6'15"7; 5. Kankkunen 6'16"5; 6. Lindholm 6'17"4; Gr.N Stohl 6'39"5

ES.10 Killeri 1 (2,23 km)
1. Makinen et Burns 1'07"9; 3. Tuohino 1'08"3; 4. Gardemeister 1'08"4; 5. C. McRae 1'08"5; 6. Kankkunen et Sainz 1'08"7; Gr.N Menzi 1'11"9

ES.11 Juupajoki (30,34 km)
1. Gronholm 15'13"8; 2. Burns 15'18"6; 3. Martin 15'24"4; 4. C. McRae 15'25"2; 5. Lindholm 15'25"8; 6. Rovanpera 15'25"9; Gr.N Paasonen 16'04"2

ES.12 Vastila (17,43 km)
1. Lindholm 8'21"7; 2. Gronholm 8'22"7; 3. Rovanpera 8'23"9; 4. Kankkunen 8'25"9; 5. Sainz 8'26"4; 6. C. McRae 8'27"6; Gr.N Galli 8'47"4

ES.13 Paijala (12,81 km)
1. Kankkunen 6'07"0; 2. Gronholm 6'09"6; 3. Rovanpera 6'10"8; 4. Lindholm 6'11"6; 5. Sainz 6'12"1; 6. C. McRae 6'12"8; Gr.N Pykalisto 6'24"0

ES.14 Ehikki 1 (19,08 km)
1. C. McRae 9'30"2; 2. Gronholm 9'31"7; 3. Lindholm 9'33"1; 4. Makinen 9'33"2; 5. Rovanpera 9'33"7; 6. Kankkunen 9'34"1; Gr.N Pykalisto 10'08"6

ES.15 Leustu 1 (23,58 km)
1. Kankkunen 11'47"1; 2. Rovanpera 11'48"7; 3. Makinen 11'49"1; 4. Gronholm 11'49"8; 5. C. McRae 11'52"2; 6. Auriol 12'00"1; Gr.N Pykalisto 12'38"4

ES.16 Ouninpohja 1 (34,21 km)
1. Gronholm 16'29"1; 2. Rovanpera 16'38"0; 3. Makinen 16'40"6; 4. Lindholm 16'42"9; 5. C. McRae 16'44"8; 6. Sainz 16'46"3; Gr.N Paasonen 17'26"4

ES.17 Vaheri 1 (25,43 km)
1. Gronholm 12'25"2; 2. Makinen 12'27"7; 3. C. McRae 12'28"1; 4. Sainz 12'29"0; 5. Rovanpera 12'31"8; 6. Kankkunen 12'32"1; Gr.N Pykalisto 13'15"4

ES.18 Killeri 2 (2,23 km)
1. Gronholm 1'08"7; 2. Rovanpera 1'09"0; 3. C. McRae 1'09"5; 4. Makinen et Kankkunen 1'09"7; 6. Lindholm 1'10"1; Gr.N Martila 1'19"1

ES.19 Ehikki 2 (19,08 km)
1. C. McRae 9'26"3; 2. Rovanpera 9'27"1; 3. Gronholm 9'27"2; 4. Makinen 9'30"8; 5. Lindholm 9'32"3; 6. Kankkunen 9'33"8; Gr.N Stohl 10'11"7

ES.20 Moksi (14,67 km)
1. C. McRae 7'58"3; 2. Gronholm 8'02"6; 3. Sainz 8'07"6; 4. Rovanpera 8'11"0; 5. Martin 8'11"2; 6. Makinen 8'11"4; Gr.N Pykalisto 8'44"6

ES.21 Leustu 2 (23,58 km)
1. Gronholm 11'41"3; 2. Rovanpera 11'46"1; 3. C. McRae 11'48"4; 4. Kankkunen 11'48"9; 5. Makinen 11'53"9; 6. Lindholm 11'54"2; Gr.N Galli 12'50"7

ES.22 Ouninpohja 2 (34,21 km)
1. Kankkunen 16'21"3; 2. Rovanpera 16'23"9; 3. Makinen 16'25"1; 4. Gronholm 16'28"5; 5. Lindholm 16'28"8; 6. C. McRae 16'33"0; Gr.N Stohl 17'26"1

ES.23 Vaheri 2 (25,43 km)
1. C. McRae 12'13"3; 2. Makinen 12'15"8; 3. Kankkunen 12'17"3; 4. Rovanpera 12'19"4; 5. Sainz 12'21"6; 6. Martin 12'24"3; Gr.N Hotanen 13'16"9

RESULTS AND RETIREMENTS

	Driver/Co-Driver	Car	Gr.	Total time
1	Marcus Gronholm - Timo Rautainen	Peugeot 206 WRC	A	3h22m37,1s
2	Colin McRae - Nicky Grist	Ford Focus WRC	A	3h23m43,3s
3	Harri Rovanpera - Risto Pietilainen	Toyota Corolla WRC	A	3h23m46,7s
4	Tommi Makinen - Risto Mannisenmaki	Mitsubishi Lancer Evo.6	A	3h24m15,8s
5	Sebastian Lindholm - Jukka Aho	Peugeot 206 WRC	A	3h25m43,1s
6	François Delecour - Daniel Grataloup	Peugeot 206 WRC	A	3h27m42,1s
7	Pasi Hagstrom - Tero Gardemeister	Toyota Corolla WRC	A	3h27m53,6s
8	Juha Kankkunen - Juha Repo	Subaru Impreza WRC 2000	A	3h28m30,0s
9	Alister McRae - David Senior	Hyundaï Accent WRC	A	3h28m46,2s
10	Markko Martin - Michael Park	Toyota Corolla WRC	A	3h29m27,7s
16	Jani Paasonen - Jakke Honkanen	Mitsubishi Lancer Evo 6	N	3h37m25,8s

ES.2	Hamed Al Wahaibi - Tony Sircombe	Toyota Corolla WRC	A	Transmission
ES.8	Gabriel Pozzo - Amelio Rodolfo Ortiz	Mitsubishi Lancer Evo.6	N	Accident
ES.8	Petter Solberg - Phil Mills	Ford Focus WRC	A	Accident
ES.9	Sebastien Loeb - Daniel Elena	Citroën Saxo	A	Clutch
ES.11	Tony Gardemeister - Paavo Lukander	Seat Cordoba WRC Evo 3	A	Fuel pump
ES.11	Freddy Loix - Sven Smeets	Mitsubishi Carisma GT	A	Accident
ES.11	Richard Burns - Robert Reid	Subaru Impreza WRC 2000	A	Accident
ES.17	Tapio Laukkanen - Kaj Lindstrom	Ford Focus WRC	A	Engine
ES.17	Janne Tuohino - Miikka Anttila	Toyota Corolla WRC	A	Accident
ES.18	Gustavo Trelles - Jorge Del Buono	Mitsubishi Lancer Evo.6	N	Engine

EVENT LEADERS

ES.1 > ES.22   Gronholm

BEST PERFORMANCES

	1	2	3	4	5	6
Gronholm	11	5	2	3	-	-
C. McRae	4	1	3	1	5	6
Burns	4	6	1	-	-	-
Kankkunen	3	-	2	4	1	5
Makinen	1	2	3	4	2	2
Lindholm	1	-	1	3	3	5
Rovanpera	-	7	6	3	4	1
Sainz	-	1	1	2	4	2
Delecour	-	1	-	-	-	-
Solberg	-	-	1	2	1	-
Martin	-	-	1	1	1	1
Tuohino	-	-	1	-	-	-
Gardemeister	-	-	-	1	-	-
Auriol	-	-	-	-	1	1
Hagstrom	-	-	-	-	-	1

CHAMPIONSHIP CLASSIFICATIONS

Drivers
1. Marcus Gronholm — 44
2. Richard Burns — 38
3. Colin McRae — 36
4. Carlos Sainz — 27
5. Tommi Makinen — 26
6. Juha Kankkunen — 18

Constructors
1. Ford — 63
2. Subaru — 60
3. Peugeot — 54
4. Mitsubishi — 33
5. Skoda — 8
6. Seat — 7

Group N
1. Manfred Stohl — 45
2. Gustavo Trelles — 34
3. Jani Paasonen — 21

Team's Cup
1. Spike Subaru Team (Bakashab) — 32
2. Toyota Team Saudi Arabia (Bakhashab) — 26
2. Frédéric Dor Rally Team (Dor) — 26

PREVIOUS WINNERS

1973	Makinen - Liddon / Ford Escort RS 1600	1987	Alen - Kivimaki / Lancia Delta HF Turbo
1974	Mikkola - Davenport / Ford Escort RS 1600	1988	Alen - Kivimaki / Lancia Delta Integrale
1975	Mikkola - Aho / Toyota Corolla	1989	Ericsson - Billstam / Mitsubishi Galant VR4
1976	Alen - Kivimaki / Fiat 131 Abarth	1990	Sainz - Moya / Toyota Celica GT-Four
1977	Hamalainen - Tiukkanen / Ford Escort RS	1991	Kankkunen - Piironen / Lancia Delta Integrale 16v
1978	Alen - Kivimaki / Fiat 131 Abarth	1992	Auriol - Occelli / Lancia Delta Integrale
1979	Alen - Kivimaki / Fiat 131 Abarth	1993	Kankkunen - Giraudet / Toyota Celica Turbo 4WD
1980	Alen - Kivimaki / Fiat 131 Abarth	1994	Makinen - Harjanne / Ford Escort RS Cosworth
1981	Vatanen - Richards / Ford Escort RS	1995	Makinen - Harjanne / Mitsubishi Lancer Ev.3
1982	Mikkola - Hertz / Audi Quattro	1996	Makinen - Harjanne / Mitsubishi Lancer Ev.3
1983	Mikkola - Hertz / Audi Quattro	1997	Makinen - Harjanne / Mitsubishi Lancer Ev.4
1984	Vatanen - Harryman / Peugeot 205 T16	1998	Makinen - Mannisenmaki / Mitsubishi Lancer Ev.5
1985	Salonen - Harjanne / Peugeot 205 T16	1999	Kankkunen - Repo / Subaru Impreza WRC
1986	Salonen - Harjanne / Peugeot 205 T16		

www.fordracing.net
MARTINI
Valvoline
MoviStar
Sainz
Moya
6
MICHELIN

cyprus

After abstaining for two years, Sainz finally allowed himself a win. It was a slow run rally and the Spaniard's tactics did the job. Finishing ahead of McRae, it was also revenge for events in Greece.

THE RALLY

His Eminence shows signs of genius

Up there, at the foot of Mount Olympus, there seemed little point in making the climb to Selladi tou Stachtou, to crawl up through the old pine trees of Alep, just to hang onto the side of the cliffs as the cars got there one by one, shrouded in clouds of dust and smoke. Marcus Gronholm should have been the first one up there at the highest point of the island, but his 206 would never make it to his own Olympus. It was stopped eleven kilometres further down the mountain with engine and hopes both dead. It was only the sixth stage of the Cyprus Rally and already the World Championship leader was out of the running. It was an electrical problem, actually an alternator failure as the team's technical director, Michel Nandan would later confirm.

Carlos Sainz can smile. He put together his first win for two years.

There's not much to an alternator, but it is as vital as the electricity it delivers. Without it, the batteries lose all their power as quickly as Popeye deprived of spinach. So, in the middle of the first leg, Gronholm would not be peeling the backing off yet another Lion sticker, one of which was added to the car each time he won a rally. He was left with three mind you, but he had planned to extend his collection in Cyprus. "That's just the way it goes. As for the championship, what can I do? Hope that Francois Delecour and Carlos Sainz score a lot of points. Well, maybe not too many for Carlos."

The problem for the Peugeot man was that Carlos was in fine form and he was hungry for victory. Right from the start, Sainz had been spectacular, better than at any time so far this season and indeed, for much of the past few years. He was quite simply in a class of his own and monopolised the stages, going quickest on seven out of the nine. On some sections, he managed to be around one second a kilometre quicker than his rivals. Impotence reigned down the order, anger and desolation too with more than a hint of jealousy. Colin McRae for example, who was in the same sort of car, could not get near the Spaniard, even allowing for a few worries with the brakes.

The Spaniard therefore returned to Limassol with the sort of lead one rarely sees in the championship these days: 1.20.2 over second placed man Delecour, to be precise. "It's a good situation," agreed the leader, but to be honest, there have been so many incidents already and the rally is far from won."

"So many incidents" was nothing short of euphemism. The first leg had certainly been action packed. The worthy Skoda team kicked off the list of retirements with the successive and very early failures of Schwarz, who went off the road and Climent, whose engine broke.

Then it was Auriol's turn. He had been driving impeccably at the start of the day, but he had to contend with shock absorber problems and the by now traditional failure of his power steering. A bit later, his team intimated he might consider pulling out as a faulty wheel bearing meant that was precisely what his right rear wheel might do in full flight!

In the Mitsubishi camp, there were worries of a more psychological nature. Having changed the settings on Makinen's and Loix's cars, the latter finally putting in times worthy of a factory driver, the Belgian rolled his way out of the event and the Finn lost all drive to the front wheels.

That left Richard Burns. He fought hard, but it was not enough. "Yes, I know I had a spin, but that is not enough to explain the difference to Sainz. And I'm driving flat out. I don't know if Carlos is doing the same, or if he's cruising." Towards the end of the leg, the Subaru driver was even passed by a pugnacious Francois Delecour.

However, the hardest part was yet to come. All through the second stage, all the crews repeated the same mantra: "We must finish, we must finish!" Everyone just wanted to make it to Limassol, to sleep and to forget what had gone before and hope the suffering was over. The first three stages of the morning were something of an irrelevance, providing just a few skirmishes. Burns managed to get ahead of Delecour again, the Frenchman admitting he had slowed the pace a bit to spare his 206. McRae seemed determined not to let the Englishman get too far ahead, while Loix was a man transformed, finally setting his first ever fastest time at the wheel of a Mitsubishi. In the past two years, he had started 346 stages in one of these cars, but he had never shone as brightly as the diamond emblem on the bonnet. He was on form for the rest of the day and the same applied to his team leader, with Tommi Makinen setting four fastest times.

Of course, all this was going on in the wake of a very confident Carlos Sainz. "I am concentrating on not making any mistakes. I am not cutting the corners too much and I'm looking after the tyres by not driving too sideways. The Ford Focus is working really efficiently and it seems to be reliable."

Getting to the finish meant getting through the two longest sections of the event, almost 50 kilometres from start to finish. When the crews finally arrived at Asprogia, which marked the end of this section, the cars were showing signs of distress, with bodywork hanging off and steam pouring from the engine bays, the smell mixing with that of the tortured tyres, white hot metal and general effort. To no one's surprise, Sainz had confirmed his form of the previous day, while a tale of woe accompanied his rivals.

Francois Delecour was furious: "27 kilometres without brakes. S**t! I could have done a really good time, I wanted to do a really good time."

Tommi Makinen held his head in his hands: "The turbo pressure keeps dropping and my tyres are destroyed."

Juha Kankkunen slaked his thirst from a bottle of water as he stoically explained he had no shock absorbers after the twelfth kilometre. "They've seized."

Freddy Loix still managed a smile. "I had a front right puncture."

The 23rd win of his career meant the Spaniard had equalled Kankkunen's total, while the Finn looked unlikely to add to his.

CYPRUS

Richard Burns was incapable of speech. He flung his gloves and balaclava down on top of the dashboard, having dragged his Subaru home with a broken front right shock absorber.

The only one who had reason to be talkative was Colin McRae, but the Scotsman adopted his usual austerity when it came to chatty conversation. And yet, he had just pulled off a sensational feat, beating Sainz by a whopping 30 seconds and the rest of the field by around a minute. It was good enough to move him up from fourth to second overall. This meant that the two team-mates and not so friendly rivals found themselves in exactly the opposite situation to the one that existed in Greece, back in June. They were both well ahead of Delecour, who was third, more than two minutes down. What happened in the Acropolis was still fresh in the memory. Wilson issued team orders in favour of McRae; Sainz attacked nevertheless to retake the lead. The boss got in a temper and the Spaniard finally obeyed orders, but with very bad grace. In Cyprus, Sainz was waiting for what goes around to come around to keep McRae off his tail. The order never came.

So the Scotsman pushed very hard over three stage, but he soon realised that the 1.04 gap would be too vast a chasm to cross. So, the Scotsman backed off in the final three stages, thus leaving Sainz to take the win.

Behind the peerless Ford men, Francois Delecour had set off, determined to hang onto third spot. An excellent time in the first stage of the day was enough to show Burns that he would have to do something special to get ahead of "Mr. Latebrake" and his Peugeot. "I want to finish on the podium here," affirmed the Frenchman. "Mainly because I have not had it easy on this rally, what with total brake failure on the long Saturday stage, But for that, I could have chased McRae. I was running at his pace. Third place would go some way to making up for the disappointment of New Zealand, where I was leading before I retired."

In the end, the fight for the final step of the podium evaporated, when the Subaru's engine began to cut out intermittently. "After that I had no chance of catching Francois," explained a disappointed Burns. "To be honest, I am not at all happy with this fourth place, but as far as the championship is concerned, it's better than nothing." At least he picked up some points for the first time since Argentina. The Englishman was still second behind Gronholm, who was happy enough, despite the fact that Sainz had picked up a raft of points.

THE COMEBACK

With the compliments of El Rey

There was no doubt that Sainz's win was the result of intelligence and experience. He laid the groundwork for his victory in the first leg, managing to look after his tyres and his car through the two longest stages of the day. He made the difference there, driving cleanly, intelligently and without making any mistakes. It was a splendid attack, combined with a raft of fastest times in the shorter stages, which meant he then had to do no more than keep the pressure on. In the lead from start to finish, Sainz was in great form, looking after the mechanical part of the package as well as the tyres, just when it was required. He never caved in under pressure from Burns, Delecour and McRae. "The end was a bit of a struggle," commented the winner. "We have had so many bad experiences recently, that Luis (Moya, his co-driver) and I only realised we had won when we stood on the podium. But the car worked perfectly, the tyres, the team, everything." With this twenty third win, which equalled Juha Kankkunen's record, he also proved that experience counts for a lot in rallying. Indeed, comparing these two former champions, it seemed more than likely that only the Spaniard would go on to add further victories to his tally. The Finn, despite coming close on a few occasions, seemed to be sliding slowly into retirement, even though he would not hear mention of the word despite his evident lethargy in recent times.

The other determining factor was experience. In 1999 in China, another terrain which was as unknown as that in Cyprus, Didier Auriol had been on majestic form. Yet again it was another "old boy" who taught the young bloods a lesson with a display of controlled aggression.

Sainz was back in the winner's circle for the first time in twenty six months, his previous win dating back to New Zealand in 1998. He had managed to mix it with the youngsters like Gronholm and Burns, who are tugging on the tailcoats of the past masters as they try and assert their reputation in the twenty first century.

38 years old, after twenty years in rallying, eleven uninterrupted seasons of competition in the world championship, with two world titles under his belt in 1990 and 1992, the winner in Cyprus could not be that far from retirement. He knows it and worries about it. If everything had gone well at Toyota in 1998 and '99, if he had managed to take a third world title, Sainz's career could have taken a different direction. Nothing in his career had dented his enthusiasm for the sport. "Year after year, I feel exactly the same. I have always had the same level of motivation and I really hope that I will be competitive in the remaining four rallies of this season. I am near the top of the classification, not leading, but close all the same. The 2000 title is still within my grasp, although it will be difficult. But I have to be realistic, so let's wait and see." There was no way he was going to make the same embarrassing mistake as in 1998, when he had T-shirts made, trumpeting a third world championship, before his Corolla expired, just 300 metres from the finish of the final rally of the season in Great Britain.

THE ANALYSIS

Cyprus passes the test

The Cyprus event got onto the calendar despite much ill feeling (see Argentinian Rally:) most of the teams and drivers left it very happy with the way it had gone. But it took a bit of time to get going. To start with, the French fishermen had blockaded the port of Marseille, which made life difficult before the start. The practice cars arrived so late, that the recce had to be delayed by 24 hours. So rather than starting on Sunday, the crews had to wait until the Monday afternoon before the rally, to start getting to know the challenge awaiting them on this, the tenth round of the world championship. Not ideal, given this was the first time Cyprus had featured on the world rally championship calendar. This was the case for all the runners except Armin Schwarz, who had won this event on the Mediterranean island in the past. It would prove no great advantage, as the over enthusiastic German would not trouble the scorer. He threw his Skoda Octavia off the road on the second stage. In his defence, he had little time to get to grips with modifications made to his car prior to the rally. For the rest of the field, Cyprus drew a favourable response. For starters, it was not as hot as had been feared. The last day was the hottest, with the temperature in Limassol hitting 37 degrees Celsius, but only thirty in the hills which were home to the stages, although the ground temperature did climb as high as forty.

On top of that, everyone from the FIA officials, the drivers, teams and media, all agreed that the rally was very well organised, with only a few minor details in need of a little tidying up. Carlos Sainz had evidently become something of a fan, even though some sections did not please everyone. "It's true that some sections are very slow (average speeds ranged from 52.97 to 100.90 km/h) but that is one of the characteristics of the event, just as high speeds are typical in Finland." Strange when one recalls that Sainz and his co-driver Luis Moya were originally virulent in their opposition to this event.

The final result was that Cyprus passed the test with flying colours. It was already scheduled to be run again from 15th to 17th June 2001. Coming two weeks after the Acropolis and three before Kenya, the calendar looked set for a prolonged hot spell. ■

For its first appearance on the world championship calendar, the Cypriot event proved worthy of its place in the upper level of the sport.

CYPRUS

CYPRUS

It was essential to look after the car and tyres on this slow but car breaking event and that's exactly what Carlos Sainz did. He made the most of his Ford and nursed it to the end. It put him at the top of the podium, out of reach of the rest.

Before the rally started, Subaru signed a contract with Markko Martin for 2001. This meant the Estonian was making one of his last appearances at the wheel of his Toyota Corolla WRC. He was not the only one joining the blue team, as Petter Solberg was also on the books for the following year.

CYPRUS

Even though they are very tough, rally tyres are powerless when drivers ask too much of them. They can be the targets of abuse but work perfectly when the car's road holding allows them. While the Mitsubishis chewed up their Michelins, the Fords were very well balanced on the same rubber.

CYPRUS

28th CYPRUS RALLY

10th leg of the 2000 world rally championship for constructors and driversrs 2000
10th leg of the production car drivers' and team's world cups
Date 08 - 10 september 2000
Route: 1227,82 km divided into 3 legs,,
23 special stages on dirt roads (348,41 km.)
1st leg: Friday 8 september: Limassol - Troodos - Limassol, 9 stages (145,16 km)
2nd leg: Saturday 9 september: Limassol - Paphos - Limassol, 8 stages (114,50 km)
3rd leg: Sunday 10 september: Limassol - Limassol, 6 stages (88,75 km)
Starters - Finishers: 52 - 27
Conditions: good weather and very hot, narrow and dusty dirt roads.

Simon Jean-Joseph continued his apprenticeship on the loose, taking part at the wheel of a private Subaru in which he finished tenth.

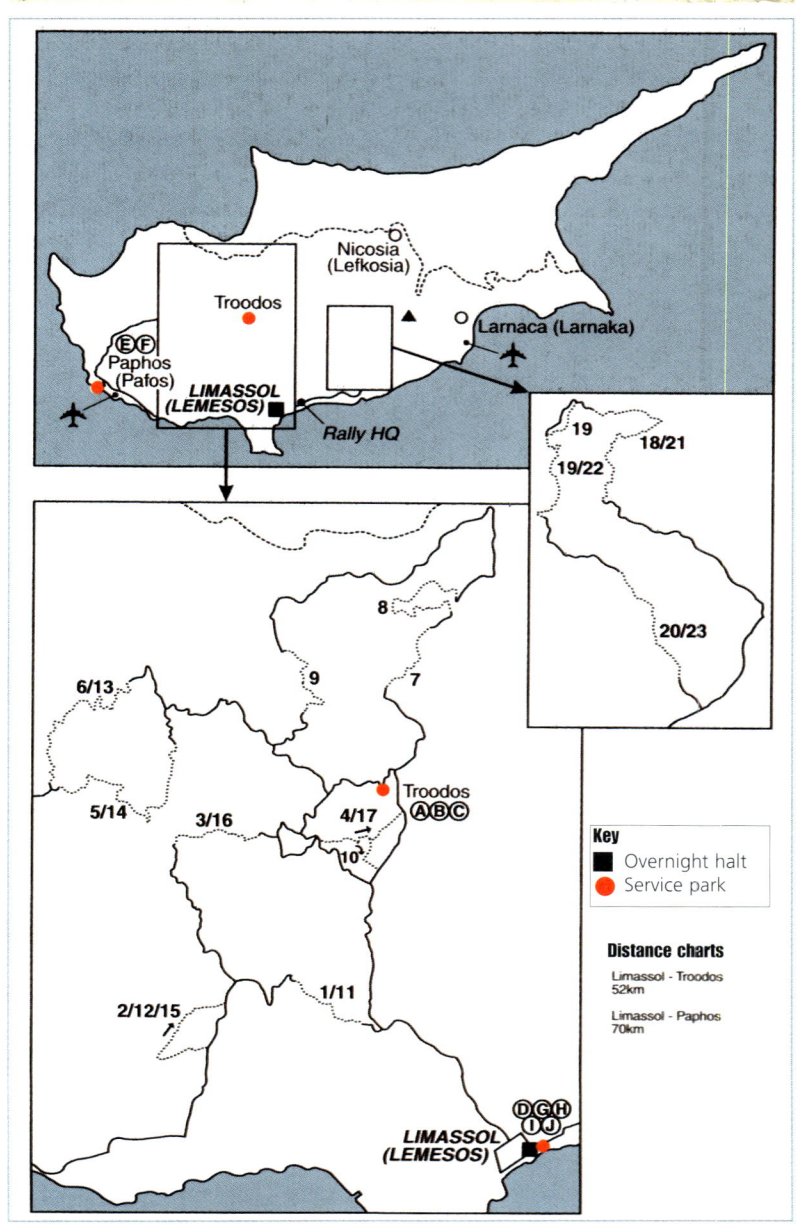

TOP ENTRIES

1 Tommi Makinen - Risto Mannisenmaki
 MITSUBISHI LANCER Evo 6

2 Freddy Loix - Sven Smeets
 MITSUBISHI CARISMA GT

3 Richard Burns - Robert Reid
 SUBARU IMPREZA WRC 2000

4 Juha Kankkunen - Juha Repo
 SUBARU IMPREZA WRC 2000

5 Colin McRae - Nicky Grist
 FORD FOCUS WRC

6 Carlos Sainz - Luis Moya
 FORD FOCUS WRC

7 Didier Auriol - Denis Giraudet
 SEAT CORDOBA WRC Evo 3

8 Toni Gardemeister - Paavo Lukander
 SEAT CORDOBA WRC Evo 3

9 François Delecour - Daniel Grataloup
 PEUGEOT 206 WRC

10 Marcus Gronholm - Timo Rautiainen
 PEUGEOT 206 WRC

11 Armin Schwarz - Manfred Hiemer
 SKODA OCTAVIA WRC

12 Luis Climent - Alex Romani
 SKODA OCTAVIA WRC

16 Petter Solberg - Phil Mills
 FORD FOCUS WRC

17 Markko Martin - Michael Park
 TOYOTA COROLLA WRC

18 Toshihiro Araï - Roger Freeman
 SUBARU IMPREZA WRC

19 Krzysztof Holowczyc - Jean Marc Fortin
 SUBARU IMPREZA WRC

20 Abdullah Bakhashab - Bob Willis
 TOYOTA COROLLA WRC

21 Frédéric Dor - Didier Breton
 SUBARU IMPREZA WRC

22 Simon Jean Joseph - Jacques Boyère
 SUBARU IMPREZA WRC

23 John Papadimitriou - Nikos Petropoulos
 SUBARU IMPREZA WRC

24 Manfred Stohl - Peter Muller
 MITSUBISHI LANCER Evo 6

25 Gustavo Trelles - Jorge Del Buono
 MITSUBISHI LANCER Evo 6

26 Hamed Al-Wahaibi - Tony Sircombe
 SUBARU IMPREZA WRC

27 Claudio Menzi - Edgardo Galindo
 MITSUBISHI LANCER Evo 6

28 Gabriele Pozzo - Rodolfo Ortiz
 MITSUBISHI LANCER Evo 6

Key
■ Overnight halt
● Service park

Distance charts
Limassol - Troodos
52km
Limassol - Paphos
70km

SPECIAL STAGE TIMES

ES.1 Alassa - Agios Therapon 1 (6,22 km)
1. Sainz 4'34"7; 2. C. McRae 4'36"3; 3. Burns 4'37"1; 4. Auriol 4'38"7; 5. Loix 4'39"9; 6. Delecour 4'40"7; Gr.N Stohl 4'57"9

ES.2 Prastio - Pachna 1 (11,06 km)
1. Burns 6'40"0; 2. C. McRae 6'41"3; 3. Sainz 6'41"4; 4. Delecour 6'43"3; 5. Kankkunen 6'44"2; 6. Gronholm 6'45"6; Gr.N Trelles 7'22"4

ES.3 Agios Nikolaos - Foini 1 (11,30 km)
1. Sainz 10'04"0; 2. Burns 10'06"6; 3. Delecour 10'06"9; 4. C. McRae 10'08"6; 5. Makinen 10'09"6; 6. Gronholm 10'10"8; Gr.N Trelles 10'45"2

ES.4 Platres - Kato Amiantos 1 (11,99 km)
1. Sainz 9454"0; 2. C. McRae 9'59"6; 3. Gronholm 10'00"7; 4. Martin 10'05"3; 5. Delecour 10'06"4; 6. Makinen 10'07"1; Gr.N Trelles 10'35"7

ES.5 Mylikouri - Monashilakas 1 (31,87 km)
1. Burns 36'05"6; 2. Gronholm 36'12"4; 3. Sainz 36'14"2; 4. Delecour 36'14"3; 5. Makinen 36'17"4; 6. C. McRae 36'20"3; Gr.N Trelles 37'44"6

ES.6 Panagia - Selladi Tou Stachtou 1 (19,52 km)
1. Sainz 17'33"8; 2. Burns 17'36"1; 3. Loix 17'37"5; 4. Kankkunen 17'49"4; 5. Delecour 17'51"0; 6. Makinen 17'51"2; Gr.N Trelles 18'36"7

ES.7 Kourdali - Assinou (14,92 km)
1. Sainz 16'28"9; 2. Makinen 16'38"2; 3. Martin 16'45"4; 4. Burns 16'45"5; 5. C. McRae 16'45"7; 6. Kankkunen 16'46"4; Gr.N Stohl 17'25"2

ES.8 Assinou - Nikitari (25,39 km)
1. Sainz 27'30"8; 2. Makinen 27'44"1; 3. C. McRae 27'48"0; 4. Kankkunen 27'49"9; 5. Burns et Martin 28'06"1; Gr.N Trelles 29'17"4

ES.9 Xerarkaka - Stavroulia (12,89 km)
1. Sainz 14'33"8; 2. Delecour 14'42"1; 3. Gardemeister 14'48"2; 4. Burns 14'50"0; 5. C. McRae 14'55"1; 6. Martin 14'56"3; Gr.N Pozzo 15'28"4

ES.10 Platres - Saittas (11,48 km)
1. Loix 9'46"4; 2. C. McRae 9'47"2; 3. Makinen, Burns et Sainz 9'48"0; 6. Kankkunen 9'50"8; Gr.N Menzi 10'24"3

ES.11 Alassa - Agios Therapon 2 (6,22 km)
1. Makinen 4'35"0; 2. Burns 4'35"1; 3. Kankkunen 4'35"9; 4. Loix et Sainz 4'36"3; 6. Delecour 4'38"7; Gr.N Pozzo 4'54"1

ES.12 Prastio - Pachna 2 (11,06 km)
1. Kankkunen 6'36"8; 2. Burns 6'37"3; 3. Loix 6'37"4; 4. C. McRae 6'37"8; 5. Delecour 6'39"1; 6. Makinen 6'40"9; Gr.N Menzi 7'11"1

ES.13 Panagia - Selladi Tou Stachtou 2 (19,52 km)
1. Loix 17'10"9; 2. Sainz 17'19"1; 3. Kankkunen 17'19"9; 4. Martin 17'23"7; 5. Burns 17'27"3; 6. C. McRae 17'27"4; Gr.N Trelles 18'39"5

ES.14 Mylikouri - Monashilakas 2 (31,87 km)
1. C. McRae 35'52"1; 2. Kankkunen 35'58"3; 3. Makinen 36'09"8; 4. Martin 36'25"3; 5. Sainz 36'32"4; 6. Loix 36'32"5; Gr.N Trelles 37'34"1

ES.15 Prastio - Pachna 3 (11,06 km)
1. Burns 6'34"6; 2. Loix 6'35"8; 3. McRae 6'36"3; 4. Makinen 6'36"9; 5. Sainz 6'37"1; 6. Delecour 6'37"5; Gr.N Pozzo 7'13"7

ES.16 Agios Nikolaos - Foini 2 (11,30 km)
1. Makinen 9'57"8; 2. C. McRae 9'58"7; 3. Burns 10'02"1; 4. Sainz 10'03"7; 5. Delecour 10'08"6; 6. Loix 10'09"6; Gr.N Trelles 10'46"3

ES.17 Platres - Kato Amiantos 2 (11,99 km)
1. Sainz 9'45"5; 2. C. McRae 9'45"6; 3. Makinen 9'47"2; 4. Delecour 9'47"8; 5. Loix 9'52"2; 6. Martin 9'58"7; Gr.N Trelles 10'37"4

ES.18 Vavatsinia - Mandra Tou Kambiou 1 (19,11 km)
1. Makinen 17'05"7; 2. Delecour 17'09"5; 3. Martin 17'16"5; 4. Kankkunen 17'20"5; 5. Sainz 17'22"0; 6. Loix 17'22"1; Gr.N Menzi 18'25"7

ES.19 Agios Onoufrios - Agioi Vavatsinas (18,10 km)
1. Burns 16'26"1; 2. Makinen 16'32"6; 3. C. McRae 16'41"8; 4. Delecour 16'44"4; 5. Loix 16'45"7; 6. Araï 16'48"5; Gr.N Menzi 18'04"1

ES.20 Lageia - Kalavasos 1 (9,62 km)
1. Burns 8'38"6; 2. C. McRae 8'39"9; 3. Loix 8'41"1; 4. Kankkunen 8'41"4; 5. Makinen 8'42"7; 6. Sainz 8'43"3; Gr.N Menzi 9'20"2

ES.21 Vavatsinia - Mandra Tou Kambiou 2 (19,11 km)
1. Makinen 16'58"3; 2. Kankkunen 17'08"3; 3. Burns 17'08"6; 4. Loix et Delecour 17'12"1; 6. Martin 17'13"4; Gr.N Stohl 18'22"9

ES.22 Machairas - Agioi Vavatsinias (13,19 km)
1. Burns 11'40"0; 2. C. McRae 11'50"4; 3. Loix 11'51"2; 4. Delecour 11'57"0; 5. Martin 11'59"0; 6. Kankkunen 11'59"2; Gr.N Menzi 12'50"8

ES.23 Lageia - Kalavasos 2 (9,62 km)
1. Burns 8'35"8; 2. Makinen 8'37"8; 3. Martin 8'40"3; 4. C. McRae 8'43"0; 5. Kankkunen 8'44"1; 6. Loix 8'45"0; Gr.N Stohl 9'15"1

RESULTS AND RETIREMENTS

	Driver/Co-Driver	Car	Gr.	Total time
1	Carlos Sainz - Luis Moya	Ford Focus WRC	A	5h26m04,9s
2	Colin McRae - Nicky Grist	Ford Focus WRC	A	5h26m42,2s
3	François Delecour - Daniel Grataloup	Peugeot 206 WRC	A	5h27m35,7s
4	Richard Burns - Robert Reid	Subaru Impreza WRC 2000	A	5h28m09,0s
5	Tommi Makinen - Risto Mannisenmaki	Mitsubishi Lancer Evo.6	A	5h23m03,1s
6	Markko Martin - Michael Park	Toyota Corolla WRC	A	5h29m50,3s
7	Juha Kankkunen - Juha Repo	Subaru Impreza WRC 2000	A	5h33m06,6s
8	Freddy Loix - Sven Smeets	Mitsubishi Carisma GT	A	5h34m10,6s
9	Toshihiro Araï - Roger Freeman	Subaru Impreza WRC	A	5h35m20,8s
10	Simon Jean Joseph - Jacques Boyère	Subaru Impreza WRC	A	5h48m21,0s
11	Gustavo Trelles - Jorge Del Buono	Mitsubishi Lancer Evo. 6	N	5h48m45,6s
ES.2	Armin Schwarz - Manfred Hiemer	Skoda Octavia WRC	A	Accident
ES.2	Abdullah Bakhashab - Bobby Willis	Toyota Corolla WRC	A	Accident
ES.4	Luis Climent - Alex Romani	Skoda Octavia WRC	A	Engine
ES.6	Marcus Gronholm - Timo Rautainen	Peugeot 206 WRC	A	Battery
ES.6	Didier Auriol - Denis Giraudet	Seat Cordoba WRC Evo 3	A	Rolling bearing
ES.9	Frédéric Dor - Didier Breton	Subaru Impreza WRC	A	Fire
ES.9	Krzysztof Holowczyc - Jean Marc Fortin	Subaru Impreza WRC	A	Transmission
ES.14	Tony Gardemeister - Paavo Lukander	Seat Cordoba WRC Evo 3	A	Accident

EVENT LEADERS

ES.1 > ES.23 Sainz

BEST PERFORMANCES

	1	2	3	4	5	6
Sainz	8	2	2	1	4	2
Burns	7	5	3	2	2	-
Makinen	4	4	2	1	3	3
Loix	2	1	4	2	3	4
C. McRae	1	8	3	3	2	3
Kankkunen	1	2	2	4	2	3
Delecour	-	3	1	5	5	3
Gronholm	-	1	1	-	-	2
Martin	-	-	3	3	2	3
Gardemeister	-	-	1	-	-	-
Auriol	-	-	-	1	-	-
Araï	-	-	-	-	-	1

CHAMPIONSHIP CLASSIFICATIONS

Drivers
1. Marcus Gronholm — 44
2. Colin McRae — 42
3. Richard Burns — 41
4. Carlos Sainz — 37
5. Tommi Makinen — 28
6. Juha Kankkunen — 18

Constructeurs
1. Ford — 79
2. Subaru — 64
3. Peugeot — 54
4. Mitsubishi — 35
5. Skoda — 8
6. Seat — 7

Groupe N
1. Manfred Stohl — 48
2. Gustavo Trelles — 44
3. Gabriel Pozzo — 22

Team's Cup
1. Spike Subaru Team (Araï) — 36
2. Toyota Team Saudi Arabia (Bakhashab) — 32
3. Frédéric Dor Rally Team (Dor) — 26

Richard Burns in action. He fought like mad to defend his fourth place and maintain his championship chances.

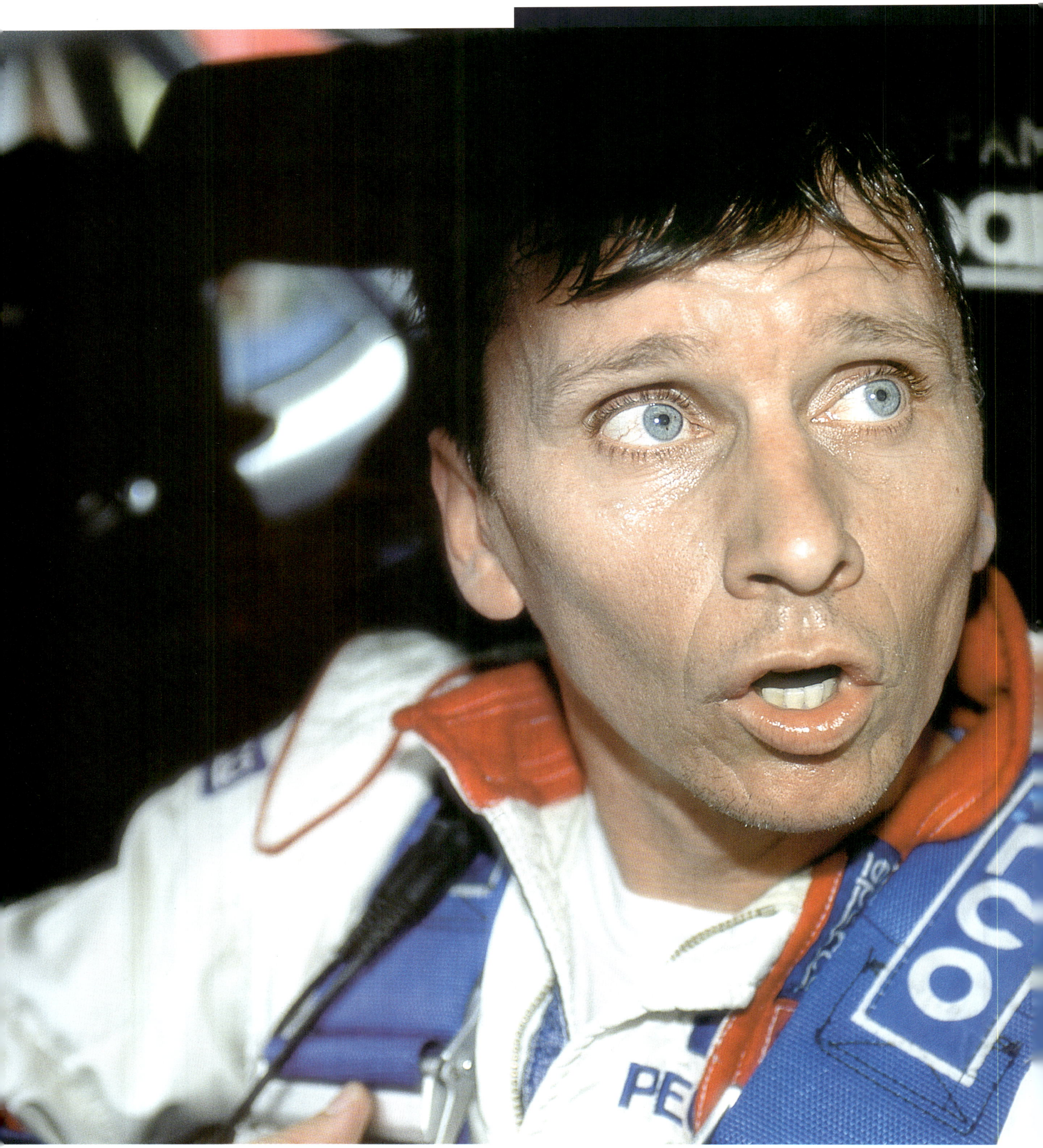

france

A first win for a dazzling Panizzi. Thanks to Delecour, it was also Peugeot's first one-two. On the island, the 206 was on a different planet to the rest.

THE RALLY

The Tour de Force

The result had been expected for a long time now and the Lion did not disappoint as it simply devoured the opposition. Finally, it produced the goods, much to the delight of its huge army of fans, which had scaled the heights of Ajaccio. Delecour and Panizzi never put a foot wrong and the expected victory was finally in the bag. While the result is straightforward, its story was hard fought.

On the morning of the first day, when the roads were dry as goat cheese, Richard Burns charged off to take the first stage in fine style, finishing 2.5 s ahead of Delecour. The Englishman must have thought he was in for an easy weekend, but he never matched that early promise during the rest of the rally. The Subaru driver's dreams would soon be shattered. On the second stage, from Lopigna to Sarrola, Panizzi was quickest and Delecour stole the lead. Burns had fired first, but he was now out of ammo. For the rest of the rally, he would not challenge for the lead. He was even out-paced by temporary team-mate Simon Jean-Joseph, whose mission was to bring his car home in the points, which he accomplished with talent and patience. Burns only really put on another spurt towards the end, when Gronholm challenged him for fourth place, although by then, the Peugeot boys had backed off.

But let us go back to that first stage. Francois Delecour and Daniel Grataloup were delighted with themselves. "I knew we would be good here," explained the driver. "The car is the way I like it, with its mechanical front and rear diffs and only the central one being electronic, making the car flow more. And as the rest has been improved, be it the brakes, the transmission, the suspension or the engine, the car is very efficient." His co-driver agreed. "I also think Francois has a bit in reserve." Maybe not too much, because at the celebrated jump at Calvese, the 206 had a very heavy landing, making worrying graunching noises. "We were really really going quickly," laughed "Mr. Latebrake." "It was a close call. But the car's alright." The noise came from the fact that on this event, the car's suspension was not really set up to deal with big jumps.

On this good opening day for the crew, that was about their only nasty moment, although there was another more amusing incident when two wild pigs decided to run across the stage. What do you expect in Corsica?

Despite their fine showing, the two men did not lead the rally, when it returned to Ajaccio. That honour fell to the Panizzi brothers. Gilles, known as the "Carbuccia Express," had timed it just right when tackling the stage of the same name. He was really enjoying this return after five months of not competing. "It does you good," he rejoiced. "I was a bit off the pace at the start of the morning, as I had to get back in the groove. But after that, I gradually picked up the pace." The end result was four fastest stage times and a devastating time on the final one, beating Makinen by 5.5. The world champion was actually delighted with the fact that his car was finally to his liking. Unfortunately, his team-mate Freddy Loix could not offer an opinion, as he had a very nasty crash at the first corner of the first stage. Could anything be dumber than that?

Faced with the incredible domination of the French team, some of the mad fans, who dashed around the Corsican countryside to cheer on the Lion, appeared to have forgotten that there were other competitors. The best of these turned out to be Carlos Sainz, who was third. "The Peugeots have definitely improved since Catalunya (the previous tarmac event)" said the Spaniard with admiration in his voice. "And I can tell you, I'm right on the limit." McRae, who was lying fifth, was of the same opinion. "Suspension, engine, tyres; who knows where their superiority comes from?" As for Burns, fourth, he admitted there was nothing he could do. "I think I'm flat out, but the 206 is much quicker than I had expected."

It was the same story on the second leg. Delecour and Panizzi were out on their own. This section was plagued with cancellations and delays, but worst of all was McRae's very nasty accident.

Win or die, so the saying goes and McRae came very close indeed to proving it correct. He managed to escape with only minor injuries after a terrible crash in the middle of the leg. Others would follow, thankfully with less damage than the Scotsman. The first one to make a faux-pas was Burns. Before tackling the first stage of this leg, Morosaglia, the Englishman got his tyre choice wrong. He opted for mixed tyres, a logical choice given that the road was still wet if not soaked, but the compound choice was not suitable. It was enough to do the damage and in 32 kilometres, he lost 29 s to the leader Gilles Panizzi, which was more than he had lost in all of the previous leg.

In the following stage, it was Makinen who suffered the most. Full of confidence, now that he felt his Mitsubishi was once again up to the required standard to deal with his not inconsiderable talent, the world champion seemed to set off on a suicide

Finally! Having come so close in the past, Panizzi drove brilliantly to take his first world championship win.

It took almost 40 minutes for the rescue crews to free Colin McRae from his Focus. He had lung and cheekbone injuries.

FRANCE

mission. The sun was out again, gradually pushing away the clouds, which were gathered round the heights of Niolo which, according to legend, is the devil's playground. In start contrast, the hills of Venaco were barren, still showing the scars of last summer's fires. Makinen apparently felt he was invincible. Sadly, he was not and broke his left front wheel against a rock that was tougher than he and his Lancer combined. As a result, he bent a steering arm and damaged a brake line. It cost him three minutes.

Finally, five kilometres into the next stage, McRae took off on the roll of his life, which is saying something, given how many times in his career he has committed a similar error. It took an age to get him out of the wreck and naturally, rumours as to his condition got ever more fanciful. McRae was finally helicoptered to the hospital in Bastia, suffering from a broken cheek bone and lung problems. The next day, he was flown to hospital in Edinburgh.

Carlos Sainz was still the only man who appeared to be able to hang onto the tails of the Peugeots. "But it's really hard, " sighed the struggling but unbeaten Spaniard. "I had a slight off on the first stage, because I was pushing like mad. But I also lost time because my set-up wasn't right for the damp conditions. My Focus doesn't seem to be as nimble or agile as the 206."

Fabrice Morel, seen here in action in his 206 and Sebastien Loeb in a Toyota Corolla started this event thanks to an FFSA initiative.

This was Simon Jean-Joseph's first rally for the works Subaru team, where he replaced Kankkunen, having been involved in the development of the Impreza P 2000.

The French team had a great day. There were only five stages; one had to be cancelled as there were too many spectators and the Peugeot drivers were quickest on all of them; three thanks to Panizzi and two for Delecour. But just when it looked as though the former would lead home this leg, he stalled at the start of the final stage and lost 10 seconds trying to re-start the beast. "I couldn't believe it! The car was dead and refused to come back to life." This meant it was left to Delecour to go quickest and take the lead by a mere two tenths of a second after two hours and thirty seven minutes of stage time.

The final leg was notable for the fact that Makinen went off, injuring a photographer. The expected duel between the two Peugeot drivers did not last long. Sainz lost his power steering and with it, 1.15. That meant he was no longer a threat and Jean-Pierre Nicolas took the immediate decision to impose team orders at the end of the Lopigna - Sarrola section. This meant that victory went to Gilles Panizzi, who had retaken the lead thanks to a demon time on the first stage of the day. At the time, he was leading Delecour by just nine tenths of a second.

It was incredible. At the start of the third day of the rally, after 3h 10m 41 on 308.42 km of stages, there was less than a second separating the Lion team-mates. The fact that Delecour officially finished 33 s behind means little, as he backed off and cruised to the end. "I have to accept the decision, but it's hard to swallow," he said. He had at least contributed to a great one-two finish for his team, who in picking up sixteen championship points were back in the title race. As for Marcus Gronholm, who had expected to lose his lead in the drivers' classification, because of his lack of experience of the route, he managed to stay in front, thanks to an impressive fifth place. It had really been a Tour de Force on the Tour de Corse for Peugeot.

THE WINNER
Panizzi at last

It made a cute picture as the little girl buried her head in her father's shoulder, trying to hide her emotion. She is only two years old, but she was ready to wipe away the tears welling in Herve Panizzi's eyes.

"We've done it at last, we won," is all Gilles' brother and inseparable co-driver coould manage. The two brothers had finally won a round of the world championship. It was a magnificent achievement and a fitting reward." Now we know what it takes to win, we have no plans to stop," laughed Gilles, with his cap at a jaunty angle. This win had taken some doing, and not just in the Corsican hills. They had fought tooth and nail and while Delecour was slowed by team orders, Panizzi had been dominant up to that point. He set eight out of seventeen fastest stage times, against four for Delecour. Philippe Bugalski, who won this event the previous year, was delighted for his successor. "Team orders were inevitable and the fact they fell at that point was a good thing." Gilles Panizzi is a real artist on tarmac, a virtuoso of the black top. The man they call Zebedee, because he is always bouncing on his toes, is a true tarmac specialist, reallly at home on the smooth roads of Corsica, Catalunya and Italy. But the world rally stage is not his ideal playground, because his progress tends to slow the moment his wheels are on the loose. Sadly for him, two thirds of the calendar are run on unmade roads.

So this win in Corsica arrived at just the right time to buck the trend of what had been a pretty disastrous year. First there had been the Monte where, of the three Peugeot drivers, Panizzi was the only one capable of matching Makinen's stunning pace. But of course, his 206 refused to fire up at the start of the second leg. In the Safari, it was not just Panizzi who was badly prepared as that criticism could be levelled at the entire Peugeot team. Zebedee got in a strop, punched another competitor, was fined 50,000 dollars by FIA and disowned by his team. Finally, there was Catalunya, where the 206 was off the pace and he finished a lacklustre sixth.

Then nothing, until this great win in Corsica. Maybe it will paint a brighter future for Panizzi, although at this time, he did not feature in Peugeot's plans for 2001. However, a winner's trophy is worth a thousand words when it comes to talks with other teams, when looking for a drive.

NICE ONE!
Loeb and Morel, the proteges

Corsica was the first of two events to feature entries for two members of the Equipe de France at the wheel of WRC cars, as part of the initiative organised by the FFSA (The French motor sport association.) It is an ambitious programme aimed at bringing young French talent to the attention of the factory teams. Fabrice Morel thus found himself back behind the wheel of the 206 WRC he had driven in Catalunya, thanks to his winning the "Volant 206," a series organised by Peugeot in 1999. As for Sebastien Loeb, who had become Didier Auriol's protege, he was entrusted with an ex-works Toyota Corolla WRC, entered by the Grifone team.

The first stage finished with Loeb in 12th place and Morel 15th after a few difficult moments. The 206 driver was taking time to find the right set-up for the diffs, but once he had done that, he started setting some promising times. Loeb made a cautious start, but then put in some great times. On average, he was losing just a second per kilometre when compared with the fastest runner. However, a slow puncture on stage five and a spin on the last one cost him precious seconds. Loeb and Morel eventually finished a respectable ninth and tenth, improving all the while. Morel was less than impressed with his inconsistency. "I would do a good time and then a bad one. I have to avoid doing that." Didier Auriol had this to say about Loeb's first event at the wheel of a WRC car. "He was learning all the time and got quicker through the event. It was a perfect performance on this treacherous rally." Grifone team manager Nik Gullino was equally pleased. "I am very impressed. Sebastien drove with intelligence and showed he has talent." Morel and Loeb would be seen again on the San Remo. ■

What can one say about Seat this year? The Spanish team never cut it. It was a sad end to the project, especially for lead driver Didier Auriol. Holding the record for the most number of wins here, (six, equal with Bernard Darniche) the best he could do was second quickest on one stage. In the pouring rain, the cars had started on slicks, but he proved that driver skill still counted for something.

FRANCE

Francois Delecour gave Gilles Panizzi a hard time. But the team asked him, quite rightly, to cool it, once Carlos Sainz was no longer a threat in the third leg. Much against his will, he let his teammate take the win without putting him under any more pressure.

Two men in new colours. Absent from the world championship since 1999, Piero Liatti joined the Ford ranks for two tarmac rallies, Corsica and San Remo, replacing Petter Solberg who was making his first appearance for Subaru in Corsica.

TOP ENTRIES

1 Tommi Makinen - Risto Mannisenmaki
   MITSUBISHI LANCER Evo 6

2 Freddy Loix - Sven Smeets
   MITSUBISHI CARISMA GT

3 Richard Burns - Robert Reid
   SUBARU IMPREZA WRC 2000

4 Simon Jean Joseph - Jacques Boyère
   SUBARU IMPREZA WRC 2000

5 Colin McRae - Nicky Grist
   FORD FOCUS WRC

6 Carlos Sainz - Luis Moya
   FORD FOCUS WRC

7 Didier Auriol - Denis Giraudet
   SEAT CORDOBA WRC Evo 3

8 Toni Gardemeister - Paavo Lukander
   SEAT CORDOBA WRC Evo 3

9 François Delecour - Daniel Grataloup
   PEUGEOT 206 WRC

10 Gilles Panizzi - Hervé Panizzi
   PEUGEOT 206 WRC

14 Kenneth Eriksson - Staffan Parmander
   HYUNDAI ACCENT WRC

15 Alister McRae - David Senior
   HYUNDAI ACCENT WRC

16 Marcus Gronholm - Timo Rautiainen
   PEUGEOT 206 WRC

17 Piero Liatti - Carlo Cassina
   FORD FOCUS WRC

18 Petter Solberg - Phil Mills
   SUBARU IMPREZA WRC 2000

20 Hamed Al-Wahaibi - Tony Sircombe
   SUBARU IMPREZA WRC

21 Serkan Yazici - Erkan Bodur
   TOYOTA COROLLA WRC

22 Gustavo Trelles - Jorge Del Buono
   MITSUBISHI LANCER Evo 6

26 Gabriel Pozzo - Fabian Cretu
   MITSUBISHI LANCER Evo 6

27 Claudio Menzi - Edgardo Galindo
   MITSUBISHI LANCER Evo 6

28 Philippe Bugalski - Jean Paul Chiaroni
   CITROEN SAXO KIT CAR

30 Jesus Puras - Marc Marti
   CITROEN SAXO KIT CAR

32 Benoit Rousselot - Xavier Panseri
   RENAULT MEGANE MAXI

33 Sebastien Loeb - Daniel Elena
   TOYOTA COROLLA WRC

34 Patrick Magaud - Guylène Brun
   FORD PUMA KIT CAR

37 Manfred Stohl - Peter Muller
   MITSUBISHI LANCER Evo 6

39 Fabrice Morel - David Marty
   PEUGEOT 206 WRC

44th RALLY OF FRANCE

11th leg of the 2000 world rally championship for constructors and driversrs 2000
11th leg of the production car drivers' and team's world cups
Date 29 september - 1st october 2000
Route: 1226,21 km divided into 3 legs,
18 special stages on tarmac roads (389.41 km) with one stage cancelled (373,27 km.)
1st leg: Friday 29 september: Ajaccio - Vignetta - Ajaccio, 6 stages (128,87 km)
2nd leg: Saturday 30 september: Ajaccio - Corte - Ajaccio, 5 stages (115,53 km)
3rd leg: Sunday 1st october: Ajaccio - Vignetta - Ajaccio, 6 stages (128,87 km)
Starters - Finishers: 121 - 80
Conditions: good weather with occasional rain showers, dry and damp roads.

On the pace once again, Carlos Sainz took third place and hoisted himself back into contention for the title. The young Norwegian hope, Petter Solberg stopped on the first stage.

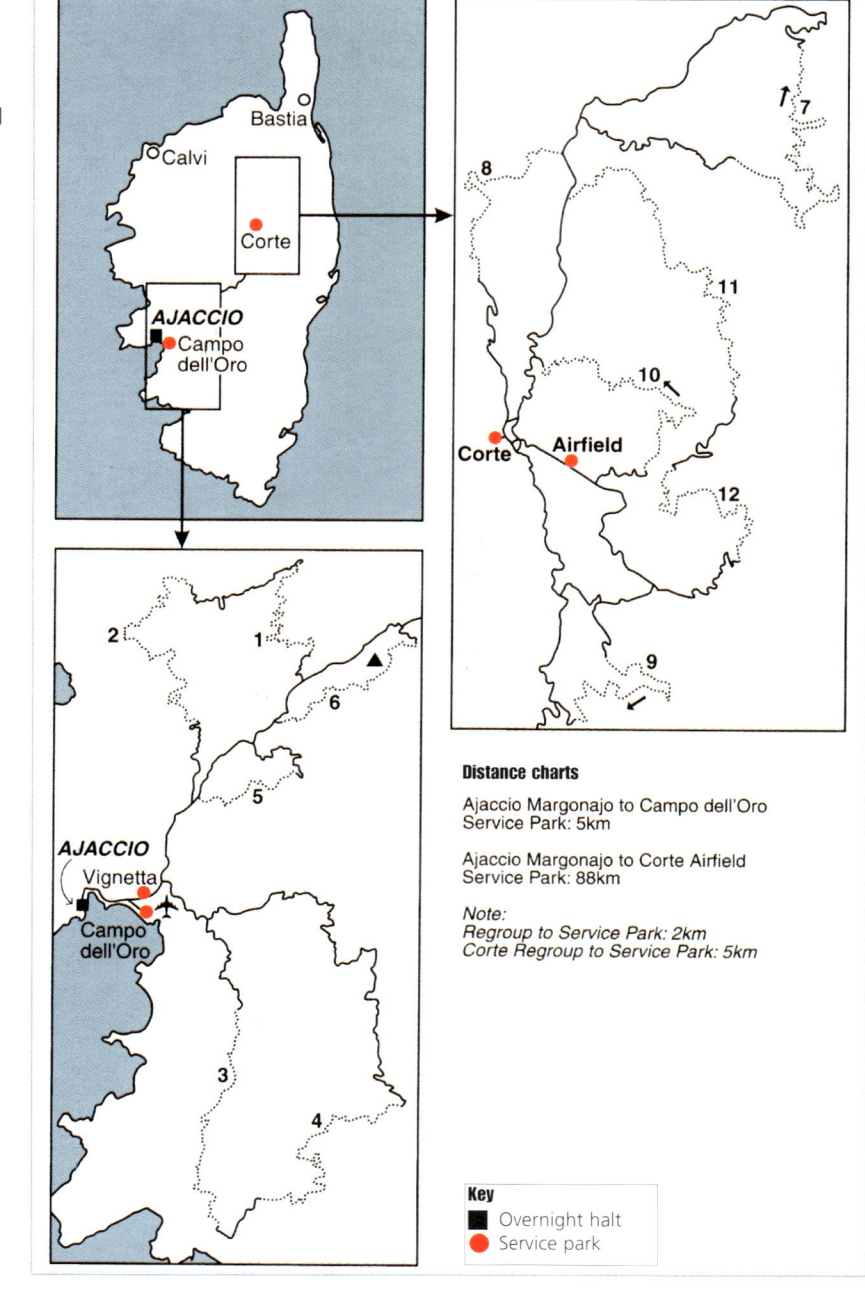

Distance charts

Ajaccio Margonajo to Campo dell'Oro
Service Park: 5km

Ajaccio Margonajo to Corte Airfield
Service Park: 88km

Note:
Regroup to Service Park: 2km
Corte Regroup to Service Park: 5km

Key
■ Overnight halt
● Service park

SPECIAL STAGE TIMES

ES.1 Vero - Pont d'azzana 1 (18,22 km)
1. Burns 12'49"6; 2. Delecour 12'52"1; 3. C. McRae 12'53"2; 4. Panizzi 12'5"37; 5. Sainz 12'53"8; 6. Makinen 12'56"1; Gr.N Stohl 13'5737

ES.2 Lopigna - Sarrola 1 (25,85 km)
1. Panizzi 19'48"9; 2. Delecour 19'49"8; 3. C. McRae 19'53"3; 4. Burns 19'54"5; 5. Sainz 19'55"0; 6. Makinen 19'56"1; Gr.N Stohl 21'33"3

ES.3 Bellevalle - Pietra Rossa 1 (20,84 km)
1. Delecour 12'16"5; 2. Makinen 12'18"0; 3. Panizzi 12'18"6; 4. Sainz 12'18"8; 5. Burns 12'19"7; 6. C. McRae 12'21"7; Gr.N Galli 13'24"0

ES.4 Filitosa - Bicchisano 1 (22,47 km)
1. Panizzi 14'07"1; 2. Delecour 14'07"8; 3. Sainz 14'08"9; 4. C. McRae 14'12"4; 5. Makinen 14'13"4; 6. Burns 14'16"0; Gr.N Galli 15'13"1

ES.5 Cuttoli - Peri 1 (17,24 km)
1. Panizzi 11'30"1; 2. Sainz 11'31"0; 3. Delecour 11'31"1; 4. C. McRae 11'32"1; 5. Burns 11'33"7; 6. Gronholm 11'35"1; Gr.N Galli 12'24"9

ES.6 Gare de Carbuccia - Tavera 1 (20,04 km)
1. Panizzi 11'51"8; 2. Makinen 11'57"3; 3. C. McRae 11'58"4; 4. Delecour 11'58"9; 5. Sainz 11'59"1; 6. Burns 12'01"2; Gr.N Galli 12'53"1

ES.7 Morosaglia - Campile (31,91 km)
1. Panizzi 21'02"8; 2. Delecour 21'05"7; 3. C. McRae 21'14"6; 4. Sainz 21'17"4; 5. Gronholm 21'23"1; 6. Liatti 21'23"9; Gr.N Stohl 22'41"8

ES.8 Taverna - Pont de Castirla (16,14 km)

Cancelled, too many spectators

ES.9 Noceta - Muracciole (16,60 km)
1. Panizzi 10'10"6; 2. Sainz 10'11"1; 3. Delecour 10'12"4; 4. C. McRae 10'17"2; 5. Liatti 10'17"8; 6. Burns 10'18"6; Gr.N Stohl 11'10"5

ES.10 Feo - Col San Quilico (26,06 km)
1. Panizzi 15'21"6; 2. Sainz 15'22"2; 3. Delecour 15'25"3; 4. Jean Joseph 15'34"2; 5. Makinen 15'35"1; 6. Burns 15'36"5; Gr.N Trelles 15'36"5

ES.11 Pont St Laurent - Bustanico (26,44 km)
1. Delecour 17'30"9; 2. Panizzi 17'31"9; 3. Sainz 17'33"9; 4. Makinen 17'39"3; 5. Gronholm 17'44"0; 6. Burns 17'42"2; Gr.N Trelles 19'04"3

ES.12 Feo - Altiani (16,52 km)
1. Delecour 10'26"3; 2. Sainz 10'31"5; 3. Liatti 10'35"4; 4. Makinen 10'35"8; 5. Gronholm 10'35"9; 6. Burns 10'38"0; Gr.N Trelles 11'22"5

ES.13 Vero - Pont d'azzana 2 (18,22 km)
1. Panizzi 13'01"4; 2. Gronholm 13'06"2; 3. Delecour 13'08"0; 4. Sainz 13'13"6; 5. Jean Joseph 13'14"5; 6. Auriol 13'17"0; Gr.N Stohl 14'11"9

ES.14 Lopigna - Sarrola 2 (25,85 km)
1. Delecour 20'17"1; 2. Panizzi 20'22"6; 3. Gronholm 20'30"7; 4. Burns 20'37"0; 5. Auriol 20'38"0; 6. Liatti 20'45"6; Gr.N Trelles 22'16"7

ES.15 Bellevalle - Pietra Rossa 2 (20,84 km)
1. Burns 12'19"2; 2. Gronholm 12'20"3; 3. Delecour 12'20"7; 4. Sainz 12'21"5; 5. Liatti 12'21"6; 6. Jean Joseph 12'22"2; Gr.N Trelles 13'27"0

ES.16 Filitosa - Bicchisano 2 (22,47 km)
1. Burns 14'03"5; 2. Sainz 14'07"7; 3. Panizz 14'09"8; 4. Liatti 14'09"8; 5. Jean Joseph 14'10"4; 6. Delecour 14'11"3; Gr.N Trelles 15'15"2

ES.17 Cuttoli - Peri 2 (17,24 km)
1. Gronholm 11'31"1; 2. Burns 11'32"2; 3. Sainz 11'33"8; 4. Liatti 11'36"1; 5. Panizzi 11'36"3; 6. Jean Joseph 11'37"5; Gr.N Ferreyros 12'41"4

ES.18 Gare de Carbuccia - Tavera 2 (20,04 km)
1. Sainz 12'55"8; 2. Auriol 12'56"1; 3. Burns 12'58"7; 4. Gronholm 13'05"3; 5. Liatti 13'05"4; 6. Loeb 13'08"4; Gr.N Trelles 13'30"0

RESULTS AND RETIREMENTS

	Driver/Co-Driver	Car	Gr.	Total time
1	Gilles Panizzi - Hervé Panizzi	Peugeot 206 WRC	A	4h02m14,2s
2	François Delecour - Daniel Grataloup	Peugeot 206 WRC	A	4h02m47,7s
3	Carlos Sainz - Luis Moya	Ford Focus WRC	A	4h03m26,8s
4	Richard Burns - Robert Reid	Subaru Impreza WRC 2000	A	4h03m45,1s
5	Marcus Gronholm - Timo Rautainen	Peugeot 206 WRC	A	4h04m11,3s
6	Piero Liatti - Carlo Cassina	Ford Focus WRC	A	4h05m08,0s
7	Simon Jean Joseph - Jacques Boyère	Subaru Impreza WRC 2000	A	4h05m23,7s
8	Didier Auriol - Denis Giraudet	Seat Cordoba WRC Evo 3	A	4h05m44,9s
9	Sebastien Loeb - Daniel Elena	Toyota Corolla WRC	A	4h09m07,4s
10	Fabrice Morel - David Marty	Peugeot 206 WRC	A	4h09m34,6s
17	Manfred Stohl - Peter Muller	Mitsubishi Lancer Evo.6	N	4h22m28,0s

ES.1	Freddy Loix - Sven Smeets	Mitsubishi Carisma GT	A	Accident
ES.1	Petter Solberg - Philip Mills	Subaru Impreza WRC 2000	A	Gearbox
ES.2	Kenneth Eriksson - Staffan Parmander	Hyundai Accent WRC	A	Accident
ES.5	Patrick Magaud - Guylène Brun	Ford Puma Kit Car	A	Engine
ES.10	Colin McRae - Nicky Grist	Ford Focus WRC	A	Accident
ES.13	Tommi Makinen - Risto Mannisenmaki	Mitsubishi Lancer Evo.6	A	Accident
ES.13	Serkan Yazici - Erkan Bodur	Toyota Corolla WRC	A	Accident

EVENT LEADERS

ES.1	Burns
ES.2 > ES.5	Delecour
ES.6 > ES.11	Panizzi
ES.12	Delecour
ES.13 > ES.14	Panizzi
ES.15 > ES.16	Delecour
ES.17 > ES.18	Panizzi

BEST PERFORMANCES

	1	2	3	4	5	6
Panizzi	8	2	2	1	1	-
Delecour	4	4	5	1	-	1
Burns	3	1	1	2	2	6
Sainz	1	5	3	4	3	-
Gronholm	1	2	1	1	3	1
Makinen	-	2	-	2	2	2
Auriol	-	1	-	-	1	1
C. McRae	-	-	4	3	-	1
Liatti	-	-	1	2	3	2
Jean Joseph	-	-	-	1	2	2
Loeb	-	-	-	-	-	1

CHAMPIONSHIP CLASSIFICATIONS

Drivers
1. Marcus Gronholm	46
2. Richard Burns	44
3. Colin McRae	42
4. Carlos Sainz	41
5. Tommi Makinen	28
6. Juha Kankkunen	18

Constructors
1. Ford	83
2. Peugeot	74
3. Subaru	69
4. Mitsubishi	35
5. Skoda	8
6. Seat	8

Group N
1. Manfred Stohl	58
2. Gustavo Trelles	50
3. Gabriel Pozzo	22

Team's Cup
1. Spike Subaru Team (Araï)	36
2. Toyota Team Saudi Arabia (Bakhashab)	32
3. Frédéric Dor Rally Team (Dor)	26

PREVIOUS WINNERS

1973	Nicolas - Vial	Alpine Renault A 110
1974	Andruet - "Biche"	Lancia Stratos
1975	Darniche - Mahé	Lancia Stratos
1976	Munari - Maiga	Lancia Stratos
1977	Darniche - Mahé	Fiat 131 Abarth
1978	Darniche Mahé	Fiat 131 Abarth
1979	Darniche - Mahé	Lancia Stratos
1980	Thérier - Vial	Porsche 911SC
1981	Darniche - Mahé	Lancia Stratos
1982	Ragnotti - Andrié	Renault 5 Turbo
1983	Alen - Kivimaki	Lancia Rally 037
1984	Alen - Kivimaki	Lancia Rally 037
1985	Ragnotti - Andrié	Renault 5 Turbo
1986	Saby - Fauchille	Peugeot 205 T16
1987	Béguin - Lenne	Bmw m3
1988	Auriol - Occelli	Ford Sierra RS Cosworth
1989	Auriol - Occelli	Lancia Delta Integrale
1990	Auriol - Occelli	Lancia Delta Integrale
1991	Sainz - Moya	Toyota Celica GT-Four
1992	Auriol - Occelli	Lancia Delta HF Integrale
1993	Delecour - Grataloup	Ford Escort RS Cosworth
1994	Auriol - Occelli	Toyota Celica Turbo 4WD
1995	Auriol - Giraudet	Toyota Celica GT-Four
1996	Bugalski - Chiaroní	Renault Maxi Megane
1997	McRae - Grist	Subaru Impreza WRC
1998	McRae - Grist	Subaru Impreza WRC
1999	Bugalski - Chiaroní	Citroën Xsara Kit Car

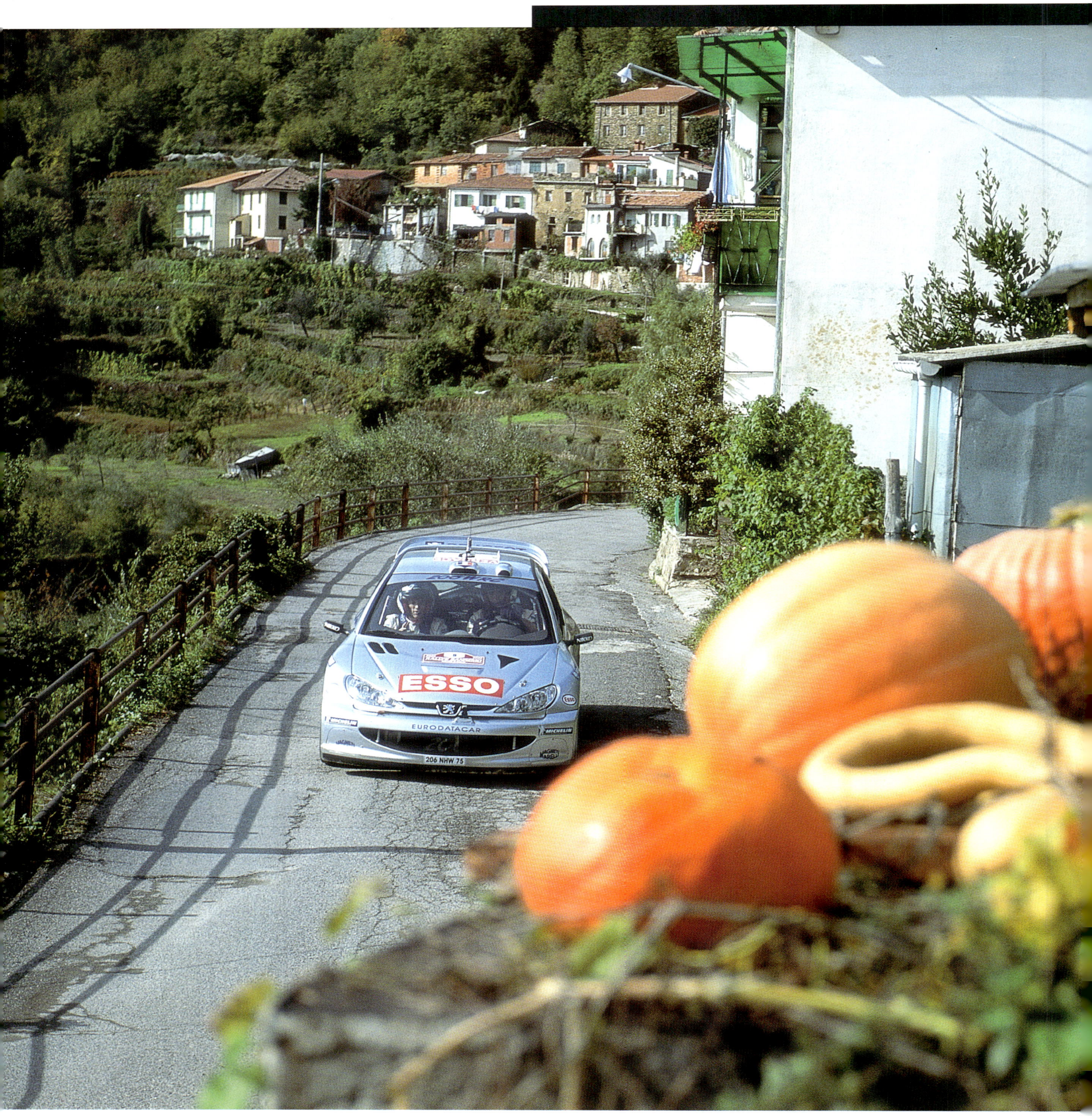
ESSO
EURODATACAR
206 NHW 75

san remo

The rally was spoilt with bickering and rumours of villainy. But once again, Panizzi won from Delecour. This promoted Peugeot to the top of the constructors's classification and once again, Gronholm was surprising on tarmac.

THE RALLY

Peugeot in style

"Bis repetita placent." Take the same and start again. The San Remo Rally did not quite stick to the script of this scholarly Latin saying, as it was not a complete carbon copy of events in Corsica. However, the first leg certainly did throw up enough similarities to recall events of three weeks earlier on the Island of Beauty. The feeling of deja-vu started with the scenery on the Italian Riviera, where the forests on the hills appeared to be on fire with the leaves turning the red colour of autumn and the resin ran from the trees through which ran wild boars.

A brave showing from Colin McRae. Just three weeks after his terrible Corsica accident, he was at the start line for the San Remo.

As for the rally, it started with Richard Burns setting fastest time on the first stage, putting his Subaru in the lead for but a brief moment, until Panizzi stole it off him on the next timed section. Then, just as in Corsica, Delecour was quickest on stage three. And again, just as in Corsica, from that point on, the two French drivers pulled away from the field.

That's where the resemblance ended. Proving that San Remo was not Ajaccio, Francois Delecour was in a blue funk with his team-mate after the two opening stages, throwing scandal into the ring with the suggestion of improper recceing by Panizzi. He added to his troubles by bursting into tears when he felt that his 206 was not quite perfect. The fault lay with a valve which controlled some anodyne part of the post-combustion system. It let go a few kilometres after the start. "The problem probably cost Francois somewhere in the region of 80 horsepower," estimated a suitably contrite Jean-Pierre Fleur, the team's engine specialist. "It's not a problem to fix, but he had to put up with it for two stages." That immediately cost him 13 seconds on Panizzi. He never stopped fighting on the six remaining stages of this leg, in order to close the gap. "When you lose time on a rally like this, it is always difficult to make it up again," he admitted. "If you compare our times, they are very similar. We have the same speed on tarmac, so a gap of this size is actually huge."

For his part, Panizzi was not about to make life easy for his team-mate. He was not as virulent in his comments about Delecour as he was at the wheel of the 206, preferring to show that actions speak louder than words. "I won't let him destabilise me," he maintained, halfway through the day. "As soon as I get back in the car, I calm down and just get on with my rally." He certainly did. Master of his art, Panizzi redoubled his efforts as the sun set over the sea, taking the last two stages and adding to his lead.

His reward was a nice 15.4s advantage. Third, over 26 seconds down was Burns, proving that no one was really capable of getting involved in the Peugeot in-house battle. It was not for lack of trying from the group of four championship contenders. The Englishman was blowing hot and cold, alternating good times with mediocre ones. "When there is nothing tricky and no damp patches, I feel totally confident," explained the Subaru man. "But I don't feel comfortable with the brakes and handling on the wet bits of road."

As for Sainz, he was wearing his moody face and biting his lip as usual. Chronic understeer and a poor set-up found him trying hard but struggling. "I'd like to be able to up the pace," explained the dejected Spaniard as he studied his 52.3 deficit to the leader at the end of the first leg.

McRae admitted he had found it hard to get back in the swing of things for the first few kilometres and he was unhappy with his lack of speed, as he too was suffering from understeer.

Gronholm completed the quartet and once again the lanky one was in sparkling form. The least at ease of the four on tarmac, he emerged unscathed at the end of the first leg. "The car is perfect, but I have not quite got the hang of it yet." The Peugeot man is a perfectionist and he had hoped to unshackle himself from the chains which he felt bound him to the tarmac. He claimed he had not managed it, but nevertheless he was in the money in sixth place.

As morning dawned for the second leg, the Panizzi brothers were keen to force home their advantage and at precisely 7.43, their 206 tore out of the village of Poggio, at the foot of Mont Moro. The bell rang, 9.47.2 later and they set off to tackle the next one at Carpasio, all 15.61 km of it.

By then, they could clearly see the damage they had inflicted on the opposition. Burns had set the second time 4 s down, while Gronholm and the others hovered around the 5 mark. It was enough to build a cushion. "I had decided to drive flat out from the start," said Zebedee. "It had to be done. First off, because I wanted to get back into a rhythm as quickly as possible, because I knew I had to extend my lead immediately."

Delecour was powerless and could do no better than the rest. He had been instructed by the team management to observe a non-aggression pact, even if he did not feel like it after the previous day's tense situation, but he did as he was told, all meek and mild. In just one morning stage, Panizzi had totally dominated the event and despite one scary moment he managed to keep the 206 on the island.

Not so Richard Burns. After he had just reached the summit of stage 10 at Monte Ceppo, he came across a left hander going way too fast. Missing his braking, the Subaru got away from him, out of shape before getting going again. But then, when he got into service, the Subaru refused to play ball. The computer plugged into its internals registered a perfect flat line on the mechanical ECG machine. The Englishman was not looking for excuses, but he was bitterly disappointed at the loss of the four points that would have been his for the third place he was occupying at the time.

Even the greats like Tommi Makinen were finding life on the Italian Riviera far from being La Dolce Vita. He set two fastest times, but it was too late by then. "It's encouraging, it's good, but the Peugeots are too far away now."

Simon Jean-Joseph was the other inspired performer on the day, setting two testing fastest times, the first of his career in the world championship arena.

Finally, we had Marcus the Magnificent, who managed to up the pace little by little, to such an extent, that right at the end of the leg, it was his turn to set a fastest time, which meant that while lying fourth, he now posed a threat to Makinen's third place.

Terrible disappointment for Richard Burns. Despite the best efforts of his mechanics, his engine refused to start up after an earlier collision.

SAN REMO

Francois Delecour passes Panizzi's 206 with a look of disdain. The two men were at daggers drawn.

ready to go again, for the shake-down two days prior to the rally. McRae was back.

If you looked closely, you could see that his left eye was still not quite right and his cheek bone looked sore and there were a few stitches on display, but otherwise he looked fit enough. The only real difference between McRae now and then, was that he had a bit more metal with him in San Remo, as he had a plate holding his cheek bone in place, which had taken three hours of micro-surgery to install, during an operation at the Edinburgh hospital on 9th October. "I think I am completely ready to start the San Remo," he told anyone who cared to listen.

It had not been easy for the bionic Scotsman. "Colin is a great specimen," said his enthusiastic physio, Bernie Shrosbee. "Seeing him on a stretcher when they brought him out of the wreck, I never thought he would get back in shape so quickly."

The medical team had done all it could. "These days you have to treat drivers like athletes," continued the English trainer. "So we asked him to spend a lot of time in a sort of tent where the atmospheric pressure is greater than at sea level. That ups the red blood cell count and speeds up the physical recovery process. Colin stayed in it for an hour one day, then two hours the next until he was spending the whole night inside." This certainly helped his injuries to heal, especially those to his lungs which had also suffered slightly in the crash.

Everyone in the team, including his "best enemy" Sainz, were delighted to see him back so soon. It was perfect timing, because despite his mistake in Corsica, the Scotsman was still in with a chance of the title.

In the end, the three days of rallying in Italy were something of a hardship. He had troubles sorting out the understeering characteristics of his Focus on these tarmac roads and he was not exactly in the best physical condition. Thus one could spot him in the service areas sleeping for a few moments with the door open, to let in some pleasantly warming rays of sunshine. "Once he is back on the stages, all the old reflexes are back," explained co-driver Nicky Grist. "But he is exhausted at the end of them." McRae's courageous performance netted him sixth place, despite being a bit off colour. It was worth another point in his pursuit of the title. It commanded and demanded respect. McRae was still McRae. ■

In fact, the gaps between the rest of the points scorers, starting with that between Panizzi and Delecour, was so big, that only this battle was of any interest in the final leg. This Finnish derby match between the reigning world champion and the best of the young pretenders, was something of a duel between the generations. It eventually went Makinen's way, after Gronholm bent a suspension arm, when he decided to test the strength of Italian rock during the first stage. At one point, he thought that Sainz might even catch and pass him.

In the end, that scenario did not materialise and Marcus could complete Peugeot's triumph: the win, the one-two, the lead in the constructors' championship, having stolen it off Ford and Gronholm increasing his advantage in the drivers' championship. What more could they have asked for?

THE ARGUMENT
Team-mates at loggerheads

I don't want to argue with him. You don't speak to an ass!" This was a major verbal off that could be heard during the first leg of the San Remo. The man doing the talking was Gilles Panizzi and the man he was talking about was Francois Delecour.

Can you spot the deliberate mistake? Yes, they both drive a Peugeot 206 WRC. They were leading the rally. What led Panizzi to make this harsh judgement? Well, it was all down to Delecour, who had been slowed from the start with technical problems, which allowed Panizzi to take the lead. Disappointed and beaten, Delecour then decided to give voice to rumours that the winner of the Tour of Corsica had carried out illicit recceing before the event. The rumours had been doing the rounds on shaky foundations along the lines that someone had seen the man, who had seen the man, who had seen Panizzi. "That's exactly what our opposition wants, by fuelling these rumours. They want to destabilise us," claimed the Peugeot management, who were furious with the deplorable media fallout from this altercation, after they had been doing so well this season.

At the first service area on the event, Delecour was all for having a pop at Panizzi before the team bosses stepped in and gave him a sharp dressing down. Whether or not he had cheated was not the issue, even if it was a terrible accusation, but more important was the fact that the most vociferous accuser was their very own Delecour, who brought the matter out into the open.

Mad with rage, Delecour was at his wits end and it took all the efforts of the team's physio, Alex Behara to coax him back into the cockpit. "I don't want to go. I don't want to do this rally," cried the overemotional lad. Panizzi tried to remain calm, affirming he had managed to maintain his concentration. However, the next day, he was still visibly shaken and had considered throwing in the towel.

But these men are both professionals and once calmed and reprimanded they went on to do what they do best; drive a rally car at speed. They had been given just one single piece of invaluable advice: don't talk to one another. Since they formed an alliance at Peugeot in 1996, Delecour and Panizzi have had a relationship that has veered from the cordial to the strained and something just snapped in San Remo. "I will never be able to be his team-mate again," affirmed the rally winner. The opposite was no doubt equally true.

A JOB WELL DONE
McRae does not lose face

In San Remo, you had to seem him to believe it. McRae was back and he looked like Colin once again and not a close relative of the Elephant Man, which is what he had resembled when he was finally hauled out of his wrecked Focus three weeks earlier. It was hard to believe that on 30th September, he had been badly hurt, his face seriously damaged with a broken cheek bone. He had been helicoptered to hospital in Bastia in a semi-conscious state after a huge crash. He did not deny that at one point he felt he had stared death in the face. But here he was

Although Freddy Loix felt more comfortable with an improved car, he was no competition for his Mitsubishi team leader, Makinen.

SAN REMO

SAN REMO

From the heights of the maritime Alps to the beauty of the blue sea in the port of San Remo, the Italian round stayed close to the Italian town which displayed all the charms of the Italian Riviera. The tight route on this year's event was not universally popular with drivers or spectators.

Marcus Gronholm was a revelation. He was expected to be off the pace on tarmac, but he defended his lead in the world championship on the two tarmac events in Corsica and San Remo. He finished fifth on the former and sixth on the latter.

Having shone on the Catalan tarmac, the Skodas were nowhere in Italy. Schwarz struggled all the way.

TOP ENTRIES

1. Tommi Makinen - Risto Mannisenmaki
   MITSUBISHI LANCER Evo 6
2. Freddy Loix - Sven Smeets
   MITSUBISHI CARISMA GT
3. Richard Burns - Robert Reid
   SUBARU IMPREZA WRC 2000
4. Simon Jean Joseph - Jacques Boyère
   SUBARU IMPREZA WRC 2000
5. Colin McRae - Nicky Grist
   FORD FOCUS WRC
6. Carlos Sainz - Luis Moya
   FORD FOCUS WRC
7. Didier Auriol - Denis Giraudet
   SEAT CORDOBA WRC Evo 3
8. Toni Gardemeister - Paavo Lukander
   SEAT CORDOBA WRC Evo 3
9. François Delecour - Daniel Grataloup
   PEUGEOT 206 WRC
10. Gilles Panizzi - Hervé Panizzi
    PEUGEOT 206 WRC
11. Armin Schwarz - Manfred Hiemer
    SKODA OCTAVIA WRC
12. Luis Climent - Alex Romani
    SKODA OCTAVIA WRC
14. Kenneth Eriksson - Staffan Parmander
    HYUNDAI ACCENT WRC
15. Alister McRae - David Senior
    HYUNDAI ACCENT WRC
16. Marcus Gronholm - Timo Rautiainen
    PEUGEOT 206 WRC
18. Piero Liatti - Carlo Cassina
    FORD FOCUS WRC
19. Petter Solberg - Phil Mills
    SUBARU IMPREZA WRC 2000
20. Michael Guest - David Green
    HYUNDAI ACCENT WRC
21. Uwe Nittel - Detlef Ruf
    TOYOTA COROLLA WRC
22. Piero Longhi - Lucio Baggio
    TOYOTA COROLLA WRC
23. Gianfranco Cunico - Luigi Pirollo
    SUBARU IMPREZA WRC
24. Henrik Lundgaard - Jens Christian Anker
    TOYOTA COROLLA WRC
25. Andréa Aghini - Dario d'Esposito
    MITSUBISHI CARISMA GT
26. Paolo Andreucci - Giovanni Bernacchini
    SUBARU IMPREZA WRC
27. Hamed Al-Wahaibi - Tony Sircombe
    SUBARU IMPREZA WRC
28. Andréa Dallavilla - Danilo Fappani
    SUBARU IMPREZA WRC
29. Serkan Yazici - Erkan Bodur
    TOYOTA COROLLA WRC
30. Markko Martin - Michael Park
    TOYOTA COROLLA WRC
31. Abdullah Bakhashab - Bobby Willis
    TOYOTA COROLLA WRC
32. Frederic Dor - Didier Breton
    SUBARU IMPREZA WRC
33. Manfred Stohl - Peter Muller
    MITSUBISHI LANCER Evo 6
35. Janusz Kulig - Jarak Baran
    FORD FOCUS WRC
36. Gustavo Trelles - Jorge Del Buono
    MITSUBISHI LANCER Evo 6
37. Gianluigi Galli - Maurizio Messina
    MITSUBISHI LANCER Evo 6
38. Gabriel Pozzo - Fabian Cretu
    MITSUBISHI LANCER Evo 6
41. Renato Travaglia - Flavio Zanella
    PEUGEOT 306 KIT CAR
42. Kris Princen - Dany Colebunders
    RENAULT MEGANE MAXI
43. Sebastien Loeb - Daniel Elena
    TOYOTA COROLLA WRC
44. Fabrice Morel - David Marty
    PEUGEOT 206 WRC
45. Philippe Bugalski - Jean Paul Chiaroni
    CITROEN SAXO KIT CAR
48. Jesus Puras - Marc Marti
    CITROEN SAXO KIT CAR
76. Alessandro Fiorio - Vittorio Brambilla
    MITSUBISHI CARISMA GT

42nd SANREMO RALLY

12th leg of the 2000 world rally championship for constructors and driversrs 2000
12th leg of the production car drivers' and team's world cups

Date 20 - 22 october 2000
Route: 1103,56 km divided into 3 legs,
17 special stages on tarmac roads (382.79 km) with one stage cancelled (344,98 km.)
1st leg: Friday 20 october: Sanremo - Sanremo, 8 stages (144,12 km)
2nd leg: Saturday 21 october: Sanremo - Sanremo, 7 stages (160,12 km)
3rd leg: Sunday 22 october: Sanremo - Sanremo, 2 stages (40,74 km)
Starters - Finishers: 116 - 62
Conditions: good weather, dry roads.

McRae was exhausted, but after this difficult event, he still managed to finish sixth. Quite an achievement!

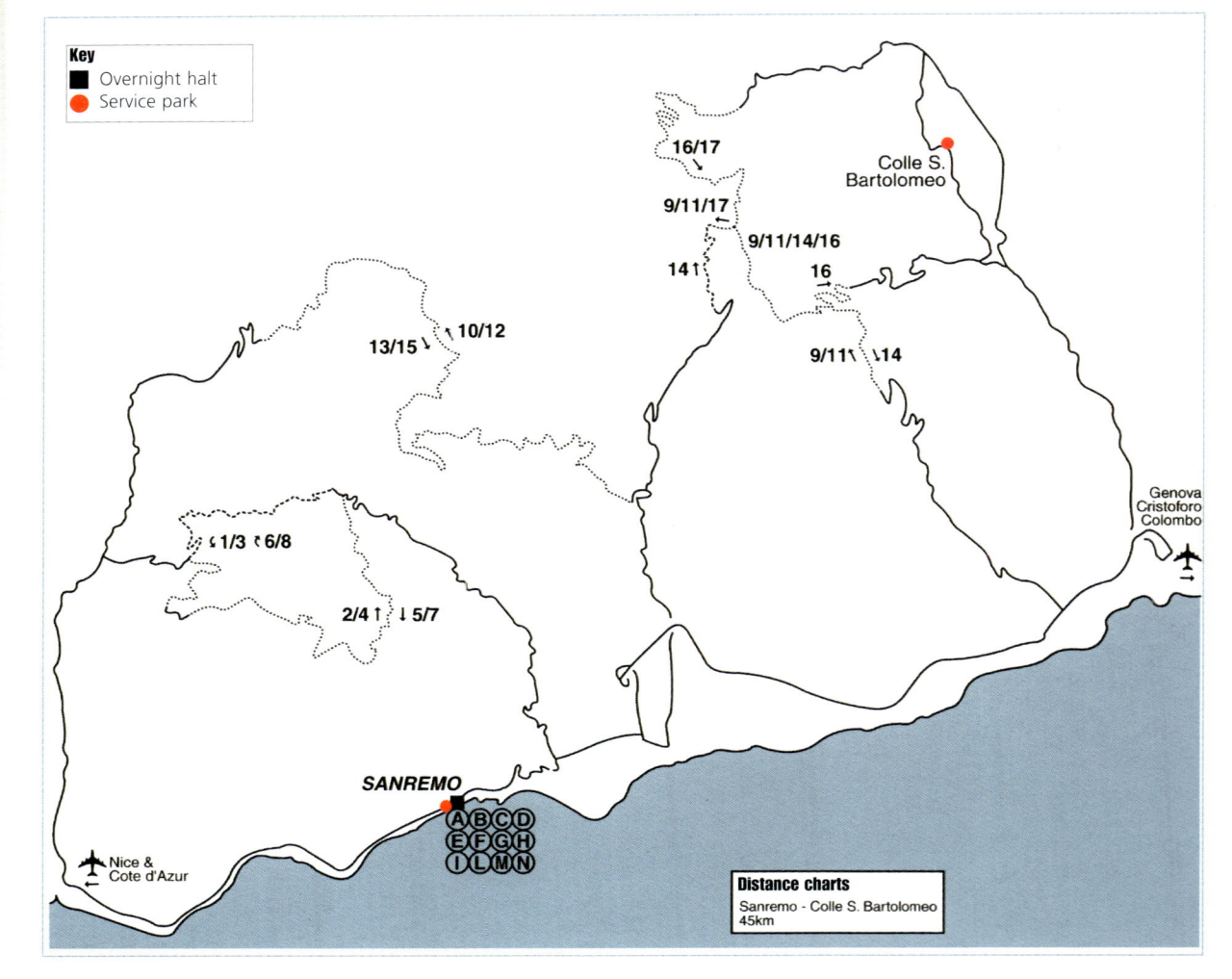

Key
■ Overnight halt
● Service park

Distance charts
Sanremo - Colle S. Bartolomeo
45km

SPECIAL STAGE TIMES

ES.1 Apricale 1 (16,73 km)
1. Burns 11'45"9; 2. Panizzi 11'46"9; 3. Gronholm 11'51"3; 4. Delecour 11'52"3; 5. Travaglia 11'52"7; 6. Makinen 11'52"8; Gr.N Fiorio 12'51"2

ES.2 Perinaldo 1 (19,30 km)
1. Panizzi 12'29"0; 2. Burns 12'33"7; 3. Longhi 12'34"1; 4. Jean Joseph 12'34"2; 5. Gronholm et Andreucci 12'35"0; Gr.N Fiorio 13'29"5

ES.3 Apricale 2 (16,73 km)
1. Delecour 11'36"9; 2. Burns 11'38"2; 3. Panizzi 11'39"0; 4. Auriol 11'40"0; 5. Longhi 11'41"7; 6. C. McRae 11'41"8; Gr.N Galli 12'39"7

ES.4 Perinaldo 2 (19,30 km)
1. Panizzi 12'13"8; 2. Longhi 12'16"1; 3. Jean Joseph 12'16"8; 4. Delecour 12'18"0; 5. Sainz 12'19"3; 6. Liatti 12'19"5; Gr.N Fiorio 13'12"6

ES.5 Ghimbegna 1 (19,30 km)
1. Delecour 12'10"0; 2. Liatti 12'12"0; 3. Burns 12'12"9; 4. Panizzi 12'13"4; 5. Sainz 12'14"6; 6. Loix 12'18"1; Gr.N Galli 13'11"9

ES.6 Baiardo 1 (16,73 km)
1. Delecour 11'38"0; 2. Panizzi 11'39"2; 3. Burns 11'40"7; 4. Sainz 11'43"3; 5. Liatti 11'44"4; 6. Auriol 11'45"9; Gr.N Galli 13'39"2

ES.7 Ghimbegna 2 (19,30 km)
1. Panizzi 12'14"0; 2. Delecour 12'14"6; 3. C. McRae 12'19"2; 4. Makinen 12'20"3; 5. Loix 12'21"0; 6. Sainz 12'21"4; Gr.N Galli 13'27"1

ES.8 Baiardo 2 (16,73 km)
1. Panizzi 11'44"0; 2. Delecour et Gronholm 11'48"6; 4. Makinen et Burns 11'49"1; 6. Liatti 11'54"2; Gr.N Galli 12'53"9

ES.9 Pantasina 1 (15,61 km)
1. Panizzi 9'47"2; 2. Burns 9'51"4; 3. Delecour et Gronholm 9'52"3; 5. Liatti 9'52"6; 6. Jean Joseph 9'52"7; Gr.N Trelles 10'36"4

ES.10 Mont Ceppo 1 (37,74 km)
1. Makinen 26'02"4; 2. Panizzi 26'04"3; 3. Delecour 26'06"5; 4. Gronholm 26'12"6; 5. Solberg 26'13"2; 6. C. McRae 26'13"3; Gr.N Galli 28'03"2

ES.11 Pantasina 2 (15,61 km)
1. Jean Joseph et Liatti 9'46"0; 3. Panizzi 9'46"5; 4. Sainz 9'46"8; 5. Solberg 9'47"2; 6. Delecour 9'48"4; Gr.N Dati 10'33"9

ES.12 Monte Ceppo 2 (37,74 km)
1. Jean Joseph 25'59"8; 2. Makinen 26'01"8; 3. Liatti 26'02"3; 4. Solberg 26'02"9; 5. Delecour 26'05"2; 6. Sainz 26'05"5; Gr.N Fiorio 27'49"5

ES.13 Langan 1 (37,81 km)
1. Makinen 26'14"0; 2. Gronholm 26'17"9; 3. Jean Joseph 26'20"1; 4. Auriol 26'20"6; 5. Delecour 26'21"2; 6. Loeb 26'22"0; Gr.N Fiorio 27'49"5

ES.14 Carpasio (15,61 km)
1. Gronholm 9'46"4; 2. Panizzi 9'49"9; 3. Sainz 9'51"6; 4. Delecour 9'51"9; 5. Makinen 9'54"2; 6. Loix 9'55"2; Gr.N Galli 10'42"4

ES.15 Langan 2 (37,81 km)
Cancelled, after an accident.

ES.16 Rezzo (25,08 km)
1. Makinen 17'16"0; 2. delecour 17'19"5; 3. Solberg 17'19"8; 4. C. McRae 17'20"1; 5. Loix 17'20"6; 6. Sainz 17'21"4; Gr.N Stohl 17'54"3

ES.17 Colle D'Oggia (15,66 km)
1. Delecour 10'44"4; 2. Gronholm 10'45"8; 3. Sainz 10'46"3; 4. Panizzi 10'46"8; 5. Makinen, Jean Joseph, ... 10'47"0; Gr.N Galli 10'47"0

RESULTS AND RETIREMENTS

	Driver/Co-Driver	Car	Gr.	Total time
1	Gilles Panizzi - Hervé Panizzi	Peugeot 206 WRC	A	3h52m07,3s
2	François Delecour - Daniel Grataloup	Peugeot 206 WRC	A	3h52m24,1s
3	Tommi Makinen - Risto Mannisenmaki	Mitsubishi Lancer Evo.6	A	3h53m00,3s
4	Marcus Gronholm - Timo Rautainen	Peugeot 206 WRC	A	3h53m09,6s
5	Carlos Sainz - Luis Moya	Ford Focus WRC	A	3h53m18,6s
6	Colin McRae - Nicky Grist	Ford Focus WRC	A	3h53m47,3s
7	Simon Jean Joseph - Jacques Boyère	Subaru Impreza WRC 2000	A	3h54m04,0s
8	Freddy Loix - Sven Smeets	Mitsubishi Carisma GT	A	3h54m30,3s
9	Petter Solberg Philip Mills	Subaru Impreza WRC 2000	A	3h54m39,0s
10	Sebastien Loeb - Daniel Elena	Toyota Corolla WRC	A	3h55m41,7s
22	Gianluigi Galli - Maurizio Messina	Mitsubishi Lancer Evo.6	N	4h09m44,6s
ES.1	Hamed Al-Wahaibi - Tony Sircombe	Subaru Impreza WRC	A	Accident
ES.2	Michael Guest - David Green	Hyundai Accent WRC	A	Accident
ES.4	Kris Princen - Dany Colebunders	Renault Megane Maxi	A	Accident
ES.5	Piero Longhi - Lucio Baggio	Toyota Corolla WRC	A	Accident
ES.7	Fabrice Morel - David Marty	Peugeot 206 WRC	A	Engine
ES.7	Philippe Bugalski - Jean Paul Chiaroni	Citroen Saxo Kit Car	A	Gearbox
ES.10	Toni Gardemeister - Paavo Lukander	Seat Cordoba Evo 3	A	Engine
ES.10	Richard Burns - Robert Reid	Subaru Impreza WRC 2000	A	Engine
ES.11	Gianfranco Cunico - Luigi Pirollo	Subaru Impreza WRC	A	Engine
ES.12	Uwe Nittel - Detlef Ruf	Toyota Corolla WRC	A	Accident
ES.12	Henrik Lundgaard - Jens Anker	Toyota Corolla WRC	A	Accident
ES.12	Piero Liatti - Carlo Cassina	Ford Focus WRC	A	Engine
ES.16	Markko Martin - Michael Park	Toyota Corolla WRC	A	Accident

EVENT LEADERS

ES.1 — Burns
ES.2 > ES.17 — Panizzi

BEST PERFORMANCES

	1	2	3	4	5	6
Panizzi	5	4	2	2	-	-
Delecour	4	3	2	3	2	1
Makinen	3	1	-	2	2	1
Jean Joseph	2	-	2	1	-	1
Gronholm	1	3	1	1	1	1
Burns	1	3	2	1	-	-
Liatti	1	1	1	-	2	2
Longhi	-	1	1	-	1	-
Sainz	-	-	2	2	2	3
Solberg	-	-	1	1	2	-
C. McRae	-	-	-	1	1	2
Auriol	-	-	-	-	2	1
Loix	-	-	-	-	2	2
Andreucci	-	-	-	-	1	-
Travaglia	-	-	-	-	1	-

CHAMPIONSHIP CLASSIFICATIONS

Drivers
1. Marcus Gronholm — 49
2. Richard Burns — 44
3. Colin McRae — 43
4. Carlos Sainz — 43
5. Tommi Makinen — 32
6. Panizzi — 21

Constructors
1. Peugeot — 90
2. Ford — 88
3. Subaru — 70
4. Mitsubishi — 39
5. Skoda — 8
6. Seat — 8

Group N
1. Manfred Stohl — 61
2. Gustavo Trelles — 54
3. Gabriel Pozzo — 22

Team's Cup
1. Toyota Team Saudi Arabia (Bakhashab) — 38
2. Spike Subaru Team (Araï) — 36
3. Frédéric Dor Rally Team (Dor) — 26

PREVIOUS WINNERS

Year	Winners	Car
1973	Thérier - Jaubert	Alpine Renault A110
1975	Waldegaard - Thorszelius	Lancia Stratos
1976	Waldegaard - Thorszelius	Lancia Stratos
1977	Andruet - Delferrier	Fiat 131 Abarth
1978	Alen - Kivimaki	Lancia Stratos
1979	Fassina - Mannini	Lancia Stratos
1980	Rohrl - Geistdorfer	Fiat 131 Abarth
1981	Mouton - Pons	Audi Quattro
1982	Blomqvist - Cederberg	Audi Quattro
1983	Alen - Kivimaki	Lancia Rally 037
1984	Vatanen - Harryman	Peugeot 205 T16
1985	Rohrl - Geistdorfer	Audi Sport Quattro S1
1986	Alen - Kivimaki	Lancia Delta S4
1987	Biasion - Siviero	Lancia Delta HF 4WD
1988	Biasion - Siviero	Lancia Delta Integrale
1989	Biasion - Siviero	Lancia Delta Integrale
1990	Auriol - Occelli	Lancia Delta Integrale
1991	Auriol - Occelli	Lancia Delta Integrale
1992	Aghini - Farnocchia	Lancia Delta HF Integrale
1993	Cunico - Evangelisti	Ford Escort RS Cosworth
1994	Auriol - Occelli	Toyota Celica Turbo 4WD
1995	Liatti - Alessandrini	Subaru Impreza
1996	McRae - Ringer	Subaru Impreza
1997	McRae - Grist	Subaru Impreza WRC
1998	Makinen - Mannisenmaki	Mitsubishi Lancer Ev.5
1999	Makinen - Mannisenmaki	Mitsubishi Lancer Ev.6

Esso
Aquabase
T. RAUTIAINEN
M. GRONHOLM
206
www.peugeot.com
Esso
Ultron
Telstra
10
clarion
CAR AUDIO & BEYOND
NGK
MONDIAL ASSISTANCE
O.Z
sparco

australia

It was a gloomy event, marred by chicanery and the disqualification of Sainz and Makinen, the latter having actually won the event on the clock. It made Peugeot's day, handing them the Constructors' title and Gronholm the win.

THE RALLY

Peugeot takes title by farce

"It's a farce!" And there is no sign of amusement on the face of the speaker, who is evidently in a very bad mood. Leaning against his Subaru, Richard Burns vents his anger in a manner that is not the norm for the well brought up Oxfordshire lad. But he cannot contain himself and does not mince his words. "It's because of the system on this rally. All day, I have been lifting off a bit to make sure there is no way I can finish in the lead. But it should not have ended up like this." The Englishman was referring to a situation that was totally idiotic and left the sport looking foolish. The degree of idiocy could be gauged from the fact that several drivers stopped in the penultimate stage of the first leg, quite simply to lose enough time so that they would not be leading. How had the rally and indeed the world championship reached this strange state of affairs?

It was quite simply down to the rules which are known to all; the FIA, the teams, the constructors and the drivers. The Australian rally, the penultimate event of the championship and therefore of vital importance was a victim of its own nature. The track surface on the stages is such that the first cars to run through them are at a disadvantage to those who are running from fifth onwards on the road.

This automatically means it is almost essential not to finish the first two legs near the front, so that one can tackle the final one with the best possible chance of winning. While the first day is always run in championship order, the final leg is run in the finishing order of the preceding one. It's crazy, but those are the rules.

But then lo and behold, the opening stage of the first leg went against the expected order of things. Gronholm had been quickest on the previous evening's super-special, but contrary to expectations, he set the best time on the first stage, despite running first on the virgin course. The Finn was as surprised as anyone at his amazing time. "I don't really understand it," he admitted. "It's very slippery. I just concentrated on driving as neatly as possibly and staying on the track."

In fact, he was just the first of many to be duped on this rally. Nobody had really attacked; neither Burns, Sainz, McRae nor Delecour, all of whom had some feeble excuse for their lack of pace.

Carlos Sainz's efforts were not rewarded, as he was disqualified after forgetting to read article 19.9 of the rules.

After eight stages, the order was thus, Gronholm, Makinen, Delecour, Kankkunen, Sainz, Burns and Laukkanen, who were all separated by 36.1 s. There were still two stages to run; Atkins and the super-special at Langley Park. Although the latter definitely counted towards everyone's cumulative time, the order for the next day's adventure would be decided according to the leader board at the end of Atkins. Why? So that the 17,000 spectators would not be faced with the spectacle of watching the best drivers come through at a crawl, allowing the less fancied runners to snatch a moment of glory.

Welcome to the land of hypocrisy!

With this in mind, Peugeot instructed Gronholm to lose thirty seconds. When Makinen got wind of this, he emitted the standard Finnish oath. "Perkele!" (S**t) and also parked up for a breather, as did Delecour and Sainz of course. Unfortunately the Spaniard chose to doze in an off-limits area and a few hours later he would pay the penalty.

The Subaru drivers were the only ones not to indulge in the game of hurry and wait. Burns was cruising but not slowly enough, whereas Kankkunen simply did not give a damn and zoomed into the lead.

It completely messed up the order, with Kankkunen now leading from Delecour, Makinen, Gronholm, Burns, Laukkanen, Gardemeister and Sainz; all eight men in 54.4. This would be the order in which they would tackle the second leg, in which we could expect the same ridiculous jockeying for position on the road.

And so it proved, making this leg no more interesting than the first. A great shame, as the scene was set for a great event with the sun, the heat and the magnificent plains and forests. The town of Collie in particular had bent over backwards to put on a show, as it hosted the mid-leg regrouping, with country singers, a fashion parade which was very Seventies, with local kids and their mums doing the modelling to some dreadfully out of tune accompaniment of municipally supplied music. Richard Burns also decided to put on a show, just as Sainz had done the previous night.

Making the most of his handy fifth place in the running order, the Englishman put on an early morning charge, which saw him take the lead immediately off his team-mate Juha Kankkunen, who had also been out to show that the fire still burned. Tommi Makinen then fought back with fastest time on the next stage. And yet the Finn shared the

Like several other competitors, Makinen was furious with the tactics of Burns and Reid (seen here.) There actions can at best be described as disturbing.

AUSTRALIA

general opinion that it was really just for show. "This day doesn't really mean much, yet again because of this business of where you run on the road," he moaned. "All of us have just got one thing on our mind and that is to be in a strong position for the start of the final leg."

Always there or thereabouts, Gronholm also ended up setting two fastest stage times. "The most important thing for me today is not to let Burns pull out too much of a lead," said the confident Peugeot man. But as it happened, the Englishman decided to let the lead slip away as evening brought a re-run of the previous night's slow bicycle race. The final chance to drop down the order came on the Murray Pines stage and all the teams had pretty flaky plans in hand. They would all be able to put a message in the small ads, saying: "For sale, throttle cable hardly used." Gronholm stopped again as did Burns and Makinen and it was the world champion who pulled off the canniest stunt. At first it looked as though he had made the mistake of winning the leg, but then he was penalised ten seconds for jumping the start of the stage. That meant he would have the advantage of running third on the road, leaving the honour of leading the field away on the final leg to Gronholm. It was a clever and well executed move.

But that was not the end of the chicanery. Before the start of the first stage, Burns had to stop and change a punctured tyre. The rules allow five minutes for the crew to do this. According to witnesses, the Englishman had deflated the tyre on the left rear himself, by ripping the valve out. So he changed the wheel and set off after Gronholm and Makinen, which gave him a clear advantage. This put the world champion in a foul mood and he offered them a sarcastic "Congratulations," as he drove past the crew fiddling with the jack. All Gronholm would say was that he wanted to finish ahead of Burns.

It never pays to put Tommi Makinen in a bad mood. In the space of two stages, he was so quick that he was now solidly in the lead and nothing that happened on the final two stages would change that.

Gronholm was running first on the road and naturally gave away some time to Burns, but only fractions. With 27.99 stage kilometres to go, only seven tenths of a second separated the two men. The Finn was quickest and it was enough to secure second place. "That was the outstanding performance on this rally," declared his boss Jean-Pierre Nicolas. "When you consider the disadvantage he was up against because of his position on the road, it must have been costing him around three tenths per kilometre." If Burns had matched these calculations, he should have fried Gronholm by nine seconds.

The Englishman was angry with himself for having missed out on doing just that. The following day, Makinen was excluded, promoting Gronholm to the position of winner, which meant Burns now trailed him by nine points in the championship. More importantly, the Mitsubishi disqualification meant that mathematically, Peugeot had won the Constructors' trophy. Fourteen years after the 205 T16, the 206 had lived up to the legend.

THE TITLE

Peugeot take it on a technicality

After all the shenanigans that had marred the rally, the final one, Makinen's exclusion, handed the lion the crown it had been after since January and it sat well on the noble beast's head. It was a legitimate award as Peugeot had won six of the thirteen rallies run thus far, including two memorable one-two finishes. In some ways, it came too early, as the Lion would have liked to take the crown after plunging its paws in the Welsh mud, rather than being honoured in some Australian outback hotel with a thick shagpile carpet. "Even if we would rather have fought for it," said the big boss, "this is still the result of a fantastic job from the team."

The result would remain a highpoint in the motor sport calendar. Since the start of the world championship, back in 1973, only one had team had managed to take the title in its first full season and that team was Peugeot. It dated back to 1985 and the fabled 205 T16, but given the opposition in this the 2000 season, the performance of the 206 WRC was even more astounding. Fifteen years earlier, its ancestor had won seven rallies, but the opposition was less intense, as it featured an Audi team which was on the way out, Lancia undergoing reconstruction and Toyota, who were only capable of going well in Africa.

The little grey car had faced much stiffer opposition. Corrado Provera had every reason to congratulate his troops. They deserved it.

"Mathematically, we are now champions," he said. "And we will try to win in Great Britain, so that we are not discredited in any way by the fact we have won the championship through the disqualification of another competitor. It is clear we have always tried to win on the road, if possible with some panache, after a season which got off to a difficult start, but finally ended in a far more positive fashion. And while Peugeot are champions, Marcus is not yet the winner in the drivers' category. He still needs two points and we will do what we can to make sure he picks up more than that. Before Makinen's exclusion, we knew we would pick up at least one title and now we are damn well going for both!"

THE PENALTIES

Would the accused please rise!

Perth, Friday 10th November 2000, 23h44. A meeting room in the Perth Sheraton Hotel. Three stewards, Mr. Brugue from Spain, their chairman, Mr. Despotopoulos and Mr. Nicol. Opposite them four Ford representatives: Carlos Sainz and Luis Moya, the accused crew, Malcolm Wilson the boss of M-Sport, the company which builds and enters the Focus for the American car giant and Martin Whitaker, boss of Ford Motorsport.

Decision No. 10. "The stewards have unanimously decided to exclude car number 6, according to article 19.9 of the general regulations of the FIA World Rally Championship 2000."

Sainz and Moya were out, leaving Ford without a car in the rally, after Colin McRae had retired with a broken engine. It was a catastrophe for these men fighting for the title and also for the team, chasing top honours, without any success since 1979.

This article 19.9, had evidently escaped the attention of most of the players, starting with the experienced Spanish crew, but it left no room for misinterpretation, as the following extract makes clear: "Stopping between the yellow warning board and the red arrival board is prohibited under pain of exclusion."

That was exactly what Carlos Sainz and Luis Moya had done at 16h32 at the end of Atkins, the ninth stage. There was nothing to be done as the incident had been captured by the television cameras. With all the evidence stacked against them, Ford reached the decision at midnight, that it was not worth appealing against the exclusion.

Ford and Sainz thus lost any chance of the title. As for Makinen, he was excluded two days later because of a turbo support on his Mitsubishi, which did not conform to the regulations. The turbo had actually been changed a few months earlier on the Japanese car. The new part was not allowed, simply because it had not been homologated, having escaped attention as the engine is assembled in Japan, before being fitted to the car in England. The stupidest aspect of this sorry affair was that the new part brought no performance advantage, its only benefit being one of cost. The FIA could see that and therefore imposed no further penalty apart from the disqualification.

Keeping a low profile, Mitsubishi explained the situation through the team manager, Phil Short, who said, they "would accept the decision of the stewards and would not appeal, in the interests of the spirit of the world rally championship." Two major exclusions in one event. Makinen had been prescient before the rally, when he said: "We are not rallying anymore, we are playing clever games." How sad that he was the victim of a stupid error, perpetrated by his own team. ∎

Tommi Makinen was really pumped up and determined to show he had lost none of his talent at the wheel of a rejuvenated Mitsubishi.

AUSTRALIA

AUSTRALIA

One rally follows another with the same result for Seat. Whether it is Toni Gardemeister, seen here, or Didier Auriol, the two drivers were thinking of their future rather than the job of driving the depressing Cordoba WRC. The Finn is expected at Ford, while the Frenchman has signed with Peugeot.

Richard Burns really went to the limit and beyond on this penultimate event. Having won here in 1999, he intended doing the same this time, but he was up against a flying Makinen and an ever improving Gronholm. The Englishman eventually had to settle for second place behind the Finn in the Peugeot.

AUSTRALIA

Once again, Francois Delecour drove a sensible rally, which resulted in a podium finish, after Tommi Makinen had been excluded. He was one of the pillars of Peugeot's championship this year. However, despite his usual ideal starting position on the road, the Frenchman hardly ever made the most of it.

AUSTRALIA

TOP ENTRIES

1. Tommi Makinen - Risto Mannisenmaki
   MITSUBISHI LANCER Evo 6
2. Freddy Loix - Sven Smeets
   MITSUBISHI CARISMA GT
3. Richard Burns - Robert Reid
   SUBARU IMPREZA WRC 2000
4. Juha Kankkunen - Juha Repo
   SUBARU IMPREZA WRC 2000
5. Colin McRae - Nicky Grist
   FORD FOCUS WRC
6. Carlos Sainz - Luis Moya
   FORD FOCUS WRC
7. Didier Auriol - Denis Giraudet
   SEAT CORDOBA WRC Evo 2
8. Toni Gardemeister - Paavo Lukander
   SEAT CORDOBA WRC Evo 2
9. François Delecour - Daniel Grataloup
   PEUGEOT 206 WRC
10. Marcus Gronholm - Timo Rautiainen
    PEUGEOT 206 WRC
14. Kenneth Eriksson - Staffan Parmander
    HYUNDAI ACCENT WRC
15. Alister McRae - David Senior
    HYUNDAI ACCENT WRC
16. Gilles Panizzi - Hervé Panizzi
    PEUGEOT 206 WRC
17. Petter Solberg - Philip Mills
    SUBARU IMPREZA WRC 2000
18. Markko Martin - Michael Park
    SUBARU IMPREZA WRC 2000
19. Tapio Laukkanen - Kaj Lindstrom
    FORD FOCUS WRC
20. Possum Bourne - Craig Vincent
    SUBARU IMPREZA WRC
22. Neal Bates - Coral Taylor
    TOYOTA COROLLA WRC
23. Michael Guest - David Green
    HYUNDAI ACCENT WRC
24. John Papadimitriou - Chris Patterson
    SUBARU IMPREZA WRC
25. Serkan Yazici - Erkan Bodur
    TOYOTA COROLLA WRC
26. Toshihiro Araï - Roger Freeman
    SUBARU IMPREZA 555
28. Manfred Stohl - Peter Muller
    MITSUBISHI LANCER Evo 6
30. Gustavo Trelles - Jorge Del Buono
    MITSUBISHI LANCER Evo 6
34. Gabriele Pozzo - Rodolfo Ortiz
    MITSUBISHI LANCER Evo 6
35. Claudio Menzi - Edgardo Galindo
    MITSUBISHI LANCER Evo 6
40. Erik Comas - Jean Paul Terrasse
    MITSUBISHI LANCER Evo.6

13th RALLY AUSTRALIA

13th leg of the 2000 world rally championship for constructors and drivers
13th leg of the production car drivers' and team's world cups
Date 09 - 12 november 2000
Route: 1283,23 km divided into 3 legs
21 special stages on dirt roads (391.17 km.)
Prologue: Thursday 9 november: Perth - Perth, 1 stage (2,20 km)
1st leg: Friday 10 november: Perth - Mundaring - Perth, 9 stages (147,76 km)
2nd leg: Saturday 11 november: Perth - Collie - Perth, 8 stages (141,19 km)
3rd leg: Sunday 12 november: Perth - Sotico - Perth, 4 stages (100,02 km)
Starters - Finishers: 83 - 50
Conditions: good weather, hot, dusty dirt roads covered with round gravel, so that order on the road is important.

The veteran Kenneth Eriksson has lost none of his pace and he drove brilliantly in the Accent WRC.

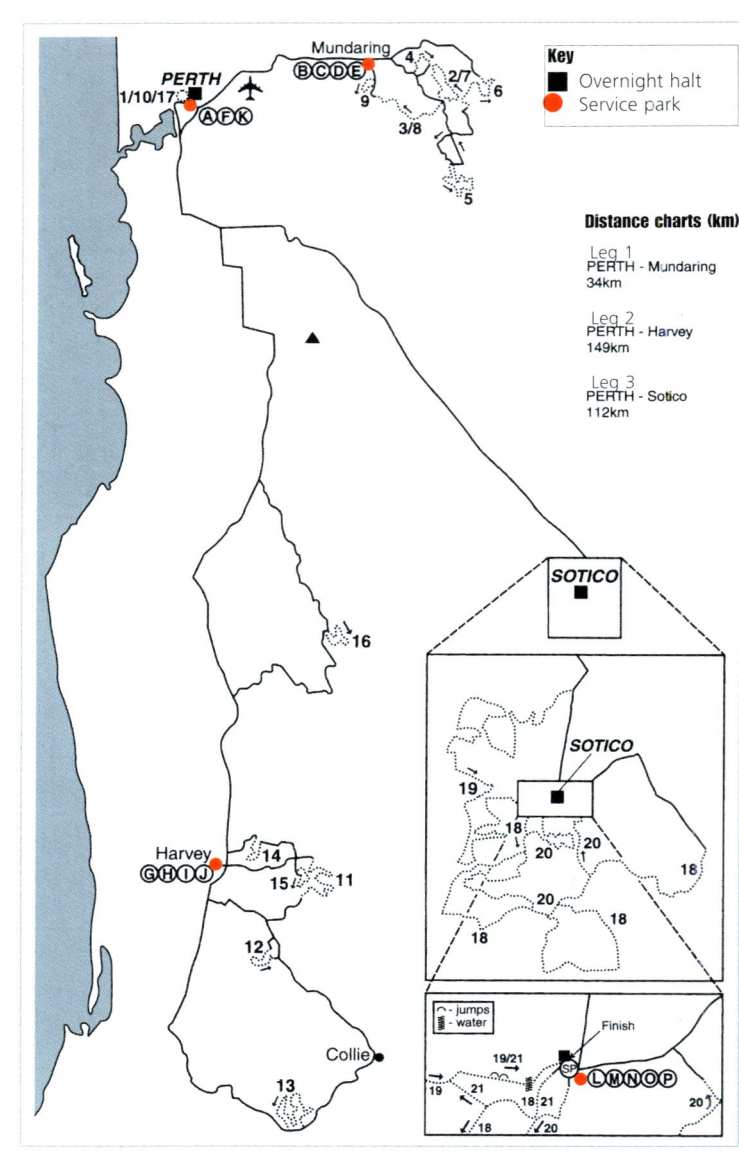

Key
■ Overnight halt
● Service park

Distance charts (km)
Leg 1
PERTH - Mundaring
34km

Leg 2
PERTH - Harvey
149km

Leg 3
PERTH - Sotico
112km

SPECIAL STAGE TIMES

ES.1 Langley Park Super 1 (2,20km)
1. Gronholm 1'31"6; 2. Delecour 1'32"3; 3. Kankkunen et Auriol 1'32"5; 5. McRae et Solberg 1'32"8 Gr.N Pozzo 1'37"4

ES.2 Helena North 1 (24,14 km)
1. Gronholm 15'27"4; 2. Sainz 15'32"1; 3. Eriksson 15'32"7; 4. Makinen 15'34"2; 5. Delecour 15'34"7; 6. Solberg 15'34"7; Gr.N Paasonen 16'13"3

ES.3 Helena South 1 (18,43 km)
1. Kankkunen 9'50"0; 2. Delecour 9'51"4; 3. A.McRae 9'52"1; 4. C. McRae 9'53"2; 5. Makinen 9'53"4; 6. Gronholm 9'53"5; Gr.N Paasonen 10'23"8

ES.4 New Kev's (9,56 km)
1. Solberg 6'10"9; 2. Sainz et Gronholm 6'11"5; 4. Makinen 6'11"9; 5. A. McRae 6'13"3; 6. Laukkanen 6'13"9; Gr.N Trelles 6'31"8

ES.5 New Beraking (26,46 km)
1. Gronholm 46'44"7; 2. Makinen 46'49"4; 3. Sainz 46'50"6; 4. Delecour 46'59"1; 5. C. McRae 46'59"5; 6. Kankkunen 47'028; Gr.N Stohl 50'11"9

ES.6 Flynns Short (19,98 km)
1. Solberg 12'03"8; 2. Laukkanen 12'07"8; 3. Kankkunen 12'11"7; 4. Gronholm 12'12"0; 5. Sainz 12'13"4; 6. Makinen 12'14"3; Gr.N Trelles 12'51"7

ES.7 Helena North 2 (24,14 km)
1. Delecour 1'39"0; 2. Gronholm 13'39"1; 3. Solberg 13'39"4; 4. Makinen 13'43"8; 5. Burns 13'44"0; 6. Kankkunen 13'44"2; Gr.N Stohl 14'39"5

ES.8 Helena South 2 (18,43 km)
1. Makinen 9'42"5; 2. Kankkunen 9'43"9; 3. Burns 9'44"3; 4. Delecour 9'45"1; 5. Gronholm 9'49"0; 6. Sainz et Auriol 9'50"1; Gr.N Trelles 10'26"1

ES.9 Atkins (4,42 km)
1. Eriksson 3'00"3; 2. Burns 3'01"0; 3. Auriol et Gardemeister 3'01"1; 4. ; 5. Kankkunen 3'02"2; 6. A. McRae 3'02"8; Gr.N Trelles 3'10"6

ES.10 Langley Park Super 2 (2,20 km)
1. Makinen et Delecour 1'31"8; 2. Panizzi 1'32"1; 4. Kankkunen 1'32"4; 5. Bourne 1'32"6; 6. Sainz 1'33"4; Gr.N Herridge 1'36"8

ES.11 Stirling East (35,48 km)
1. Burns 20'01"3; 2. Gronholm 20'08"4; 3. A. McRae 20'19"5; 4. Eriksson 20'20"2; 5. Makinen 20'23"5; 6. Kankkunen 20'24"5; Gr.N Paasonen 21'25"0

ES.12 Brunswick (16,63 km)
1. Makinen 9'16"3; 2. Gronholm 9'19"2; 3. Kankkunen 9'20"4; 4. Burns 9'21"4; 5. Eriksson 9'25"4; 6. A. McRae 9'27"2; Gr.N Trelles 10'11"8

ES.13 Wellington Dam (45,42 km)
1. Burns 25'37"7; 2. Makinen 25'57"4; 3. Eriksson 26'00"0; 4. Delecour 26'03"1; 5. Laukkanen 26'09"9; 6. Gronholm 26'11"2; Gr.N Trelles 27'48"8

ES.14 New Harvey Weir (7,04 km)
1. Gronholm 3'51"8; 2. Makinen 3'54"8; 3. Gardemeister 3'55"6; 4. Burns 3'56"6; 5. A. McRae 3'57"1; 6. Kankkunen 3'57"5; Gr.N Stohl 4'13"5

ES.15 Stirling West (15,89 km)
1. Gronholm 9'31"2; 2. Makinen 9'39"1; 3. Auriol 9'39"7; 4. Eriksson 9'42"0; 5. Burns 9'42"7; 6. Laukkanen 9'43"4; Gr.N Manfrinato 10'18"3

ES.16 Murray Pines (18,53 km)
1. Eriksson 11'10"8; 2. Auriol 11'15"0; 3. Gardemeister 11'20"4; 4. Makinen 11'20"7; 5. Panizzi 11'21"0; 6. Delecour 11'22"7; Gr.N Ordynski 11'53"1

ES.17 Langley Park Super 3 (2,20km)
1. Burns 1'33"7; 2. Delecour 1'33"9; 3. Auriol 1'34"3; 4. Panizzi 1'34"6; 5. Gronholm 1'34"7; 6. Bourne 1'35"0; Gr.N Caldani 1'37"7

ES.18 Bannister West (35,29 km)
1. Makinen 17'33"0; 2. Burns 17'41"3; 3. Gronholm 17'43"0; 4. Delecour 17'48"9; 5. Laukkanen 17'56"3; 6. Gardemeister 18'11"4; Gr.N Ordynski 19'19"2

ES.19 Bannister North (36,84 km)
1. Makinen 19'44"6; 2. Burns 19'54"7; 3. Gronholm 19'54"9; 4. Delecour 20'02"1; 5. Laukkanen 20'09"1; 6. Eriksson 20'16"4; Gr.N Stohl 21'54"3

ES.20 Bannister South (25,16 km)
1. Gronholm 15'04"3; 2. Burns 15'04"5; 3. Makinen 15'08"4; 4. Eriksson 15'14"5; 5. Delecour 15'17"2; 6. Auriol 15'19"4; Gr.N Herridge 16'32"8

ES.21 Michelin TV Stage (2,73 km)
1. Gronholm 1'33"9; 2. Burns 1'35"7; 3. Makinen 1'36"2; 4. Auriol 1'37"1; 5. Laukkanen 1'37"5; 6. Panizzi 1'38"3; Gr.N Stohl 1'45"4

RESULTS AND RETIREMENTS

	Driver/Co-Driver	Car	Gr.	Total time
1	Marcus Gronholm - Timo Rautiainen	Peugeot 206 WRC	A	3h43m57,2s
2	Richard Burns - Robert Reid	Subaru Impreza WRC 2000	A	3h43m59,9s
3	François Delecour - Daniel Grataloup	Peugeot 206 WRC	A	3h45m30,1s
4	Kenneth Eriksson - Staffan Parmander	Hyundaï Accent WRC	A	3h46m17,8s
5	Tapio Laukkanen - Kaj Lindstrom	Ford Focus WRC	A	3h46m28,1s
6	Tony Gardemeister - Paavo Lukander	Seat Cordoba WRC Evo 3	A	3h46m46,5s
7	Possum Bourne - Craig Vincent	Subaru Impreza WRC	A	3h48m30,7s
8	Didier Auriol - Denis Giraudet	Seat Cordoba WRC Evo 3	A	3h51m51,8s
9	Neal Bates - Coral Taylor	Toyota Corolla WRC	A	3h53m04,0s
10	Katsuhiko Taguchi - Bob Willis	Mitsubishi Lancer Evo 6	A	3h57m43,8s
12	Gustavo Trelles - Jorge Del Buono	Mitsubishi Lancer Evo.6	N	4h01m36,1s
ES.2	Markko Martin - Michael Park	Subaru Impreza WRC 2000	A	Transmission
ES.3	Freddy Loix - Sven Smeets	Mitsubishi Carisma GT	A	Transmission
ES.6	Colin McRae - Nicky Grist	Ford Focus WRC	A	Engine
ES.8	Petter Solberg - Phil Mills	Subaru Impreza WRC 2000	A	Accident
ES.10	Carlos Sainz - Luis Moya	Ford Focus WRC	A	Expulsion
ES.14	Erik Comas - Jean Paul Terrasse	Mitsubishi Lancer Evo.6	A	Accident
ES.15	Alister McRae - David Senior	Hyundaï Accent WRC	A	Accident
ES.16	Juha Kankkunen - Juha Repo	Subaru Impreza WRC 2000	A	Steering
ES.19	Michael Guest - David Green	Hyundaï Accent WRC	A	Electrical
After rally	Tommi Makinen - Risto Mannisenmaki	Mitsubishi Lancer Evo.6	A	Disqualified turbo unconform

PREVIOUS WINNERS

1989	Kankkunen - Piironen Toyota Celica GT-Four		1995	Eriksson - Parmander Mitsubishi Lancer Ev.2
1990	Kankkunen - Piironen Lancia Delta Integrale		1996	Makinen - Harjanne Mitsubishi Lancer Ev.3
1991	Kankkunen - Piironen Lancia Delta Integrale		1997	McRae - Grist Subaru Impreza WRC
1992	Auriol - Occelli Lancia Delta HF Integrale		1998	Makinen - Mannisenmaki Mitsubishi Lancer Ev.5
1993	Kankkunen - Grist Toyota Celica Turbo 4WD		1999	Burns - Reid Subaru Impreza WRC
1994	McRae - Ringer Subaru Impreza			

EVENT LEADERS

ES.1 > ES.8	Gronholm
ES.9 > ES.10	Kankkunen
ES.11 > ES.15	Burns
ES.16 > ES.17	Gronholm
ES.18 > ES.21	Makinen
Finish	Gronholm

BEST PERFORMANCES

	1	2	3	4	5	6
Gronholm	6	4	2	2	2	2
Makinen	6	3	2	4	2	1
Burns	3	5	1	2	2	-
Delecour	2	3	-	4	1	2
Eriksson	2	2	1	3	1	1
Solberg	2	-	1	-	2	-
Kankkunen	1	1	3	1	2	2
Auriol	-	1	4	1	-	2
Sainz	-	1	2	-	1	2
Laukkanen	-	1	-	-	4	3
Gardemeister	-	-	3	-	-	1
A. McRae	-	-	2	-	2	2
Panizzi	-	-	1	1	1	1
C. McRae	-	-	-	1	1	-
Bourne	-	-	-	-	1	1
Bates	-	-	-	-	-	1

CHAMPIONSHIP CLASSIFICATIONS

Drivers
1. Marcus Gronholm	59
2. Richard Burns	50
3. Colin McRae	43
4. Carlos Sainz	43
5. Tommi Makinen	32
6. FranÁois Delecour	23

Constructors
1. Peugeot	104
2. Ford	88
3. Subaru	76
4. Mitsubishi	39
5. Seat	11
6. Skoda	8

Group N
1. Manfred Stohl	65
2. Gustavo Trelles	64
3. Grabriel Pozzo	22

Team's cup
1. Spike Subaru Team (Araï)	42
2. Toyota Team Saudi Arabia (Bakashab)	32
3. Frédéric Dor Rally Team (Dor)	26

Tapio Laukkanen jumped into the Ford seat left vacant by Petter Solberg, which Pierro Liatti occupied on the tarmac events.

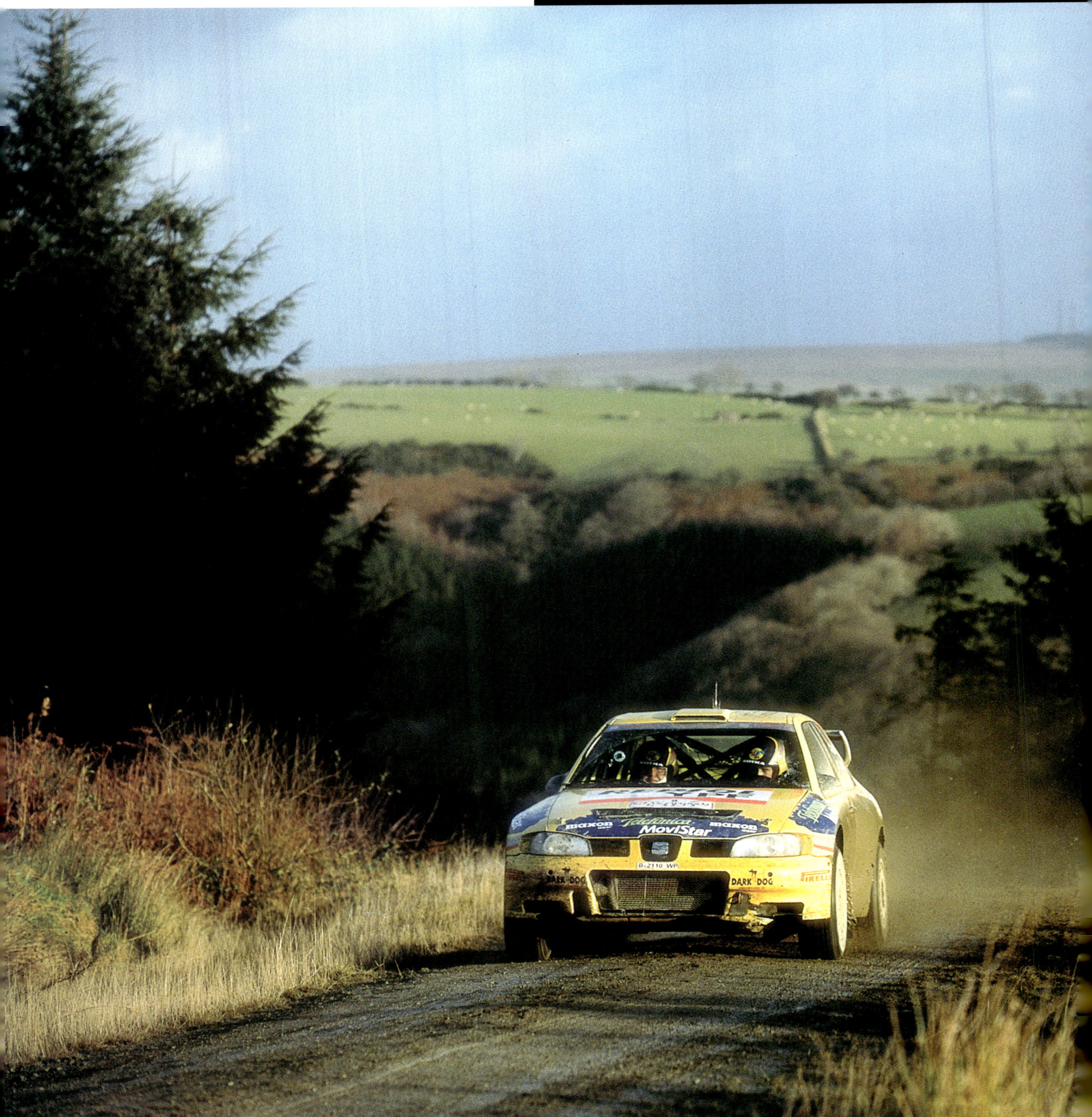
Telefonica
MoviStar
DARK DOG
PIRELLI
B-2110 WP

great britain

THE RALLY
Burns wins but loses

With the constructors' championship already decided in Australia, the rules of engagement for the final round could not have been simpler. To take the title, Burns had to win and hope that Gronholm did no better than sixth. Any other scenario would result in the lanky blonde Peugeot man taking the crown that Makinen had worn since 1996.

The suspense would not last long and ended on a sad little road, which emerged from the mist that swirled around the flat-topped hills which linked the dark little villages with their grey houses sporting the odd early festive decoration. Down below ran a river, equally dark with its coal black water, reflecting the lifeblood of these valleys. It was called Rhondda Fawr. In the rain, it lacked any charm, even if the stages running above it had been spectacular enough. Here, down below, more mundane matters needed attending to, as far as Richard Burns found to his cost.

Down on one knee, protected from the road surface by a jacket gallantly loaned by a spectator, so that his overalls would not get dirty, the driver turned mechanic was fettling his machine. A wheel was lying on the road and co-driver Robert Reid was relaying instructions from the team. Calm and methodical, Burns tied up the rear hub as best he could with some straps and replaced the wheel. The two men then jumped back into the car, did up their belts and headed off in a crab-like motion to tackle the seventy kilometres to the service area. For the Impreza duo, as they handed over their broken car to the specialists, it had been a very close call.

The incident actually happened just one kilometre into the second stage of the event. On a flyer, Burns turned into a left hander and the rear wheel hit a rock. He admitted it was his fault. "I made a mistake. I went in too deep and we hit something which damaged the rear end. We managed to get through the three stages and get to service, but it was a close thing to be honest." It meant that with three stages gone, he was already 57.2 s behind leader Colin McRae, but at least he was still in the rally, which was quite an achievement on the opening day.

Sainz was a regular visitor to the ditches, while McRae practised his pirouettes. As for Makinen, his roof mounted air intake was full of branches, after encountering a tree which was not in his notes-understandable really as he was off the road at the time. Delecour was struggling with a bad tyre choice, but Panizzi was a front runner on the loose for the first time, while by some miracle, Auriol got his Seat up to third for a while, until the Spanish coupe starting running on three cylinders.

Gronholm had exciting tales to tell, after the rear of his 206 made contact with a rock and the front with a sheep. "There were three on the stage and I managed to avoid two of them." However, he had made a phenomenal start to the rally, taking the lead for a while, when he did not really need to. But McRae was on a charge and coupled with the fact the Finn eased off, the Scotsman took the first leg, although Burns had fought his way back up to fifth, around one minute down.

With a solid lead, McRae set off on the second leg with the bit firmly between his teeth. But the wind in the Welsh hills seemed to push him on a bit too quickly and he abused his talent with a roll which eliminated him from the event. The "McCrash" label just won't come off! "This is not what we needed," cursed Francois-Xavier Demaison, Marcus Gronholm's engineer. Sure, it promoted his driver to the lead, but he neither could nor wanted to contain the incredible Burns comeback. The Englishman was taking seconds everywhere thanks to the good form of his Subaru. After just five stages on this second leg, the Englishman had a 10.8 s lead. "I've realised what I've got to do and that's to take the lead," he explained at the end of the second leg. "Now, I've just got to concentrate on my target which is to win. It's the only thing I still have some control over."

With the Englishman leading the Finn as they went into the final leg, these two men had proved once again that they were the undoubted class of the field this year; the quickest, the safest and the most consistent. They were both up for a final showdown, to be played out in the mountains, the mud and the clouds. After thirteen rallies and two legs in Wales, it would all come down to this final section. They had covered 5,600 kilometres over 240 stages and Makinen's successor would now be decided over the final 84.19 kilometres of the last three stages.

It was not easy, but in the end, both men did what they had to do. "It was very tough keeping the car on the road with all this mud and trying not to make any mistakes over the three days," said the weary Peugeot man. Burns therefore had to settle for winning the rally, while Gronholm did enough to take the title. The Finn did it in calm and determined fashion, never putting a foot wrong and never getting distracted by "strange noise syndrome" which affects so many drivers as they listen to every little sound their car makes on the final run to the finish and glory.

If he had any doubts at all, they came on the final stage, run in unexpected sunny weather, through the immaculate park surrounding Margam castle. "Of course we had decided not to take any risks all day," related co-driver Timo Rautiainen. "But on this tricky surface, it is sometimes easier to attack, so as not to get the braking points wrong. In the last stage, I felt that Marcus was braking harder than usual and I thought it might get dangerous. I had to push him along a bit and then, just before the final corner, I told him we were almost there. 'You can brake now if you like!'" The crown awaited and what a crown! It was worn by a man who had shown bravery, panache and modesty all season long.

Juha Kankkunen and Tommi Makinen knew the score. They parked their cars at the end of the stage, got out and waited. The 206 of the new champions hove into view. The old guard pounced on the car, dragged Gronholm out and hugged him long and hard as they celebrated another championship for that little country that has produced so many stars of this sport. It was a Finnish moment. Welcome to the club Marcus, you are one of us now, the sons of Suomi who have been crowned champion.

DOUBLE WHAMMY
Show time for Peugeot!

The Peugeot camp had been here before and they knew what to do, so that the final moments of the season followed a well worn pattern. At the centre of attention were the two bosses, Corrado Provera and Jean-Pierre Nicolas, who were glued to the radios for any news of their drivers, especially Gronholm. The mechanics got on with their work in subdued silence. They seemed reluctant to indulge in their usual waiting games in the service area, where boredom is often the mood of the moment. In the trucks, the engineers tried to disguise the air of tension, their eyes glued to their computer screens. The atmosphere was charged with emotion and the fans had gathered, as had the journalists, friends of the family and an army of Finns. They were all forced to shelter under the truck awnings as the Welsh heavens opened yet again to dampen their enthusiasm in the Bridgend service area, located in a huge car park bearing allegiance to Ford!

The radio crackled into life: "We are through the stage okay," said Timo Rautiainen calmly. His gravelly

End of the road, end of the championship: the star of the season took the title. Well done Marcus Gronholm!

GREAT BRITAIN

After an extraordinary start to the event, Colin McRae ended his 2000 season just as he did a year earlier: with an accident!

voice was the signal they had been waiting for and there was an immediate explosion of relief, hugs and even tears. For some, the moment was too much to bear and they went off in their own little corner. Jean-Pierre Nicolas, thanked the crew, his eyes damp and red. "Thank you, thank you!" came the response from the Finns. Then Corrado Provera grabbed the radio. "Is the duck still alive?" For the past few events this had been the code used between car and team to discuss the state of health of the alternator. Now, these words served as a call to victory. "Yes, of course," confirmed Gronholm.

It was party time. French and Finnish flags were hung all over the final service area, in anticipation of the triumphal entry of their car and some of the mechanics painted their faces in national colours with pennants hanging off their ears, while despite the rain, most of the team changed into T-shirts with the words, "World Champions" emblazoned across their chests.

Then everyone ran across the car park to welcome the 206. It was time for the first interviews and more embraces. Giant blue and white flags appeared from nowhere, with one on the ground where the car was due to park up. There was no end to it as joy was unconfined. Mobile phones were in constant use. Automobiles Peugeot boss Frederic Saint-Geours was called up with the good news. He had arrived for a lightning visit on Saturday, but had to return to France to look after his wife who had broken a shoulder. Mates and girlfriends back home had to be told and then, amidst the general pandemonium, the photographers wanted their pound of flesh. So the entire team was hastily assembled around the car. Smiles were set, click-click went the shutters. "Come on, we have to go," shouted Gronholm, as he still had to drive the final road section back to Cardiff and the night time podium ceremony at the foot of the majestic City Hall. The old Victorian building would resound once again to the cheers of the crowd, as they proved that it was not only in the sport of Rugby that the French flag could fly high in Wales.

THE BEATEN WINNER
Burns, no regrets

Richard Burns might not have won the concours d'elegance this year, either in terms of his appearance or his demeanour, given that his occasional arrogance and somewhat non-sporting behaviour meant he was not particularly popular with his fellow drivers. But he will always be a good, a great driver, finishing as he did, second in the world championship for the second consecutive year. "At least I know what I have to do here this year," he explained before the start. "I must win. I know I can do it. But after that, the final outcome is not totally in my control and that actually takes off some of the pressure in terms of the championship."

Burns did a great job of fulfilling his side of the bargain, despite going off the road on the second stage. This time, unlike on several previous occasions, he was lucky enough to be able to limp into the following service area. He won his home event, helped in part by the departure of Colin McRae. Richard Burns was also the first Brit to achieve the hat trick, previously the preserve of just two men, the Swede Eric Carlsson and the Finn Tommi Makinen. It was a job well done.

However, thanks to his second place, Marcus Gronholm robbed the Englishman of any chance he had of taking the world championship title, which had not gone to a Brit since McRae did it for the first and only time in 1995.

"What can I say about Marcus?" asked the Subaru driver, once the 2000 season was done and dusted. "He drove really well, not just here in this rally, but in Australia too. Even if I am disappointed at not having won the title, I have to admit he was the better driver in the end. He stood up to the pressure amazingly well and he deserves the championship." He went on to admit that he had not held out much hope at the start of this the final rally. "I am happy to have won," he concluded. "I just concentrated on what I had to do. Winning the title was a bit optimistic. I didn't think about it too much. I was nine points down before the event, so I can't claim to be too disappointed." Finally, it was down to Marcus Gronholm to pay homage to his rival. "Next year, the fight with Richard will be even closer." The Englishman's time will come. He deserves it. ∎

Richard Burns was very lucky to get his car to the service area early in the rally, after damaging the rear axle.

GREAT BRITAIN

Carlos Sainz enjoyed the early part of the event. What followed was not so much fun, as he had to give best to a charging Makinen, who pipped him to the final spot on the podium. However, once again, the Spaniard was a front runner, finishing third in the championship and helping his employers at Ford to take second place.

Farewell Mr. Kankkunen. The Rally of Great Britain might have marked more than just the end of the season for the Finn. Mister K hoped to drive in 2001, but no deal was in place. This year, the great man did not shine, but he is still a four times world champion.

GREAT BRITAIN

The final kilometres of the final stage of the final rally which Francois Delecour would drive in Peugeot colours, took place in front of Margam castle. A few hours after the finish, he was given his marching orders by the Lion, his seat going to Finland's Harri Rovanpera.

GREAT BRITAIN

56th RALLY OF GREAT BRITAIN

14th leg of the 2000 world rally championship for constructors and drivers
14th leg of the production car drivers' and team's world cups
Date 23 - 26 november 2000
Route: 1509,48 km divided into 3 legs,
17 special stages on dirt roads (380,80 km.)
Prologue: Thursday 23 november: Cardiff - Cardiff, 1 spéciale (2,43 km)
1st leg: Friday 24 november: Cardiff - Builth Wells - Cardiff, 7 stages (127,76 km)
2nd leg: Saturday 25 november: Cardiff - Swansea - Cardiff, 6 stages (166,42 km)
3rd leg: Sunday 26 november: Cardiff - Pembrey - Cardiff, 3 stages (84,19 km)
Starters - Finishers: 150 - 79
Conditions: rain and heavy winds. Very muddy and slippery forest roads.
Running order does not matter.

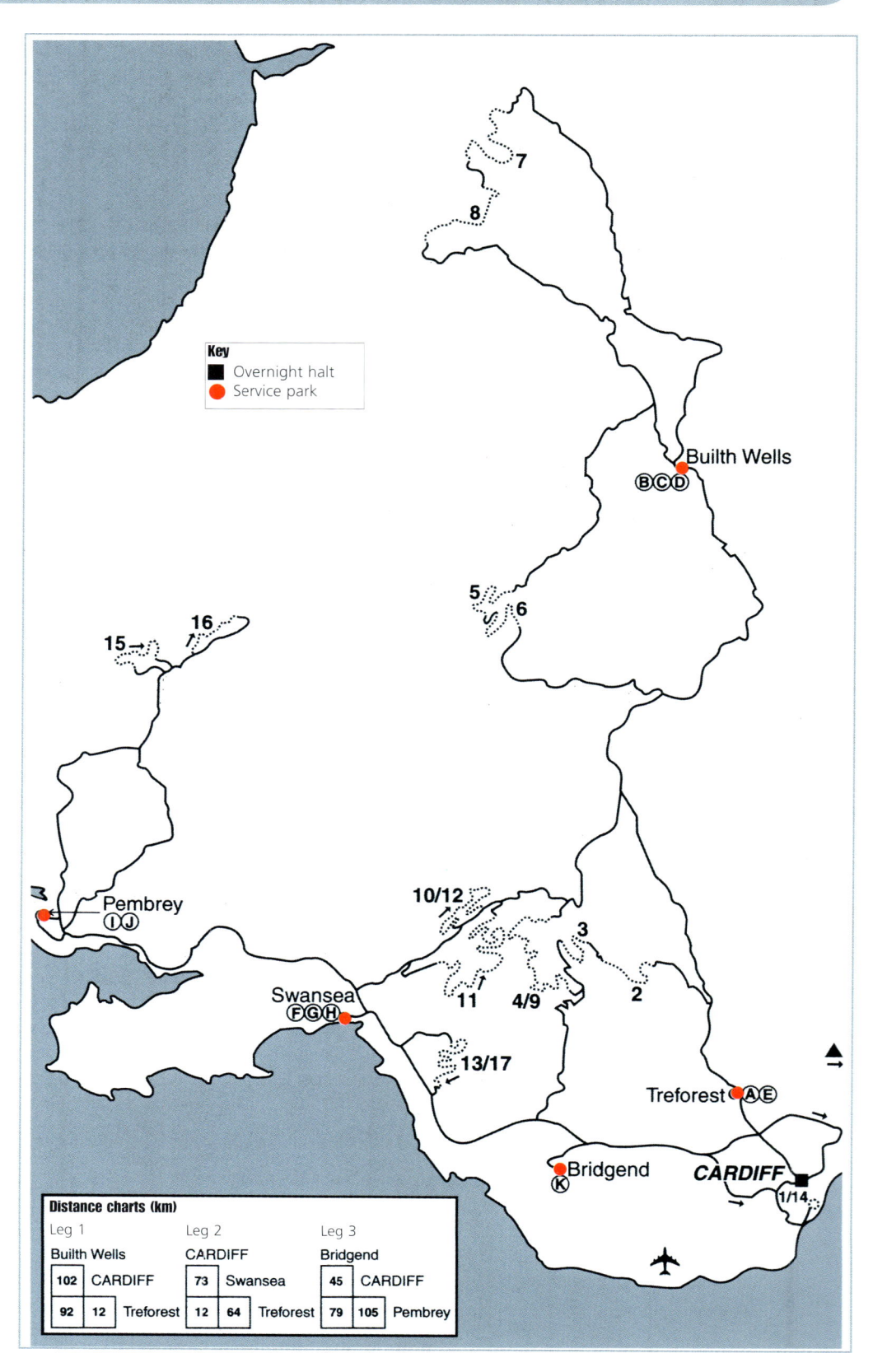

TOP ENTRIES

1 Tommi Makinen - Risto Mannisenmaki
MITSUBISHI LANCER Evo 6

2 Freddy Loix - Sven Smeets
MITSUBISHI CARISMA GT

3 Richard Burns - Robert Reid
SUBARU IMPREZA WRC 2000

4 Juha Kankkunen - Juha Repo
SUBARU IMPREZA WRC 2000

5 Colin McRae - Nicky Grist
FORD FOCUS WRC

6 Carlos Sainz - Luis Moya
FORD FOCUS WRC

7 Didier Auriol - Denis Giraudet
SEAT CORDOBA WRC Evo 3

8 Toni Gardemeister - Paavo Lukander
SEAT CORDOBA WRC Evo 3

9 François Delecour - Daniel Grataloup
PEUGEOT 206 WRC

10 Marcus Gronholm - Timo Rautiainen
PEUGEOT 206 WRC

11 Armin Schwarz - Manfred Hiemer
SKODA OCTAVIA WRC

12 Luis Climent - Alex Romani
SKODA OCTAVIA WRC

14 Kenneth Eriksson - Staffan Parmander
HYUNDAI ACCENT WRC

15 Alister McRae - David Senior
HYUNDAI ACCENT WRC

16 Petter Solberg - Philip Mills
SUBARU IMPREZA WRC 2000

17 Harri Rovanpera - Risto Pietilainen
SEAT CORDOBA WRC Evo 3

18 Tapio Laukkanen - Kaj Lindstrom
FORD FOCUS WRC

19 Gilles Panizzi - Hervé Panizzi
PEUGEOT 206 WRC

20 Gwyndaf Evans - Howard Davies
SEAT CORDOBA WRC Evo 3

21 Markko Martin - Michael Park
TOYOTA COROLLA WRC

22 Toshihiro Araï - Roger Freeman
SUBARU IMPREZA WRC

23 Janne Tuohino - Petri Vihavainen
TOYOTA COROLLA WRC

25 Henning Solberg - Ola Floene
TOYOTA COROLLA WRC

28 Gustavo Trelles - Jorge Del Buono
MITSUBISHI LANCER Evo 6

29 Neil Wearden - Trevor Agnew
VAUXHALL ASTRA KIT CAR

30 Manfred Stohl - Peter Muller
MITSUBISHI LANCER Evo 6

32 Stig Blomqvist - Ana Goni
MITSUBISHI LANCER Evo 6

34 Pernilla Walfridsson - C Thorszelius-Bab
MITSUBISHI LANCER Evo 6

36 Hamed Al-Whahaibi - Tony Sircombe
SUBARU IMPREZA WRC

37 John Papadimitriou - Chris Patterson
SUBARU IMPREZA 555

38 Frédéric Dor - Didier Breton
TOYOTA COROLLA WRC

43 Achim Warmbold - Antony Warmbold
TOYOTA COROLLA WRC

45 Mark Fisher - Gordon Noble
PEUGEOT 206 WRC

62 Sebastien Loeb - Daniel Elena
CITROEN SAXO VTS

Distance charts (km)

Leg 1			Leg 2			Leg 3		
Builth Wells			CARDIFF			Bridgend		
102	CARDIFF		73	Swansea		45	CARDIFF	
92	12	Treforest	12	64	Treforest	79	105	Pembrey

SPECIAL STAGE TIMES

ES.1 Cardiff 1 (2,43 km)
1. Kankkunen 2'19"5; 2. Tuohino 2'19"5; 3. Sainz 2'19"8; 4. Laukkanen 2'20"0; 5. P. Solberg 2'20"4; 6. C. McRae 2'20"5; Gr.N Stohl 2'23"8

ES.2 St Gwynno (13,67 km)
1. P. Solberg 6'46"3; 2. Panizzi 6'49"1; 3. Makinen 6'49"5; 4. C. McRae 6'49"5; 5. Sainz 6'50"4; 6. Kankkunen 6'51"3; Gr.N Ferreyros 7'27"1

ES.3 Tyle (10,58 km)
1. Gronholm 5'48"2; 2. C. McRae 5'49"5; 3. Burns 5'51"8; 4. Sainz 5'52"2; 5. Auriol 5'53"9; 6. Makinen 5'54"5; Gr.N Clark 6'23"2

ES.4 Rhondda 1 (26,47 km)
1. Gronholm 14'26"5; 2. C. McRae 14'29"9; 3. Martin 14'40"8; 4. Panizzi 14'42"3; 5. Auriol 14'42"5; 6. Sainz 14'42"7; Gr.N Stohl 16'03"7

ES.5 Crychan (15,57 km)
1. Gronholm 9'09"4; 2. Makinen 9'09"8; 3. Auriol 9'14"9; 4. Kankkunen 9'15"1; 5. Martin 9'15"7; 6. Delecour 9'16"0; Gr.N Stohl 9'57"9

ES.6 Halway (17,45 km)
1. Burns 10'09"8; 2. Gronholm 10'11"8; 3. Delecour 10'12"9; 4. Auriol 10'15"0; 5. Panizzi 10'19"2; 6. Sainz 10'20"6; Gr.N Stohl 11'04"3

ES.7 Hafren (27,23 km)
1. C. McRae 16'36"9; 2. Burns 16'41"0; 3. Sainz 16'47"2; 4. Makinen 16'54"3; 5. Gronholm 16'57"6; 6. Delecour 16'58"4; Gr.N Stohl 18'56"1

ES.8 Myherin (16,79 km)
1. C. McRae 9'54"8; 2. Burns 9'59"6; 3. Sainz 10'01"8; 4. Gronholm 10'09"3; 5. Auriol 10'11"0; 6. Makinen 10'12"0; Gr.N Stohl 10'04"7

ES.9 Rhondda 2 (26,47 km)
1. Burns 14'36"1; 2. Gronholm 14'38"0; 3. C. McRae 14'39"5; 4. Makinen 14'46"9; 5. Auriol 14'47"8; 6. Delecour 14'48"7; Gr.N Stohl 16'08"1

ES.10 Rehola 1 (31,47 km)
1. C. McRae 17'50"7; 2. Burns 17'50"8; 3. Gronholm 18'05"0; 4. Panizzi 18'05"2; 5. Kankkunen 18'07"1; 6. Rovanpera 18'10"6; Gr.N Ferreyros 19'41"5

ES.11 Resolfen (46,45 km)
1.C.McRae 25'15"7; 2. Burns 25'16"9; 3. Delecour 25'27"0; 4. Gronholm 25'28"4; 5. Makinen 25'30"0; 6. Kankkunen 25'32"3; Gr.N Stohl 27'51"8

ES.12 Rehola 2 (31,47 km)
1. Burns 17'51"3; 2. P. Solberg 17'53"5; 3. Kankkunen 17'59"0; 4. Gronholm 17'59"3; 5. Delecour 18'01"1; 6. Martin 18'02"1; Gr.N Ferreyros 19'42"8

ES.13 Margam 1 (28,13 km)
1. Burns 17'10"0; 2. Sainz 17'17"4; 3. Kankkunen 17'17"7; 4. P. Solberg 17'21"1; 5. Gronholm 17'23"8; 6. Delecour 17'25"7; Gr.N Backlund 19'25"5

ES.14 Cardiff 2(2,43km)
1. P.Solberg 2'18"5; 2. Burns 2'22"6; 3. Kankkunen 2'23"0; 4. Laukkanen 2'23"6; 5. Schwarz 2'23"8; 6. Panizzi 2'24"4; Gr.N Anderson 2'30"0

ES.15 Brechfa (29,80 km)
1. Burns 17'32"7; 2. Delecour 17'33"5; 3. P.Solberg 17'36"3; 4. Sainz 17'40"4; 5. Kankkunen 17'41"5; 6. Gronholm et Laukkanen 17'49"6; Gr.N Walfridsson 19'24"7

ES.16 Trawscoed (26,26 km)
1. Makinen 16'17"8; 2. Burns 16'26"0; 3. Delecour 16'28"3; 4. Gronholm 16'32"2; 5. Sainz 16'34"1; 6. Auriol 16'34"9; Gr.N Cox 18'05"5

ES.17 Margam 2 (28,13 km)
1. Makinen 16'57"7; 2. Martin 17'03"9; 3. Kankkunen 17'11"2; 4. Sainz 17'15"0; 5. Delecour 17'15"2; 6. Burns 17'17"2; Gr.N Walfridsson 18'53"9

RESULTS AND RETIREMENTS

	Driver/Co-Driver	Car	Gr.	Total time
1	Richard Burns - Robert Reid	Subaru Impreza WRC 2000	A	3h43m01,9s
2	Marcus Gronholm - Timo Rautiainen	Peugeot 206 WRC	A	3h44m07,5s
3	Tommi Makinen - Risto Mannisenmaki	Mitsubishi Lancer Evo 6	A	3h44m16,9s
4	Carlos Sainz - Luis Moya	Ford Focus WRC	A	3h45m35,4s
5	Juha Kankkunen - Juha Repo	Subaru Impreza WRC 2000	A	3h44m48,8s
6	FranÂois Delecour - Daniel Grataloup	Peugeot 206 WRC	A	3h44m50,4s
7	Markko Martin - Michael Park	Toyota Corolla WRC	A	3h46m26,3s
8	Gilles Panizzi - Hervé Panizzi	Peugeot 206 WRC	A	3h46m37,5s
9	Didier Auriol - Denis Giraudet	Seat Cordoba WRC Evo 3	A	3h47m29,4s
10	Harri Rovanpera - Risto Pietilainen	Seat Cordoba WRC Evo 3	A	3h48m12,0s
17	Manfred Stohl - Peter Muller	Mitsubishi Lancer Evo 6	N	4h07m45,3s
ES.2	Freddy Loix - Sven Smeets	Mitsubishi Carisma GT	A	Accident
ES.3	Janne Tuohino - Petri Vihavainen	Toyota Corolla WRC	A	Electronics
ES.4	Kenneth Eriksson - Staffan Parmander	Hyundai Accent WRC	A	Engine
ES.9	Gwyndaf Evans - Howard Davies	Seat Cordoba WRC Evo 3	A	Clutch
ES.9	Achim Warmbold - Antony Warmbold	Toyota Corolla WRC	A	Withdraw
ES.11	Mark Fisher - Gordon Noble	Peugeot 206 WRC	A	Mechanics
ES.12	Colin McRae - Nicky Grist	Ford Focus WRC	A	Accident
ES.12	Stig Blomqvist - Ana Goni	Mitsubishi Lancer Evo 6	A	Mechanics
ES.13	Toshiro Arai - Roger Freeman	Subaru Impreza WRC	A	Fire
ES.16	Petter Solberg - Phil Mills	Subaru Impreza WRC 2000	A	Accident
ES.16	Tapio Laukkanen - Kaj Lindstrom	Ford Focus WRC	A	Accident

EVENT LEADERS

ES.1	Kankkunen and Tuohino
ES.2	Solberg
ES.3 > ES.4	C. McRae
ES.5 > ES.6	Gronholm
ES.7 > ES.11	C. McRae
ES.12	Gronholm
ES.13 > ES.17	Burns

BEST PERFORMANCES

	1	2	3	4	5	6
Burns	5	6	1	-	-	1
C.McRae	4	2	2	-	-	1
Gronholm	3	2	2	3	2	1
Makinen	2	1	1	2	1	2
P. Solberg	2	-	1	1	1	-
Kankkunen	1	1	3	1	2	2
Tuohino	1	-	-	-	-	-
Sainz	-	1	3	3	2	2
Delecour	-	1	3	1	1	4
Martin	-	1	1	-	2	-
Panizzi	-	1	-	2	1	2
Auriol	-	-	-	1	4	1
Laukkanen	-	-	-	-	2	1
Schwarz	-	-	-	-	1	-
Rovanpera	-	-	-	-	-	1
H. Solberg	-	-	-	-	-	1

CHAMPIONSHIP CLASSIFICATIONS

Drivers
1. Marcus Gronholm — 65
2. Richard Burns — 60
3. Carlos Sainz — 46
4. Colin McRae — 43
5. Tommi Makinen — 36
6. François Delecour — 24

Constructors
1. Peugeot — 111
2. Ford — 91
3. Subaru — 88
4. Mitsubishi — 43
5. Seat — 11
6. Skoda — 8
   Hyundai — 8

Group N
1. Manfred Stohl — 75
2. Gustavo Trelles — 64
3. Grabriel Pozzo — 22

Team's cup
1. Spike Subaru Team (Araï) — 42
2. Toyota Team Saudi Arabia (Bakashab) — 38
3. Team Atakan (Yazici) — 33

PREVIOUS WINNERS

1974	Makinen - Liddon, Ford Escort RS 1600
1975	Makinen - Liddon, Ford Escort RS
1976	Clark - Pegg, Ford Escort RS
1977	Waldegaard - Thorszelius, Ford Escort RS
1978	Mikkola - Hertz, Ford Escort RS
1979	Mikkola - Hertz, Ford Escort RS
1980	Toivonen - White, Talbot Sunbeam Lotus
1981	Mikkola - Hertz, Audi Quattro
1982	Mikkola - Hertz, Audi Quattro
1983	Blomqvist - Cederberg, Audi Quattro
1984	Vatanen - Harryman, Peugeot 205 T16
1985	Toivonen - Wilson, Lancia Delta S4
1986	Salonen - Harjanne, Peugeot 205 T16
1987	Kankkunen - Piironen, Lancia Delta HF
1988	Alen - Kivimaki, Lancia Delta Integrale
1989	Airikkala - McNamee, Mitsubishi Galant VR4
1990	Sainz - Moya, Toyota Celica GT-Four
1991	Kankkunen - Piironen, Lanica Delta Integrale
1992	Sainz - Moya, Toyota Celica Turbo 4WD
1993	Kankkunen - Piironen, Toyota Celica Turbo 4WD
1994	McRae - Ringer, Subaru Impreza
1995	McRae - Ringer, Subaru Impreza
1996	Schwarz - Giraudet, Toyota Celica GT-Four
1997	McRae - Grist, Subaru Impreza WRC
1998	Burns - Reid, Mitsubishi Carisma GT
1999	Burns - Reid, Subaru Impreza WRC

2000 World Championship for Drivers

	DRIVERS	Monte-Carlo	Swedish	Safari	Portugal	Catalunya	Argentina	Greece	New Zealand	Finland	Cyprus	France	Italy	Australia	Great Britain	TOTAL
1	Marcus Gronholm (FIN)	0	10	0	6	2	6	0	10	10	0	2	3	10	6	65
2	Richard Burns (GB)	0	2	10	10	6	10	0	0	0	3	3	0	6	10	60
3	Carlos Sainz (E)	6	0	3	4	4	0	6	4	0	10	4	2	0	3	46
4	Colin McRae (GB)	0	4	0	0	10	0	10	6	6	6	0	1	0	0	43
5	Tommi Makinen (FIN)	10	6	0	0	3	4	0	0	3	2	0	4	0	4	36
6	François Delecour (F)	0	0	-	2	0	0	0	0	1	4	6	6	4	1	24
7	Gilles Panizzi (F)	0	-	0	-	1	-	-	-	-	-	10	10	0	0	21
8	Juha Kankkunen (FIN)	4	1	6	0	0	3	4	0	0	0	-	-	0	2	20
9	Harri Rovanpera ((FIN)	-	0	-	3	-	-	-	-	4	-	-	-	-	0	7
10	Petter Solberg (NOR)	-	-	2	0	0	1	0	3	0	0	0	0	0	0	6
11	Kenneth Eriksson (S)	-	0	-	0	0	0	0	2	0	-	0	0	3	0	5
12	Didier Auriol (F)	0	0	4	0	0	0	0	0	0	0	0	0	0	0	4
	Toni Gardemeister (FIN)	3	0	0	0	0	0	0	0	0	0	0	0	1	0	4
	Toshihiro Arai (J)	-	-	1	-	0	-	3	0	-	0	-	-	0	0	4
	Freddy Loix (B)	1	0	0	1	0	2	0	0	0	0	0	0	0	0	4
16	Thomas Radstrom (S)	-	3	-	0	-	-	-	-	-	-	-	-	-	-	3
17	Bruno Thiry (B)	2	-	-	-	-	-	-	-	-	-	-	-	-	-	2
	Armin Schwarz (D)	0	-	0	0	0	-	2	-	-	0	-	0	-	-	2
	Sebastian Lindholm (FIN)	-	-	-	-	-	-	-	-	-	2	-	-	0	-	2
	Tapio Laukkanen (FIN)	-	-	-	-	-	-	-	-	-	-	-	-	2	0	2
21	Abdullah Bakashab (SA)	-	0	-	0	0	-	1	-	0	0	-	0	-	-	1
	Possum Bourne (NZ)	-	-	-	-	-	-	-	1	-	-	-	-	-	-	1
	Markko Martin (EST)	-	-	-	0	0	-	0	-	0	1	-	0	-	0	1
	Piero Liatti (I)	-	-	-	-	-	-	-	-	-	-	-	1	0	-	1

2000 World Championship for Constructors

	CONSTRUCTORS	Monte-Carlo	Swedish	Safari	Portugal	Catalunya	Argentina	Greece	New Zealand	Finland	Cyprus	France	Italy	Australia	Great Britain	TOTAL
1	PEUGEOT	0	11	0	9	3	6	2	10	13	4	16	16	14	7	111
2	FORD	6	4	3	4	14	0	16	10	6	16	4	5	0	3	91
3	SUBARU	4	5	16	10	6	13	4	0	2	4	5	1	6	12	88
4	MITSUBISHI	12	6	0	2	3	6	0	0	4	2	0	4	0	4	43
5	SEAT	3	0	4	0	0	0	0	0	0	0	1	0	3	0	11
6	SKODA	1	-	3	1	0	-	3	-	-	0	-	0	-	0	8
	HYUNDAI	-	0	-	0	0	1	0	3	1	-	0	0	3	0	8

REGULATIONS : DRIVERS' CHAMPIONSHIP : All results count. 1st - 10 points, 2nd - 6 points, 3rd - 4 points, 4th - 3 points, 5th - 2 points, 6th - 1 point.
CONSTRUCTORS' CHAMPIONSHIP : To be eligible, the constructors who have registered with FIA, must take part in all the events with a minimum of two cars. The first two cars score the points according to their finishing position. All results are taken into consideration. Points scale is the same as for the drivers.

World Championship for Constructors

1973	Alpine-Renault	1987	Lancia
1974	Lancia	1988	Lancia
1975	Lancia	1989	Lancia
1976	Lancia	1990	Lancia
1977	Fiat	1991	Lancia
1978	Fiat	1992	Lancia
1979	Ford	1993	Toyota
1980	Fiat	1994	Toyota
1981	Talbot	1995	Subaru
1982	Audi	1996	Subaru
1983	Lancia	1997	Subaru
1984	Audi	1998	Mitsubishi
1985	Peugeot	1999	Toyota
1986	Peugeot	2000	Peugeot

World Championship for Drivers

1977	Sandro Munari (I)	1989	Miki Biasion (I)
1978	Markku Alen (SF)	1990	Carlos Sainz (E)
1979	Bjorn Waldegaard (S)	1991	Juha Kankkunen (SF)
1980	Walter Rohrl (D)	1992	Carlos Sainz (E)
1981	Ari Vatanen (SF)	1993	Juha Kankkunen (SF)
1982	Walter Rohrl (D)	1994	Didier Auriol (F)
1983	Hannu Mikkola (SF)	1995	Colin McRae (GB)
1984	Stig Blomqvist (S)	1996	Tommi Makinen (SF)
1985	Timo Salonen (SF)	1997	Tommi Makinen (SF)
1986	Juha Kankkunen (SF)	1998	Tommi Makinen (SF)
1987	Juha Kankkunen (SF)	1999	Tommi Makinen (SF)
1988	Miki Biasion (I)	2000	Marcus Grönholm (SF)

1977-1978 : FIA Cup for Drivers

2000 Production Car Championship for Drivers (Group N)

	DRIVERS	Monte-Carlo	Swedish	Safari	Portugal	Catalunya	France	Argentina	Greece	New Zealand	Finland	Chine	Italy	Australia	Great Britain	TOTAL
1	Manfred Stohl (A)	10	3	4	6	4	0	4	10	4	3	10	3	4	10	75
2	Gustavo Trelles (ROU)	6	-	-	0	6	10	6	6	0	10	6	4	10	0	64
3	Gabriel Pozzo (RA)	-	-	0	0	0	6	10	0	0	6	0	0	0	-	22
4	Jani Paasonen (FIN)	-	10	-	-	1	-	-	-	10	-	-	-	0	-	21
5	Claudio Menzi (RA)	-	-	10	0	2	0	0	0	0	4	0	-	1	-	17
	Ramon Ferreyros (PE)	-	-	-	4	0	3	3	-	-	-	2	2	0	3	17
7	Uwe Nittel (D)	0	-	-	0	10	0	0	-	0	-	-	-	-	-	10
	Roberto Sanchez (RA)	-	-	6	0	0	4	-	-	-	-	-	-	-	-	10
9	Toshihiro Arai (J)	-	-	-	-	-	-	-	-	-	-	-	-	6	0	6
10	Reece Jones (NZ)	-	-	-	-	-	-	-	4	-	-	-	-	-	0	4

REGULATIONS: The classification is based on the total number of rallies minus one. At least one rally outside Europe has to be entered. Points scored as follows; 1st - 10 points, 2nd - 6 points, 3rd - 4 points, 4th - 3 points, 5th - 2 points, 6th - 1 point. The points are added with those scored in the different capacity classes (up to 1300cc; 1301-2000cc, over 2000cc) on the following scale: 1st - 3 points, 2nd - 2 points, 3rd - 1 point. Class points are only attributed to drivers finishing in the top six of the production car classification.

2000 FIA Team's Cup

	TEAMS	Monte-Carlo	Swedish	Safari	Portugal	Catalunya	Argentina	Greece	New Zealand	Finland	Cyprus	France	Italy	Australia	Great Britain	TOTAL
1	SPIKE SUBARU TEAM	-	-	10	-	6	-	10	0	-	10	-	-	6	0	42
	Toshihiro Arai															
2	TOYOTA SAUDI ARABIA	-	6	-	0	10	-	6	-	10	0	-	6	0	-	33
	Abdullah Bakhashab															
3	TEAM ATAKAN	-	-	-	0	0	10	3	-	-	-	0	10	10	-	33
	Serkan Yazici															
4	ARAB WORLD RALLY TEAM	-	-	-	-	-	-	0	10	0	0	10	0	0	10	30
	Hamed Al-Wahaibi															

REGULATIONS : To be eligible to score points each team must take part in 7 Cup rallies with at least one outside Europe, with a maximum of 2 cars (Group A or Group N) per team. Only the best placed car can score points according to its position relative to the other cup competitors, on the same scale of points as the FIA world rally championship.

Group N Cup Winners

- 1987 Alex Fiorio (I)
- 1988 Pascal Gaban (B)
- 1989 Alain Oreille (F)
- 1990 Alain Oreille (F)
- 1991 Grégoire de Mevius (B)
- 1992 Grégoire de Mevius (B)
- 1993 Alex Fassina (I)
- 1994 Jesus Puras (E)
- 1995 Rui Madeira (P)
- 1996 Gustavo Trelles (ROU)
- 1997 Gustavo Trelles (ROU)
- 1998 Gustavo Trelles (ROU)
- 1999 Gustavo Trelles (ROU)
- 2000 Manfred Stohl (D)

FIA Team's Cup

- 1998 H.F. Grifone
- 1999 Valencia Terra Mar - Luis Climent
- 2000 Spike Subaru Team - Toshihiro Arai

DRIVERS WHO HAVE WON WORLD CHAMPIONSHIP RALLIES FROM 1973 TO 2000

DRIVERS	Numbers of WINS	RALLIES
Andrea Aghini (I)	1	1992 I
Pentti Airikkala (SF)	1	1989 GB
Markku Alen (SF)	20	1975 P 1976 SF 1977 P **1978** P-SF-I 1979 SF 1980 SF 1981 P 1983 F-I 1984 F 1986 I-USA 1987 P-GR-SF 1988 S-SF-GB
Alain Ambrosino (F)	1	1988 CI
Ove Andersson (S)	1	1975 EAK
Jean-Claude Andruet (F)	3	1973 MC 1974 F 1977 I
Didier Auriol (F)	19	1988 F 1989 F 1990 MC-F-I 1991 I 1992 MC-F-GR-RA-SF-AUS 1993 MC 1994 F-RA-I 1995 F 1998 E 1999 C
Fulvio Bacchelli (I)	1	1977 NZ
Bernard Beguin (F)	1	1987 F
Miki Biasion (I)	17	1986 RA 1987 MC-RA-I **1988** P-EAK-GR-USA-I **1989** MC-P-EAK-GR-I 1990 P-RA 1993 GR
Stig Blomqvist (S)	11	1973 S 1977 S 1979 S 1982 S-I 1983 GB **1984** S-GR-NZ-RA-CI
Walter Boyce (CDN)	1	1973 USA
Philippe Bugalski (F)	2	1999 E-F
Richard Burns (GB)	9	1998 EAK 1999 Gr-AUS-GB 2000 EAK-P-RA-GB
Ingvar Carlsson (S)	2	1989 S-NZ
Roger Clark (GB)	1	1976 GB
Gianfranco Cunico (I)	1	1993 I
Bernard Darniche (F)	7	1973 MA 1975 F 1977 F 1978 F 1979 MC-F 1981 F
François Delecour (F)	4	1993 P-F-E 1994 MC
Ian Duncan (EAK)	1	1994 EAK
Per Eklund (S)	1	1976 S
Mikael Ericsson (S)	2	1989 RA-SF
Kenneth Eriksson (S)	6	1987 CI 1991 S 1995 S-AUS 1997 S-NZ
Tony Fassina (I)	1	1979 I
Guy Frequelin (F)	1	1981 RA
Marcus Gronholm (SF)	4	**2000** S-NZ-F-AUS
Sepp Haider (A)	1	1988 NZ
Kyosti Hamalainen (SF)	1	1977 SF
Mats Jonsson (S)	2	1992 S 1993 S
Harry Kallstom (S)	1	1976 GR
Juha Kankkunen (SF)	23	1985 EAK-CI **1986** S-GR-NZ **1987** USA-GB 1989 AUS 1990 AUS 1991 EAK-GR-SF-AUS-GB 1992 P **1993** EAK-RA-SF-AUS-GB 1994 P 1999 RA-SF
Anders Kullang (S)	1	1980 S
Piero Liatti (I)	1	1997 MC
Colin McRae (GB)	20	1993 NZ 1994 NZ-GB **1995** NZ-GB 1996 GR-I-E 1997 EAK-F-I-AUS-GB 1998 P-F-GR 1999 EAK-P 2000 E-GR
Timo Makinen (SF)	4	1973 SF-GB 1974 GB 1975 GB
Tommi Makinen (SF)	20	1994 SF **1996** S-EAK-RA-SF-AUS **1997** P-E-RA-SF **1998** S-RA-NZ-SF-I-AUS **1999** Mc-S-NZ-I 2000 Mc
Shekhar Mehta (EAK)	5	1973 EAK 1979 EAK 1980 EAK 1981 EAK 1982 EAK
Hannu Mikkola (SF)	18	1974 SF 1975 MA-SF 1978 GB 1979 P-NZ-GB-CI 1981 S-GB 1982 SF-GB **1983** S-P-RA-SF 1984 P 1987 EAK
Joaquim Moutinho (P)	1	1986 P
Michèle Mouton (F)	4	1981 I 1982 P-GR-BR
Sandro Munari (I)	7	1974 I-CDN 1975 MC 1976 MC-P-F **1977** MC
Jean-Pierre Nicolas	5	1973 F 1976 MA 1978 MC-EAK-CI
Alain Oreille (F)	1	1989 CI
Gilles Panizzi (F)	2	2000 F-I
Rafaelle Pinto (P)	1	1974 P
Jean Ragnotti (F)	3	1981 MC 1982 F 1985 F
Jorge Recalde (RA)	1	1988 RA
Walter Rôhrl (D)	14	1975 GR 1978 GR-CDN **1980** MC-P-RA-I **1982** MC-CI 1983 MC-GR-NZ 1984 MC 1985 I
Bruno Saby (F)	2	1986 F 1988 MC
Carlos Sainz (E)	23	**1990** GR-NZ-SF-GB 1991 MC-P-F-NZ-RA **1992** EAK-NZ-E-GB 1994 GR 1995 MC-P-E 1996 RI 1997 GR-RI 1998 MC-NZ 2000 CY
Timo Salonen (SF)	11	1977 CDN 1980 NZ 1981 CI **1985** P-GR-NZ-RA-SF 1986 SF-GB 1987 S
Armin Schwarz (D)	1	1991 E
Kenjiro Shinozuka (J)	2	1991 CI 1992 CI
Joginder Singh (EAK)	2	1974 EAK 1976 EAK
Patrick Tauziac (F)	1	1990 CI
Jean-Luc Thèrier (F)	5	1973 P-GR-I 1974 USA 1980 F
Henri Toivonen (SF)	3	1980 GB 1985 GB 1986 MC
Ari Vatanen (SF)	10	1980 GR **1981** GR-BR-SF 1983 EAK 1984 SF-I-GB 1985 MC-S
Bjorn Waldegaard (S)	16	1975 S-I 1976 I 1977 EAK-GR-GB 1978 S **1979** GR-CDN 1980 CI 1982 NZ 1983 CI 1984 EAK 1986 EAK-CI 1990 EAK
Achim Warmbold (D)	2	1973 PL-A
Franz Wittmann (A)	1	1987 NZ

A: Austria - AUS: Australia - BR: Brazil - C : China - CDN: Canada - CI: Ivory Coast - CY : Cyprus - E: Spain - EAK : Kenya - F: France - GB: Great Britain - GR: Greece - I: Italy - MA: Marocco - MC: Monte-Carlo - NZ: New Zealand - P: Portugal - PL: Poland - RA: Argentina - RI: Indonesia - S: Sweden - SF: Finland - USA : United States of America